Postcolonial Public Theology

Postcolonial Public Theology

Faith, Scientific Rationality, and Prophetic Dialogue

PAUL S. CHUNG

Foreword by Lois Malcolm

CASCADE *Books* · Eugene, Oregon

POSTCOLONIAL PUBLIC THEOLOGY
Faith, Scientific Rationality, and Prophetic Dialogue

Cascade Books
An Imprint of Wipf and Stock Publishers
199 W. 8th Ave., Suite 3
Eugene, OR 97401

www.wipfandstock.com

PAPERBACK ISBN 13: 978-1-62564-902-7
HARDCOVER ISBN 13: 978-1-4982-8531-5

Cataloging-in-Publication data:

Chung, Paul S., 1958–

Postcolonial public theology : faith, scientific rationality, and prophetic dialogue /
Paul S. Chung ; foreword by Lois Malcolm.

xviii + 234 p. ; 23 cm. —Includes bibliographical references and index.

ISBN: 978-1-62564-902-7 (paperback) | ISBN: 978-1-4982-8531-5 (hardback)

1. Postcolonialism—Religious aspects—Christianity. 2. Postcolonial theology.
3. Public theology. I. Malcolm, Lois, 1959–.

BT83.57 .C48 2016

Manufactured in the U.S.A.   02/01/2016

Dedicated to my family:
life companion, supporter, and strength, Jane,
and my daughters, Beth and Heidi

Contents

Foreword

I write this foreword having just returned from China. Thirty-three members of my extended family had attended the seventieth anniversary of the liberation of the Weihsien Internment Camp, where two thousand expatriates—including my mother's missionary family—were interned by the Japanese during the Second World War. As I read the proofs of Paul Chung's *Postcolonial Public Theology* while on the plane coming back to the United States, my mind was fresh with images not only of the camp and the no-longer-existing colonial world it represented but also of the myriad ways in which the Chinese cities we had visited during our trip—Beijing, Yantai, and Weifang—were now clearly being marked by the expansive forces of global capitalism and rapid technological innovation.

Reflecting on these images, I found myself drawing parallels between Chung's postcolonial proposal for public theology and Langdon Gilkey's account of his experience at Weihsien. Gilkey, a young English teacher during his internment, would later become a theology professor who—like Chung—would bring classic Reformation insights about creation, sin, and grace to bear on contemporary analyses of society and history. In addition, he would—again like Chung—attend to the relationship between science and religion, on the one hand, and interreligious and pluralist dialogue, on the other. However, Gilkey is probably best known for his book *Shantung Compound: The Story of Men and Women under Pressure* (1966), an account of how the prisoners at Weihsien had created a civil society of sorts within the internment camp. Addressing not only the indifference, injustice, prejudice, and even cruelty that can surface when people live together in such close quarters and extreme circumstances, *Shantung Compound* also discusses the resilience of the human spirit and the way the grace and forgiveness of God create a space for healthy relationships and a creative concern for the world around us and for our neighbors.

Like the internees in the Weihsien camp, we too face the question of how we will organize our lives together in a world that is rapidly becoming even more interconnected. And although the colonial world represented by the camp's motley group of expatriates no longer exists, it continues to affect our lives together, emerging in ever new "neo-colonial" and "post-colonial" permutations in which the powerful who have access to knowledge, power, wealth, and technological resources continue to exclude and take advantage of the weak and dispossessed.

Chung is uniquely equipped to address this world in which we find ourselves. A true cultural and intellectual hybrid, Chung has throughout his theological career consistently sought to bring together domains of theory and practice we often keep separate. Yet if his hybridity leads him to be a deeply *analogical* thinker who notes similarities across diverse worlds, then it also leads him to be incorrigibly *dialectical*, identifying points of dissonance and dissimilarity we tend to gloss over or ignore. True to form, his *Postcolonial Public Theology* sets in conversation European, American, and Asian voices from both the past and the present. Linking not only Christian theology, hermeneutics, and ethics, but also issues and themes related to scientific rationality and interreligious dialogue, Chung seeks throughout this book to articulate a truly "public" Christian theology in a world increasingly affected by economic globalization. Nonetheless, he does this from a distinctive "postcolonial" stance: grounded in the subversive memory of Jesus, he stands in solidarity with those who are victimized and marginalized by that world.

Chung's public theology has been deeply influenced by David Tracy, who was a colleague of Gilkey's at the University of Chicago Divinity School. Reinterpreting Christian symbols in relation to philosophical hermeneutics and critical social theory, Tracy's proposal for public theology seeks a mutually critical correlation of the Christian confession of faith and analyses of our contemporary situation; deeply analogical, it seeks similarities in difference even as it appropriates, critiques, and reconstructs worlds of meaning. Although Chung locates his proposal in relation to Tracy's public theology, he revises it by placing more emphasis on difference and dissimilarity. With his focus on what is "irregular" in our shared life together, Chung articulates a distinctive voice that brings together a confluence of Reformation and Asian themes.

At the heart of Chung's theology are two classic Reformation themes: the *viva vox evangelii* (the living voice of the gospel that embodies God's living discourse) and the *theologia crucis* (the theology of the cross). Nonetheless, Chung radicalizes and contextualizes these themes in relation to a Korean minjung theology rooted in Jesus' solidarity with the *massa perditionis*—the public sinners and tax collectors—which Chung also calls the *ochlos* (meaning "crowd" in Greek) or *minjung* (meaning "masses" in Korean). In his solidarity with the *ochlos-minjung*, Jesus not only suffers with others but also embodies—through his social relations and personal biography—the disclosure of the gospel of God's coming kingdom of justice and mercy in their midst. For Chung, Jesus is neither merely an exemplar for social change (as in some earlier versions of minjung theology) nor merely one whose vicarious death is expunged of its deeply prophetic and social-critical import (as in Kazoh Kitamori's theology of the cross). Rather, what Chung seeks to highlight is the way Jesus' embrace of all who are vulnerable, broken, and victimized discloses God's creative and reconciling discourse—precisely within the radical plurality of our social and natural worlds.

Emmanual Levinas' distinction between "saying" (living discourse) and "said" (written text) provides Chung with an important conceptual resource for depicting how God's infinite "saying" speaks through the "face" that discloses the otherness of the Other. If God's living Word in Jesus embraces and addresses all suffering, sin, and injustice with a creative and reconciling word, then it is possible to discern how this Word speaks a critical and emancipatory address from, through, and for those who have been victimized by history. In his interpretation of the fusion of multiple horizons that emerges when intra-textual biblical narratives are juxtaposed against the extra-biblical narratives of our social worlds, Chung seeks to incorporate an "irregular" moment into public theology. Focusing on the "irregular" that emerges in this fusion of horizons, Chung attempts an "archeological" rewriting of the "otherness" of the vulnerable, fragile, and victimized because it is precisely there, he argues—in Jesus' solidarity with the *massa perditionis* or *ochlos-minjung*—that we can perceive and anticipate God's just and merciful eschatology, the reign of God, in our midst. Thus, even though Chung appropriates Tracy's "analogical" approach to public theology, he revises it in terms of what he calls an "analectical" method that replaces the "logos" in the word "ana*logy*" with a "dia*lectics*" that seeks to bring to the fore the *dissimilarity* in the social discourse of those on the margins through whose "face" God continues to address.

In this way, Chung's "analectical" method incorporates into public theology a postcolonial archeological strategy that seeks to unearth the narratives of those marginalized by the double effects of the legacy of colonialism and the rapid expansion of economic globalization. Two thinkers aid him in developing this archeological strategy: Edward Said, who seeks to demystify Western representations of the "Orient" based on binary contrasts between the "superior" West and the "inferior" East, and Michel Foucault, who seeks to uncover the complex interplay of power and knowledge deeply embedded in religious, political, and cultural institutions.

Yet if Chung seeks to incorporate an irregular ("postcolonial") moment into public theology, then—true to his own analogical and dialectical method—he also seeks to incorporate a constructive ("public") moment into postcolonial discourse. Against Said, he argues that victims need not merely remain passive as they rewrite their history of suffering: their archeological rewriting of history can be done in a spirit of *metanoia* (repentance) and responsible agency grounded in God's creative justice and promise of new creation. Against Foucault, he argues that the critique of *parrhesia* (truth-telling) so identified with his approach need not merely be epistemic, solely rooted in the interplay of language, knowledge, and power: it can be rooted in a social ontology open to the irruption of God's kingdom in our midst. In this way, Chung seeks to develop a postcolonial public theology grounded in a theological humanism that attends to basic needs, distributive justice, and the integrity of life. Like William Schweiker, who also makes a case for theological humanism in our time, Chung seeks to counter both a post-modern *anti-humanism* that negates the human capacity to make claims about truth and justice and a modern *over-humanization* that fails to grasp, especially in the face of environmental degradation, the limits of human finitude.

Chung, therefore, takes very seriously the need to relate his postcolonial public theology to an account of scientific rationality. Unlike some liberation theologians, who have a primarily negative view of science and technology, Chung seeks to cultivate what he describes as a "transmodern"—as opposed to a "modern"—approach for developing an "integral" rationality that can enter into dialogue with science and technology even as it attends to the poor in both society and nature (what he calls the "new poor"). Such an integral rationality would address the limit questions raised by science and technological progress. These include, on the one hand, ethical questions that emerge in the face of such things as war, poverty, and environmental sustainability and, on the other hand, epistemological questions that emerge once we take seriously the social worlds of those who construct or are affected by scientific and technological development. Although Ted Peters does not explicitly address postcolonial discourse in his work, his proleptic theology provides Chung with a platform for cultivating such a transmodern and integral rationality. Deeply rooted in a Lutheran theology of promise, Peters develops an eschatological theology centered in the promise of new creation embodied in Jesus' life, death, and resurrection that establishes points of contact with contemporary science even as it seeks to establish the grounds for perceiving and creating a just and sustainable global community in our time.

Finally, Chung locates his proposal for a postcolonial public theology in the practical task of interreligious dialogue where representatives and practitioners of the world's major religions engage one another in conversation about the moral and ethical issues facing our shared world. In order to develop a conceptual framework for approaching this task, Chung rethinks Ernst Troeltsch's relativistic approach to the historical study of religions by critically revising it in view of Hans-Georg Gadamer's ontologically grounded hermeneutics and Jürgen Habermas' critical social theory. Such revision, Chung argues, enables public theology to shift away from a Eurocentric modern rationality that tends to presuppose, in Max Weber's words, the "disenchantment" of nature. Instead, this kind of interreligious dialogue can enable public theology to cultivate a "transmodern" rationality that can enable us to become more aware of our coexistence with other creatures and of our responsibility in that coexistence for sustaining the natural and social worlds in which we find ourselves. As an exemplification of the kind of "transmodern" rationality that can emerge from such dialogue, Chung discusses Christian and Buddhist approaches to economic justice and ecological sustainability, drawing on Dietrich Bonhoeffer's poems on the *theologia crucis* and Buddhist texts on compassion and wisdom.

Given this reframing of the practical task of public theology, Chung critically engages Max Stackhouse's framework for relating a biblical and theological vision of economic stewardship to the forces of economic globalization affecting our shared public life. Although Chung shares much of the theological vision that informs Stackhouse's public theology, he nonetheless seeks to sharpen its critique of global capitalism from a postcolonial perspective. Informed by Ulrich Duchrow's reflections on the church's responsibility to stand for economic justice in the face of economic globalization, Chung seeks to relate God's justifying grace to a prophetic *diakonia* that witnesses to God's economy (i.e., *oikonomia*, which entails both *oikos*, household, *and nomos*, law or management) in the midst of market forces that degrade human dignity and harm the natural world. In a similar vein, he turns in his epilogue to yet another major concern: ecological sustainability. Engaging Confucian and Christian sources he seeks to deepen our sense, from a Christian perspective, of God's presence as the *topos* of the world that sustains our commitment to ecological justice and the healing of creation.

Although we are not interned in a camp (like the prisoners of Weihsien), we nonetheless find ourselves in a world that is becoming increasingly interconnected. We cannot ignore the reality of economic globalization. We also cannot be oblivious to the ongoing effects of the history of colonialism, which are often intertwined with the effects of globalization on the most vulnerable in our world. Chung's proposal for a postcolonial public theology addresses these challenges in ways that neither simply acquiesce to market forces nor merely criticize them without inspiring repentance and responsible action. Saturated in the biblical witness to God's creative and reconciling Word in Jesus Christ and the new creation it ushers in amidst our suffering, sin, and injustice, Chung calls us to engage others—especially those with the least power—so that within the fecundity and fullness of God's pluriform creation we can together not only perceive God's merciful solidarity and creative justice in our midst but also embody it in the face of forces and powers that threaten human dignity and the integrity of our natural world.

Lois Malcolm
Luther Seminary
St. Paul, Minnesota
August 23, 2015

Acknowledgments

Postcolonial Public Theology is a study to shape a postcolonial approach to public theology. It incorporates scientific insights and prophetic dialogue, while contextualizing Western systematic theology, social ethics, and postmodern hermeneutics. The public sphere in the American context and others becomes more and more multiculturally fused and infiltrated by the dominion of Empire linked to economic globalization. After completing *Postcolonial Imagination: Archeological Hermeneutics and Comparative Religious Theology* (2014), I begin to realize how significant it is to elaborate a postcolonial shaping of rationality in interaction with the scientific theory of evolution and other scientific insights and postmodern holism.

Ted Peters provided valuable comments and guidance for me to incorporate discourse of theistic evolution in interaction with Darwinian evolutionary theory into shaping public scientific rationality in a postcolonial-hermeneutical frame of reference. I thank him for all he has done for me. I seek to advance interreligious dialogue in terms of prophetic dialogue in which inculturation, economic justice, and *diakonia* come into focus. Interreligious dialogue in the aftermath of colonialism requires an archeological reading strategy concerned with deciphering and recovering the prophetic side of religious classics to liberate them from the colonial discourse and scholarship imposed upon them.

This said, I express my gratitude to Ulrich Duchrow, who takes a groundbreaking approach to overcome limitations and setbacks of Western modernity and its neocolonialist economic discourse in terms of the integration of theology, economic justice in a global context, and interreligious study for the sake of a transmodern notion of the Second Axial Age. I also thank Craig L. Nessan for friendship and solidarity during both joyful and difficult times, always encouraging my theological creativity in postcolonial relief. I also appreciate Professor Lois Malcolm, who accompanies my theological journey by way of the foreword. I extend my gratitude to Charlie

Collier, editor at Wipf and Stock, who has accepted this book for publication under the Cascade imprint. I dedicate my book to Korean Lutheran Church and Holy Shepherd Lutheran Church, Orinda, California, which remain friendly, supportive, and encouraging to my vocation as a parish pastor and a public intellectual scholar.

I also would like to thank the editors of the journal Ching Feng for permission to reprint, in a modified form, the following article: Paul S. Chung, "Engaging Dietrich Bonhoeffer in Comparative Ethical Study," *Ching Feng*, n.s., 11.2 (2012) 123–44.

Regarding chapter 5, "Faith, Scientific Rationality, and Evolution," I extend gratitude to the Christian Study Centre on Chinese Religion and Culture, which allowed me to revise my chapter "Postcolonial Imagination, Scientific Rationality, and Evolution," in *Postcolonial Imagination: Archeological Hermeneutics and Comparative Religious Theology*, by Paul S. Chung.

Paul S. Chung
Berkeley, California,
Reformation Day, October 31, 2014

Abbreviations

BC   *The Book of Concord: The Confessions of the Evangelical Lutheran Church*. Minneapolis: Fortress, 2000.

LW   American edition of Luther's Works. Philadelphia and St. Louis, 1955–.

WABr   *D. Martin Luthers Werke: Briefwechsel*. 15 vols. Weimar, 1930–78.

WATr   *D. Martin Luthers Werke: Tischreden*. 6 vols. Weimar, 1912–21.

Introduction

This book will advance a threefold project in order to articulate a public theology for postcolonial people: Christian confession, the relationship between science and religion, and comparative religious study. In an attempt to integrate a postcolonial perspective with public theology, I undertake a hermeneutical-constructive endeavor to articulate public, religious, and cultural issues ensuing in the aftermath of colonialism. Colonialism marks the historical process for the West to systematically exclude the cultural uniqueness and value of the non-West. The aftermath of colonialism generates cultural hybridity grounded in the double relation between the colonial past and the postcolonial present. In the age of global capitalism, the public sphere is embedded with nationalism, social movement of global civil society, and the neocolonial reality of domination.

Public theology is a theological-philosophical endeavor to provide a broader frame of reference to facilitate the responsibility of the church and theological ethics for social, political, economic, and cultural issues. It investigates public issues, developing conceptual clarity and providing social-ethical guidance of religious conviction and response for them. The biblical notion of *oikonomia*, which implies the whole inhabited world, propels Christian theology to articulate its public dimension and ethical responsibility as it participates in social discourse of the political, economic structure of the world.

Seen in light of God's Future, a biblical notion of God's *oikonomia* helps us to renew a modernist reduction of religion, ethics, and moral values into the private, personal, and subjective sphere of life and to renew a public theology in terms of a social holistic view on politics, economics, and culture. Having said this, public theology is required to enforce a reformulation of forms of knowledge and social structure authorized by colonialism, because colonial legacies remain unquestioned until recently.

1

Public Theology in Postcolonial Reorientation

Public theology needs to incorporate a postcolonial critique and Christian eschatology of God's Future, combined with social sciences and natural scientific findings, in an ecumenical, global, interreligious, and pluralistic context.[1] Furthermore, public theology is conceptualized in terms of the correlation between Christian theology and philosophical reflection. Seen in the correlational revisionist frame of reference, eschatological theology of hope or prolepsis can be incorporated into a public theology that advocates critical social theory in the fashion of Jürgen Habermas in commitment to the struggle for social justice and agapeic love.[2]

For this task, David Tracy draws upon our anticipation of God's future kingdom of justice for our commitment to justice in the present. In the prophetic and apocalyptic hope, we commit ourselves to the reality of God's reign for the struggle for justice now. The radical self-sacrificial love is disclosed in the cross of the Crucified One, who expresses the gospel as agapeic gift, commanding us to live in radical equality with every human being.[3]

Public theology in this regard integrates scientific empirical data, critical social analyses of colonialist modernity, and ethical responsibility in protest to the colonization of lifeworld. The *postcolonial* continues to exist as an aftermath infiltrated into the life of the world, generated by the previous dominion of colonialism.

Such an integrative perspective is hermeneutically informed and practically driven in the reinterpretation of Christian symbols through a creative alliance between critical social theory and philosophical hermeneutics. It also seeks to make the arguments in society, the academy, and the church relevant to all rational people. Public theology is best conceptualized as a mutually critical correlation and dialogue that brings the interpretation and praxis of the Christian faith into conversation with the interpretation and praxis of the contemporary cultural situation and with non-theological disciplines.

Given this, public theology is characterized as fundamental, systematic, hermeneutical, and practical, taking seriously the language of analogical imagination. Interpretation, envisioned in the process of an ever new and ongoing process, allows the present horizon of the reader to be vexed, provoked, and challenged by the claim of the text, generating a surplus of

---

1. Stackhouse, *Public Theology and Political Economy*, 1–15.
2. Tracy, *Blessed Rage for Order*, 245.
3. Tracy, *Analogical Imagination*, 434–35.

meaning.[4] Interpretation mediates past with present and translates what is performed within the effective history of a tradition in order to retrieve meaning through a fusion of horizons. This perspective also facilitates critical distance from the ideologically distorted system of language or colonialist discourse and also from excessively privileged modernist reason. At the heart of an analogical imagination is our participatory act in the ongoing meaning event and self-distancing from the limitations of tradition and history through the self-constituting claim of critical reflection in a postcolonial direction. It also provides the profound similarities-in-difference in all reality of public discourses imbued with history, society, and culture. This repudiates the modernist notion of metanarrative, by resisting all homogenization of the difference of the colonized Other into binary opposites.

I find it helpful to advance a linguistic notion of analogical imagination based on the similarity-in-difference by which to articulate a postcolonial notion of hermeneutics with more emphasis on the difference or dissimilarity in terms of analectical method and social discourse. I coin the term "analectical" by replacing logos with dialectics for integration between analogy and social discourse, such that I cut through scholastic and hierarchical notions of analogy, with attention to social location and dissimilarity of language and discourse in the life of those on the margins, through whose face God continues to address.

Analectical Method, Eschatology, and Postcolonial Epistemology

Analectical method begins with the social discourse of the Other, discovering the analogical character of the Other. Theologically, *dabar* in a Hebrew manner qualifies the analogy to take an attitude of trust toward the Other. Emmanuel Levinas's distinction of the said from the saying is helpful for us to conceptualize God's saying through the world and in the otherness of the Other.[5] This strengthens postcolonial epistemology in repudiation of the post-Enlightenment metanarrative through the fashion of God's Infinite Saying through the face of the Other and the innocent victims in the natural and historical world. This characterizes analectical method in public ethical orientation toward God's act of speech in the life of those subalterized.

Furthermore, *dabar* means a speaking event in self-revelation (or self-showing) in relation to the God of promise, transcendence, hope, and future. God in the biblical context is defined in terms of the promise of the

---

4. Ibid., 105.

5. Levinas, *Otherwise than Being*, 6, 46–47.

eschatological kingdom of God, because God is a word of promise, hope, and indwelling with people on the promised new creation, a new Heaven and a new Earth (Rev 21:3; Isa 65:17–19).

Creation, seen in light of *dabar*, implies goodness and emancipation, which reflects the historical experience of Israel from the Babylonian captivity (Gen 1:1—2:4), in which the biblical narrative of creation in the Elohist fashion shows itself as emancipation from the Babylonian mythical power structure.[6] As an articulation of ontological dependence of the world upon God, *creatio ex nihilo* is historically mediated toward God's act of emancipation through the resurrection of Jesus, whose coming future inspires and awakens us to challenge the reality of powers and principalities in the present neocolonial reality.

The creation in the biblical context reflects an imperative toward respect for the integrity of life, regard for the enemy, and emancipation from sin (forgiveness of sin). It grounds our commitment to enhance life in distributive and restorative justice and responsible politics which transcends the logic of retribution. God's grace of reconciliation in Christ does not eradicate the right of the creation in the classic sense of the first function of the law, but bolsters it through God's act of speech to the reconciled world in anticipation of the coming of God's kingdom.

In the integrative metaphor of creation and reconciliation, it is important to take into account a proleptic theology in "provolutionary" character, which seeks to embody God's will for the consummate future proleptically in the present.[7] In the proleptic vision of God's Future, the human being as *imago Dei* is inseparably connected with Jesus Christ, because the human being becomes a new creature in Christ through the grace of justification and reconciliation. God's promise of new creatures in Christ, who is the prototype and ground of humanity as *imago Dei*, encourages us to develop a theological humanism in striving for justice, equality, and emancipation. This perspective counters the problem of overhumanization in the modernist project (causing ecological devastation) as well as the postmodern malnutrition of anti-humanism.

The metaphor of creation as grace implies that self and other exist under God's blessing for an account of abundance and fecundity. This is such that the pluralistic character of creation becomes manifest in Jesus's life and ministry engaged with the social discourse of *massa perditionis* (public sinners and tax collectors), analectically witnessing to the kingdom of God.

---

6. Küng, *Beginning of All Things*, 115.

7. Peters, *God—the World's Future*, 378–79.

Given this, it is substantial to consider the analectical horizon and discursive dimension of biblical language and symbols. Analogy is a language for talking about God, helping to eschew idolatry and upholding people's experience of God in a social, concrete way (Hos 12:10). Analogy in Jesus's language of the parables stands in his socio-biographical solidarity with *massa perditionis*, as explicit in his gospel about the coming kingdom of God. The analectical aspect in disclosure of the analogical discourse and social life of the Other recognizes that differences decipher a history for a privileging of the standpoint of history's forgotten and foreclosed Other. Jesus utilizes secular parables and discourses of those on the margins to bear witness to the in-breaking kingdom of God, entailing a protest of all forms of idolatry, religious self-justification, and absolutism. Analectical method considers the social discourse of the dissimilarity of the life of those who are vulnerable, fragile, and victimized through whose face God continues to address the church in our midst, awakening the church's responsibility for the Other. Jesus as the anticipatory-analectical embodiment of God's Future is the Lamb of God, a victimized scapegoat in the religious mechanism of self-justification and violence.[8] The church (or people) has an imperative to break through the inherited system of violence and sacrifice, just as the cross also annihilates it. We realize and anticipate God's eschatology in our midst through the life of Jesus in solidarity with the public sinners and tax collectors and his promise about his Future.

To develop a thick description of history and society in terms of similarity-in-difference, our current history and society, seen in light of *similarity*, must be comprehended in an archeological rewriting of the *dissimilarity* of the silenced and marginalized history. A postcolonial strategy of archaeology is an interpretation of history by unearthing the marginalized narratives of those victimized in the aftermath of colonialism.

The *postcolonial* describes a form of social critique addressing the unequal and uneven process of representation that is framed in Western scholarship and politics regarding the once-colonized countries. It does not direct our attention away from present inequalities and dominion in the global system of the Empire in matters of political, cultural, economic, and discursive structure. The umbrella term *postcolonial* signifies changes in power structures in the aftermath of colonialism, while unraveling the continuing effects of colonialism related to political rhetoric of self-justification and social cultural mechanism of scapegoating the Other and the different.

Given this, I use the term *postcolonial* as a critical and analytical epistemology that enables us to overcome limitations of the Western project of

---

8. Girard, *Things Hidden*, 159–64.

Enlightenment embedded within the nexus between knowledge and power,[9] while framing the public theology in terms of analectical method and social discourse in reference to the in-breaking reality of God's eschatology in the life of those subalterized.

Social Discourse and Archeological Hermeneutics

To present social discourse in connection with archeological hermeneutics, first of all, I pay attention to the reality of globalization, which causes a deterritorialization of culture, enabling a hybrid, relational complex embedded within cultures. Through the transnationalization of production the process of production is globalized, crossing over the barriers of nation-states. Challenging the distinction between the First and Third Worlds, it leads to multiple ethnic cultures in pluralistic society, thus creating hybridity in a networked world.

The global reality of the Empire affects and infiltrates public dimensions of religion and social cultural issues in an interconnected manner, generating the new imperial order that controls its subjects and creates a global imaginary and reality in the suppression of the subaltern. In confrontation with the Western discourse of Orientalism in its representation of the non-Western, postcolonial theory advances a methodology of refusal, deconstruction, and difference as it comes to the arguments about the truth that is entrapped with a colonialist discourse of representation, hegemony, and binary opposition between the colonizer and the colonized. A poignant question—"can the subaltern speak?"—is an attempt to create a larger space for the subaltern to speak for themselves.[10]

Along these lines, a new geography of Christianity is of polycentric character. Christianity became contextualized in a different direction from the Christian center of early Christianity, which was commingled with Greco-Roman civilization and then with Germanic traditions.[11] In a shift from Eurocentric historiography toward a polycentric historiography, a postcolonial public theology takes interest in archeological hermeneutics in deciphering and reinterpreting the forgotten and irregular side of church history to emphasize *metanoia* toward the kingdom of God. It also undertakes a creative dialogue with the past for the problem of the present and in projection of the future in light of God's eschatology.

9. Mongia, *Contemporary Postcolonial Theory*, 2.

10. See Westhelle, *After Heresy*.

11. González, *Changing Shape of Church History*, 12–16.

In matters of archeological hermeneutics, a social critical theory of language helps us better understand the mutual dependence of culture and language. Contextual issues, such as ethnic stratification, gender, race, social inequality, and political representation, are related to social judgments of language and language contacts. As social discourse, language can critique misrepresentations of the dominant group, characterizing an idea of postcolonial hermeneutics of intertextuality in historical effectiveness and social location, as well.

In inquiry of the global reality under the spell of Empire, a linguistic dimension of a postcolonial reality integrates a critical-dialectical notion of analogy with social discourse that is imbued with the power-knowledge interplay (social cultural formation) and with economic material formation (labor, capital, reification, and market).[12]

Postcolonial critical methodologies are delineated by interpolation, mimicry, archeology, magical realism, palimpsest, and re-presentation.[13] Notions of interpolation, archeology, and re-presentation retain a strong demand for rewriting and re-presenting the lost and buried history. This perspective helps us to correct the shortcomings of Edward Said's logic of Orientalism in his wholesale rejection of discourse of representation,[14] underlying a constructive horizon of postcolonial public theology. Postcolonial public theology entails a renewed interest in investigating history, culture, and traditional religious resources, because such an investigation does not necessarily mean nostalgia for the previously colonized past or as a self-Orientalizing exercise, as postcolonial deconstructionists argue.[15]

Postcolonial public theology assuming transformative ethical activity is future-oriented, sharpening its ethical direction in the spirit of *metanoia* from the wrongdoing in the past toward God's promised new activity in our midst. History is open for the God of promise to bring new saving activity through Jesus's prophetic anamnesis. This is retrospectively connected with God's activity of exodus and refers also to God's promised future of a new exodus, resurrection, and a new Heaven and a new Earth whose temple is the Lord God the Almighty and the Lamb in the shining glory of the Holy Spirit (Rev 21:22). God as the source of the whole of time has the promised new *topos* that inspires us to make the public sphere, life arrangements, and ecological world a better place in analectical and social praxis in anticipation of God's Future.

12. Chung, *Hermeneutical Theology*, 288.
13. Ibid., 48–59.
14. Said, *Orientalism*.
15. Nakashima Brock et al., *Off the Menu*, 16.

A notion of interpolation backs up Lamin Sanneh's model of mission as translation, which is an antidote to Western theological hegemony. At issue here is an articulation of the indigenous discovery of the Christian religion by critically uncovering the missionary-colonial gospel implanted in a previous era.[16] Indigenizing the faith calls for the decolonization of Western Christianity and theology toward the project of inculturation and emancipation. The metaphor "taking off one's shoes" is raised when approaching the cultural-religious place of the Other. Honoring the place of the Other as a holy place shows a new appreciation of others.[17]

Furthermore, archeology performed with a palimpsest is undertaken to unearth indigenous forms of culture buried by the colonial experience. A palimpsest is originally a piece of manuscript on which the previous entry has been rubbed out and replaced by another. No inscription is indelible. A place may be re-appropriated and given new meaning by the people who continue to live.[18] Through an archeological work, magical or extraordinary elements can be derived from the traditional past for the sake of making the present world better.

Hence, postcolonial hermeneutics is of an archeological-transformative character, entailing a substantial moment of decentering the centered narrative and knowledge-power system and critically analyzing economic material formation. This perspective renews Foucault's strategy of archeology in terms of a hermeneutical notion of preunderstanding, history of effect, and transformative praxis in orientation to God's Future. Foucault's archeology, which is unilaterally based on discursive statement as social *episteme*, needs to be clarified in connection with social ontology embedded with history, society, and praxis of a better life for the present in light of God's Future.

For this direction, Walter Benjamin remains an inspiration for the emancipatory project of engaging in the lost side of history with an emphasis on an archeological-anamnestic reasoning of not-forgetting the mass suffering of innocent victims.[19] A hermeneutical archeologist abides in a conviction for the spark of hope, because "*even the dead* will not be safe from the enemy if he wins. And this enemy has not ceased to be victorious."[20] In the history of the victors the historical process appears to be unitary. However, the vanquished cannot see the historical process in the

16. Sanneh, *Whose Religion Is Christianity?*, 10.

17. Bevans and Schroeder, *Constants in Context*, 259.

18. Ingleby, *Beyond Empire*, 54.

19. Ibid., 57.

20. Benjamin, *Illuminations*, 255.

same fashion, because their own affairs and struggles have been violently cancelled and erased from the collective memory. Given this, I sharpen an archeological-anamnestic reasoning in light of God's promised indwelling with God's people, the innocent victims from whose eyes God will wipe every tear. "Death will be no more; mourning and crying and pain will be no more, for the first things have passed away" (Rev 21:4).

This perspective corrects limitations of the psychological notion of mimicry, because it tends to suppress the politics of difference as hybridity in an emancipatory-prophetic relief. Postcolonial intellectuals refer to the politics of mimicry or hybridity uniformly regarding their relation to the First World, generating constitution of the world according to their self-image and justification. However, they are beneficiaries rather than victims in the context of global capitalism.[21]

Public Theology and Scientific Rationality

Faith seeks understanding. In other words, faith and understanding are driven and refined in a hermeneutical circle, which qualifies a scientific and critical investigation of the biblical narrative. This perspective is applied in the science-religion dialogue. A theology of nature engages with natural scientific findings and argument in a critical-constructive framework, while attending to the contribution of other religious perspectives on scientific and environmental issues. In such interaction, a classic epistemology, such as faith in search of understanding, can be pursued in a broader context embedded within science and religion. Public theology in this regard appreciates a model of interaction underlying the critical and revisionist relationship between science and theology, such that mutual questioning and enrichment can be undertaken for the sake of enhancing integrity of life in humanity and nature.[22]

The first stage of the scientific-technological project was engaging and fascinating. Then, wars have come in which science and technology revealed their unimaginable capacity for destruction. Nuclear, chemical, and biological weapons have become a great potential for apocalypse in the history of the world. We have to find alternatives to unlimited scientific-technological progress initiated since the Enlightenment project. It is certain that scientific rationality and discourse are shaped by their social, historical, political,

---

21. Arif Dirlik, "The Postcolonial Aura," in Mongia, *Contemporary Postcolonial Theory*, 304–5, 313.

22. Küng, *Beginning of All Things*, 41.

and cultural contexts, which interact with the biological ground of human rationality.

In the tradition of Galileo, Descartes, and Isaac Newton, the scientific conceptual framework pictured the world as a perfect machine governed by exact mathematical laws—thereby linked to values of competition, expansion, and domination generally associated with Western men.[23] In the political development of the theory of evolution, the name of Darwin is ideologically connected with the social Darwinism of Herbert Spencer and Francis Galton (the eugenics movement), who incorporated the "white man's burden" (Rudyard Kipling's phrase) into the developmental model of racism and colonialism. This fatal ramification found a historical climax in the unimaginable horrors of the Holocaust.[24]

Limit questions in scientific progress emerge in the face of poverty, hunger, armament, war, and ecological sustainability, suspicious of credulity in absolutizing science and technology. The limit questions cannot be answered by scientific method per se, because they transcend it. Correlated with science, religious questions arise at the horizons or limit situations of human experience. Two kinds of limit questions in science may be seen in ethical issues in the use of science for the integrity and enhancement of life in the aftermath of colonialism and also in epistemological conditions for the possibility of scientific inquiry.

Political independence has not brought economic emancipation and freedom to the previously colonized countries, such that these countries entail a right to speak out against the neocolonial reality in the aftermath of colonialism.

The recovery of the religious and mystical dimensions of political inspiration can be found in view of the crisis of the paradigm of modernity, which is spurred by the knowledge of domination for the sake of wealth by exploitation and colonialism. Religion has the voice of a consciousness and conscience in taking issue with scientific description of the world that sacralizes the established order of things. The religious-utopian project of liberation theology is to critically transcend the status quo for emancipation.[25]

Insofar as scientific research and facts arise out of an entire constellation of human perception, values, and interest, scientists are accountable for their research both at the intellectual level as well as the ethical level. All scientific concepts and theories are limited and approximate in dealing with the universe as a dynamic web of interrelationship, because the truth cannot

23. Capra, *Web of Life*, 10.
24. Peters and Hewlett, *Evolution from Creation*, 52–58.
25. Boff, *Ecology and Liberation*, 60.

be pursued in terms of a precise and literal correspondence between reality and description. Theological critical realists acknowledge the metaphorical dimension of human language in theological and scientific inquiries, assuming non-literal and referential correspondence of truth with reality. Models and theories of symbol system are taken seriously in a metaphorical sense.[26]

However, I am interested in breaking through such epistemology of critical realism by way of historical effectiveness and social discourse to avoid its representational way of thinking in the correspondence theory of truth. Scientific research and method are conducted in a social historical life connection, which shapes and influences the position of the researcher. Scientific knowledge is a historically constituted system that is imbued with institutional support and power structure in a social context. Socio-historical relations need to be considered in the production of a knowledge system to reinforce epistemological dynamism in interaction with scientific reasoning.

This perspective finds a postfoundational rationality helpful, which is driven by a fusion of epistemological and hermeneutical concern.[27] It facilitates a postcolonial approach to scientific rationality for the sake of an alternative transmodernity concerned with the life of the poor and nature (new poor), which upholds a postcolonial form of integral rationality in transcending the limitation of modernity. A notion of integral transmodernity seeks to de-center the subject as the epistemological foundation, in recognition of the social and contextual resources of shaping rationality. It challenges a totalizing metanarrative of scientism, based on representational knowledge, atomic individualism, and technical control and domination.

In Ian Barbour's project of theology of nature, some traditional doctrines need to be reformulated in light of current scientific advancement. Barbour endorses the process thought of Alfred North Whitehead (1861–1947) who extends the idea of interdependence into what may be called a social ecological view of reality. It implies a highly integrated and dynamic pattern of interdependent events in interaction with every event within a given context.[28] This train of thought finds parallel systems of thought which maintain that the living system emerges out of the interaction and relationship among the parts. In other words, it is comprehended only within the context of the larger whole, in the framework of the parts and the whole.[29]

---

26. Barbour, *Myths, Models, and Paradigms*, 38.

27. Van Huyssteen, *Shaping of Rationality*, 33.

28. Barbour, *Religion and Science*, 284–93.

29. Capra, *Web of Life*, 9–10.

But a question remains to whether God in process identifies Godself as a creative movement forward, but without a goal or a climax—thereby a lack of metaphysics of God's Future. The God of process theology fails to provide sufficient grounds for hope regarding God who raised Jesus from the dead.[30]

Ted Peters presents a notion of proleptic theology in terms of provolution creating advent shock. It seeks to project future visions of a just and sustainable global community and then uses present resources to actualize that vision for posterity. Our present reality proleptically anticipates the new creation yet to come from God's Future, grounding the liberation process of the oppressed and victims of injustice and poverty through faith in God's Future (Rev 21:1).[31]

Engaged in science-religion dialogue, we need to conceptualize public ethics for transformative activity in an endeavor to make the world a better place. We advocate for the Judeo-Christian notion of the promised new creation that has already occurred ahead of time in the life, death, and resurrection of Jesus Christ, an embodiment of God's promised new creation. We must develop an ethically responsible project of internal solidarity and internal modernity to restrict the harm done by science and technology and to guarantee the dignity of people and ecological sustainability.

Science and technology are seen as forms of human capital accumulated over generations, therefore as essentially social and political in character. Consequently, they are the main weapons for upholding political dependence and ensuring economic dominance over nations and their populations.

This said, science and technology should be set within the triangle formed by the satisfaction of basic needs, distributive justice for society, and integrity of life. This perspective challenges the technological utopianism (the gospel of technocracy) of the ruling system, which purports to give everyone more than abundant food, housing, medical care, and leisure. Against this technological dream, a new paradigm in the context of liberation theology is proposed in the holistic, ecological, and spiritual framework.[32]

To be sure, the liberation perspective is future oriented in the transformation of the present system of structural violence. However, focusing excessively on mysticism and the environment tends to romanticize nature, disparaging science and technology, refusing to analyze the potential of science and technology to move us toward overcoming environmental threats.

30. Polkinghorne, *Faith of a Physicist*, 68.

31. Peters, *God—the World's Future*, 388–89.

32. Boff, *Ecology and Liberation*, 76.

Third-world liberation theologies, for the most part driven by a deep ecological movement, tend to conflate science with technology, which is condemned as the weapon for destroying the environment as well as exploiting
the third world.

Cutting through such antipathy, it is important to adopt a critical constructive approach to the roles of science and technology, placing them in
the service of social, political, and ecological action for the sake of God's Shalom and life-enhancing emancipation. This perspective aims at overcoming
divisions due to race, ethnicity, gender, nation, or any other divisive identity
caused by the legacies of colonialism, pursuing a harmony between civilization and the ecosphere. Such a vision postulates an alternative modernity
as integral transmodernity for the good of all humanity and ecological life
in an enhanced awareness of a common destiny and benefit. This seeks to
transcend the global reality of binary opposition, constructing the present
and future better in analectical accordance with God's reign on earth. Theological visions of the future new creation based upon God's promise and
reconciliation contribute to postcolonial imagination in overcoming the
reality of binary contradiction in terms of an integral transmodernity, in
collaboration with science and technology for peace, social justice, political
freedom, and a sustainable ecological web of life. Thus, postcolonial public
theology is driven by the endless approximation of the second petition of
the Lord's Prayer: "Thy will [the promised new creation] be done on earth
as it is in heaven."

Comparative Religious Study and
Prophetic Dialogue

Foucault's strategy of bio-power becomes a guiding principle for understanding political, cultural, and institutionalized discourse in the analysis
of the interplay between knowledge and power in the colonist discourse
of Orientalism. Said's Orientalism becomes the watershed of postcolonial
theory in an attempt to demystify the cultural representation of the Orient
which was undertaken by the Western authorities in the colonial period.
The orientalists have disregarded the views of those who they actually study,
imposing their own intellectual superiority and dominion over them. Associated with ideological and financial support for institutionalizing power
and dominion over the colonized, Western depiction of the Orient has
constructed an inferior world, a place of backwardness, irrationality, and
wildness, while the West is identified with the opposite characteristics—
progressive, rational, and civil.

However, Said's limitation lies in his excessive emphasis on the pas-
sivity of the colonized. He does not discuss the ways in which Indigenous
people of the East have constructed their critical response to colonialism in
interpretation of their own religious classics. When studying non-Western
religious, ethical, and philosophical materials, it is substantial to transcend
the limitations of Foucault's relativistic anti-representationalism tied to
Said's logic of Orientalism.[33]

As previously noted, the integrative model of creation and reconciliation, imbued with God's act of speech in light of God's Future, becomes a
theological metaphor advocating the comparative study of religions in the
framework of interreligious dialogue. A theological notion of pluralism,
oriented toward respecting and enhancing the integrity of life, receives its
impulse from creation in which God provides the bounty of life even to the
enemy and the ungrateful. Creation as a pluralistic reality is connected with
the concept of *creatio continua*, which refers to God's creative activity in
sustaining and enhancing life in creation. Seen in light of *creatio continua*,
creation is the world with which God is reconciled in Christ. God's act of
speech in the fashion of Infinite Saying assumes plural and multiple horizons in the reconciled world through the world of other religions.

Sociologists have studied religion as a central theoretical problem in
the understanding of social action, as they deal with the relation between
religion and other areas of social life, such as economics, politics, and social
class, including religious roles, organizations, and movement. Max Weber's
thesis on the influence of the Protestant ethic on modern society remains
a classic example of the relationship between religious factors and ethical
disposition and behavior.[34]

Comparative work in the field of religions has been much criticized
for the attempt to typify whole religious traditions, such as Christianity,
Buddhism, and Islam, and then to compare them with each other in broad
terms, which results in gross simplifications. Otherwise, such comparative
study has been undertaken in an apologetic manner.

Aware of these limitations, I seek a public religious theology in critical-constructive correlation of one religious tradition with another religion.
Public religious theology is undertaken as a normative, constructive, and
revisionist procedure, while appreciating the methods of comparison, the
findings, and results emerging out of the philosophical and sociological
study of religion. A revisionist and constructive procedure facilitates a viable lens for the public religious theology to develop a reading strategy in

---

33. King, *Orientalism and Religion*, 95.
34. Weber, *The Protestant Ethic and the Spirit of Capitalism*.

interpreting the meaning and truth claims of one tradition in critical cor-relation with other religious traditions and their text resources.[35]

For this task, I find it important to critically explore and revise Ernst Troeltsch's insight into the historical-critical approach and the study of re-ligions for public religious theology. It is significant to utilize the history of religions methods to comprehend the holistic webs of belief and practice in rich historical and cultural context. More than that, I am interested in incorporating the hermeneutical-dialogical approach, which uses intercul-tural moral theorizing and praxis involving the quest for cross-cultural un-derstanding and the fusion of diverse moral and religious horizons.[36] This perspective critically revises Troeltsch's triadic method based on analogy, critique, and correlation, incorporating its critical insight into public reli-gious theology in postcolonial relief.

In interreligious dialogue we observe that representatives of the world's major religious traditions have pursued dialogue about substantial moral is-sues of general concern to the peoples of the world. Interreligious dialogue offers to public religious theology a more persuasive rationale, agenda of issues, and practical orientation. By the same token, public religious theol-ogy offers to interreligious dialogue a number of critical tools and methods that could enhance the sophistication and effectiveness of its practical work.

A narrative approach undertakes comparative storytelling and com-parative spirituality. This is founded on the assumption that our understand-ing of good and evil is primarily shaped by the kind of story we tell. Ethical insights occur and are communicated within religious traditions through story, community biographies, and ritual rather than theory. We live in an interconnected world where people are often deeply shaped not only by their own traditions but also by those of others. For example, Gandhi's ethi-cal views were shaped not only by his own Hinduism but also by Tolstoy's writings on the Sermon on the Mount, and Martin Luther King Jr.'s ethical views were deeply shaped by Gandhi's insights into the *Bhagavad Gita*. A narrative approach advocates passing over into the religions and cultures of others in order to finally come back with new insight into one's own.[37]

A religious tradition, and also every human life, is more complex than one root metaphor: "Many metaphors are necessary and actually exist in a moral lexicon, while none alone exhausts the meaning of life and its worth."[38] This aspect provides a larger framework for undertaking a multidi-

35. Clooney, *New Comparative Theology*, x–xiii.

36. Twiss and Grelle, *Explorations in Global Ethics*, 1.

37. Fasching and deChant, *Comparative Religious Ethics*, 1–10.

38. Schweiker, *Theological Ethics and Global Dynamics*, 214.

mensional theological-ethical analysis and response to global dynamics for
public religious theology. This comparative religious perspective improves
on the inadequacy and poverty of ethics caused by the modern banishment
of religion from the public sphere.

Human existence is thoroughly historical or linguistically grounded in
the world. We can never escape our historical context, or lifeworld, because
of our *situatedness* in the world, tradition, and language. In a hermeneutical
conversation with the Other, we can anticipate experiencing a new meaning
that emerges, helping dialogue partners to understand their own traditions
better. In an encounter of different horizons a new meaning can be acquired,
so that interpretation is driven in an open-ended and dynamic manner.[39]

This perspective incorporates a historical-critical method and postcolonial theory of religion and moral teaching into hermeneutical epistemology underlying the practice of appreciation, deconstructive critique, and
reconstruction, which characterizes public religious theology. Interreligious
moral dialogue has a reasonably persuasive rationale and postcolonial
reasoning which calls the world to shared responsibility for the alleviation
of suffering and oppression. Thus, contextual-constructive interpretation
of Christian narrative and symbols remains a substantial task in shaping
postcolonial public theology within the framework of comparative religious
study and prophetic dialogue.

Given the postcolonial reframing of public theology, part I articulates
the impulses of Reformation theology for public theology by undertaking a
contextual-constructive interpretation of Martin Luther and Dietrich Bonhoeffer (Part I, chapters 1 and 2). I approach Luther and Bonhoffer through
the postcolonial lens, inter-religious dialogue, and public ethics. My theological and hermeneutical exploration of contemporary issues for Lutheran
theological inquiry finds its impetus in the reformation imperative of gospel
as the *viva vox evangelii*, the living voice of God. Reformation theology finds
its voice not with insular or pedantic approaches to other faiths. Rather it
emphasizes its confessional-prophetic contribution toward contemporary
issues through a fusion of horizons with religious, socioeconomic, and cultural others, deepening the universal dimension of the gospel.

Then chapter 3 explores Karl Barth's analogical theology and public witness regarding the theology-science dialogue, including his major
theological achievements such as theological-critical epistemology, divine
action, creation, and eschatology. Barth's hermeneutic cannot be separated
from Luther's notion of gospel as the *viva vox evangelii*. Barth's analogical
imagination finds a dialogue with the theory of critical realism, such that I

39. Gadamer, *Truth and Method*, 306–7.

shall look into the implication of Barth for natural science, divine action, and postcolonial theology.

Part II deals with postcolonial imagination, postmodernity, and recognition of the Other, critically examining the unfinished project of the Enlightenment. I seek postcolonial imagination in terms of postmodern constructive theory and the issue of inculturation tied to recognition of the Other. In so doing I pursue a postcolonial contour of rationality in the sense of integral transmodernity (chapter 4). Then we will pursue theological dialogue with scientific rationality in light of faith seeking understanding. An appraisal of the relationship between creation and evolution comes to focus, developing the hermeneutical dimension of the theology-science dialogue, which includes Buddhist perspectives on scientific rationality and ecology (chapter 5). Finally, I shall take Ted Peters' proleptic theology as the platform for advancing public theology in a postcolonial scientific frame of reference. The proleptic theology, framed within postmodern holism, shall be assessed in dialogue with public theology (chapter 6).

Part III is a study of dealing with public theology in the framework of comparative religious study and interreligious dialogue. Ernst Troeltsch shall be taken as an important example of a public theologian in regard to his historical critical inquiry and comparative religious study (chapter 7). Then we shall undertake a study of conceptualizing public religious theology from Buddhist-Christian dialogue, in which sociological study about religious ethos and economic justice is articulated and explored (chapter 8). Finally, Stackhouse's public theology and political economy will be critically examined for the sake of conceptualizing a biblical-prophetic notion of *diakonia* and economic justice in critically analyzing the reality of Empire. This study presents a postcolonial horizon of public theology in terms of interaction between prophetic *diakonia* and economic justice in the ecumenical and global context (chapter 9). The epilogue is an outline of what has been investigated and argued in the integration between postcolonial theory and public theology, clarifying and advancing what postcolonial public theology means in terms of confession, scientific rationality, and prophetic dialogue.

The Afterword is a reflection of articulating public theology in a social ecological frame of reference, undertaking comparative studies of Confucian moral ecology. This Afterword finds its interest in complementing the ecological horizon of public theology, which strengthens the study of postcolonial public theology.

PART I

Confession, Contextual Interpretation, and Public Issues

1

Martin Luther

Contextualization and Public Witness

This chapter undertakes a contextual and constructive interpretation of
Martin Luther's theology in reference to an East Asian reading of him
in order to radicalize his insights into public issues such as social justice
and political responsibility in the aftermath of colonialism. This perspective
entails a hermeneutical endeavor, bringing his theological insights more
meaningfully into dialogue with Asian contextual theologies, which take issue with the Western hegemonic model of self-interested individualism and
dominion embedded within the interplay between knowledge, power, and
discourse. Hence, this chapter seeks a hermeneutical and practical retrieval
of the prophetic potential of Reformation theology to set forth on radical,
new, and alternative possibilities of liberation, life for all creation in fullness,
and recognition of people of other cultures and faiths.

I begin with a critical analysis of the Japanese colonial interpretation
of Luther's theology of the cross (Kazoh Kitamori). The generalizing term
"Asian" was embedded within the Japanese colonial context. This colonial
character of "Asian" continued to shape the Japanese imperial understanding of God's pain, referencing Reformation theology. Challenging Kitamori's
imperial reading of Luther, I introduce a prophetic interreligious reading of
Luther and Buddhism in terms of the reality of the suffering of the subal-
tern/*minjung* in their political cultural context.

Furthermore, I interpret Luther's reflection on the triune God as the
source of life and emancipation, facilitating his hermeneutical-prophetic
direction in a way that is meaningful and amenable to the issues of public

witness, inculturation, and integrity of life. Thus I seek further to revive Luther's great contribution to the hermeneutics of the gospel in the sense of *viva vox evangelii*, which accords to the Hebrew manner of *dabar* in the sense of God's act of speech. Driven by the prophetic configuration of the living and emancipating word of God, it is substantial for me to reinterpret Luther's position and his public theology regarding political responsibility, economic justice, the integrity of creation, and the church's mission. This perspective, framed within a postcolonial orientation, covers new terrain in advancing the future of Luther's Reformation theology in the East Asian context.

Luther and God's Pain in Japanese Colonial Context

In a study of Christian theology in Asia,[1] we observe that the churches in Asia have attempted to maintain their identity and integrity by articulating their own theologies. The terms "Asian," "Asian sense," or "Asian method" highlight the context, relevance, characteristics, and orientation of Asian theological works. A genealogical and archeological study of the unifying term "Asian" reveals its political and colonial usage within the context of Japan's nationalism and colonialism.

The Japanese colonial discourse of "Asian" might be traced to a Japanese imperial theology and its reference to Japanese life in a post-Hiroshima context. The first attempt to read Luther in this imperial direction was undertaken in a Japanese cultural context. Hence, I critically examine Kitamori's seminal book, *The Theology of the Pain of God*.[2]

In the wake of World War II, Kitamori (1916–98) explored the suffering of God in terms of a traditional Japanese *kabuki* drama. The traditional and imperial *kabuki* drama is often shunned by those today who want to break away from Japan's reprehensible colonial past. However, Kitamori utilizes Japanese cultural terms such as *tsurasa* (vicarious suffering) in order to propose a theology of the cross. Given Luther's metaphor of "death against death" on the cross, Kitamori unfolds his theology in terms of "pain against pain." A notion of "God in pain" comes to the foreground in the sense that God embraces those who do not deserve to be embraced.[3]

---

1. Kim, *Christian Theology in Asia*, xi–xii.
2. Kitamori, *Theology of the Pain of God* .
3. Ibid., 27.

Kitamori's theology of the cross takes the way of analogy in light of pain, that is, *analogia doloris*,[4] incorporating the Japanese word *tsurasa* into the wounded heart of God.[5] Silence in God's mystery and *tsurasa* are the guiding metaphors for underscoring Kitamori's theological project, featuring God as the One who loves the unlovable through the sacrifice of Christ.

Commenting on Kitamori's theology, Kosuke Koyama has shown that "embracing and enduring *tsurasa* becomes an intercultural correspondence to Luther's concept of 'God fighting with God.'"[6] Kitamori utilizes *tsurasa*, re-rooting the Christian narrative of a theology of the cross in the Japanese cultural matrix.[7]

Certainly, Kitamori takes *deus absconditus* in Luther's thought as the theological epistemology in understanding God's pain, because the hidden God is the fundamental principle of Luther's theology from which the rest of Luther's thought emerges.[8] Emphasizing the hidden God enmeshed with God in pain, Kitamori maintains that God's eternal decision to deliver the Son to the world becomes a hermeneutical bedrock for proposing the analogy of pain, which is in contrast to the Catholic teaching of the analogy of being and the Barthian teaching of the analogy of faith.

Kitamori transforms Luther's teaching of justification into a mysticism of God's pain and silence in the fashion of the hidden God. In so doing, unfortunately, he expunges social-critical and prophetic dimensions of the grace of justification in matters pertaining to Japanese colonialism, its historical responsibility, and guilt. Kitamori sidesteps the human capacity to love and respect the righteousness and justice of *deus absconditus* only through *deus revelatus* (revealed God) in Jesus's *resignatio ad infernum* (descent into hell), thereby becoming the vicarious representative of those innocent victims. For Luther, Jesus Christ as a mirror of the Father's heart is also the firstborn among many brothers and sisters. Jesus Christ as the exemplary prototype is in solidarity with the tormented, because he is the one who suffers injustice among victims of violence and the forsaken among the forsaken.

Kitamori's book was completed at the very height of the war. Writing during the war, Kitamori idealizes and even fetishizes the tragic suffering of the Japanese people, through which he perceives and comprehends the pain of God, while completely ignoring the innocent victims who suffered under

4. Ibid., 56.
5. Ibid., 138.
6. Koyama, *Waterbuffalo Theology*, 120.
7. Ibid., 115.
8. Kitamori, *Theology of the Pain of God*, 107.

Japanese colonial politics in other Asian countries. Kitamori completely eradicates the real victims of WWII, those suffering and murdered during the period of Japanese colonization. For instance, Japanese troops committed a series of atrocities in Nanjing during the Japanese war of aggression against China. The brutal slaughter of innocent people, together with the rape and destruction of that ancient and beautiful city, occurred over a period of six weeks between December 1937 and January 1938. The God in the pain of the Japanese people remains questionable and even dangerous, because this God is mute and elusive with regard to the outcry of the real victims of the brutality of World War II.

God's Solidarity with *Minjung*

A Japanese colonial reading of God's pain has faced a radical challenge from *minjung* theology, which refines a theology of the cross in terms of Jesus's socio-biography in deep solidarity with the marginalized, oppressed, and outcast. *Minjung* theology entails a strong critique of Japanese ideology, which emulated Western civilization in terms of colonialism, scholarship, and hegemony. A *minjung* theological reading of God's pain emphasizes Jesus's life connection with the *ochlos-minjung*, in which the gospel of the kingdom of God reinvigorates the *minjung*-subaltern as the subject of history. Here Bonhoeffer's insight into a theological epistemology from below remains crucial in the radical horizon of the gospel—that is, "from the perspective of the outcast, the suspects, the maltreated, the powerless, the oppressed, the reviled—in short, from the perspective of those who suffer."[9]

Minjung theology is a postcolonial-liberative project in the study of the *minjung*-subaltern, which seeks to uncover the globalization of cultures and histories with the structural violence of Western modernity ensuing in the aftermath of colonialism. It articulates the lingering effects of the colonial aftermath while archeologically reading the previous history of the innocent victim in order to remember the forgotten for our neocolonial present. A project of inculturation in this regard endeavors to appreciate the distinctive character of culture for a thick description of the gospel narrative in the context of World Christianity. It debunks a legitimatization of a racist, paternalistic, and neocolonial system embedded within the civilization of the West. Thus inculturation as a critical and creative process aims at discovering and advancing Christian values that are already inherent in a culture. It also holds the potential of emancipation from Westerncentrism, archeologically discovering God's ongoing work in Christ and the Spirit in

9. Bonhoeffer, *Letters and Papers from Prison*, 17.

a different culture. It enhances God's presence within the people, their culture, and history.

Challenging Kitamori's Japanese cultural-imperial reading of Luther, I have presented a prophetic, interreligious hermeneutic for radicalizing Luther's theological insights in dialogue with the Asian reality of *minjung* and Buddhist compassion through social engagement.[10] Faith, gratitude, and universal compassion in the Buddhist tradition do not stand in contradiction to Christian teaching. Rather, such a perspective needs to be appreciated and applied in any translation of Reformation teaching into East Asian language, culture, and religion. In a hermeneutical circle, the meaning of the living voice of the gospel is contextualized, while at the same time keeping a critical distance from past colonial limitations and current neocolonial mistakes. Life together with the Other, grounded in faithfulness to the living and emancipatory Word of God, has priority over an individualist ontology in our prophetic project of interpretation and discipleship for ethical solidarity with the Other.[11] This theological project is grounded in our anamnestic reasoning and subversive memory of Jesus, whose socio-biology for the gospel of the kingdom of God embraces his people, the *massa perditionis* (public sinners and tax collectors, thereby *ochlos-minjung*).

Advancing this postcolonial imagination, I now seek to radicalize Luther's theological insights to be more amenable to church and theology in East Asia on behalf of emancipation, inculturation, and fullness of life in creation.

Martin Luther: The Triune God and the Church

For Luther, God is eternally a glowing oven full of love, fully revealed in Jesus Christ, "a mirror of the Father's heart." Jesus opens to us "the most profound depths of his fatherly heart and his pure, unutterable love."[12] The triune God, revealed as the fountain of love, speaks in terms of God's strange work, law, and the gospel.

In contrast to the Greek *logos*, the word in the Christian tradition is pure event, because the Word became flesh. Creation once took place through the word of God, such that the miracle of language is explained in the un-Greek notion of the creation. In his exposition of John's Prologue, Luther argues that God is the Word speaking in, with, and to God's self. God speaks because God is the Word—a force of communication—enabling

10. Chung, *Martin Luther and Buddhism.*

11. Levinas, *Otherwise than Being*, 37–38.

12. Luther, Large Catechism, in *Book of Concord* (hereafter cited as *BC*), 439, 440.

communication within God's self and for the world. Luther conceived of God as the subject of divine speaking in promise, dialogue, and relation.[13]

This perspective characterizes God as the source of life, communication, and redemption, such that Trinity means a living, relational, and emancipatory God. God as the speaking subject upholds Luther's notion of the gospel in the sense of the living voice of God. God is living, effective, life-giving, prophetic, and redemptive in the gospel, since God's Trinitarian being is framed in the internal structure of speech-event in loving communion, that is, promise, dialogue, and participation.

The Word of God mediates God *in self* with God *for us* in the sense of *verbum relationis* (the relation of the word), which comprehends faith and the life of the world as linguistic, creational, and emancipatory. The triune God comes to us in historical time: God the Creator, God the Redeemer, God the Sanctifier in God's salvific-historical drama, because "the Father gives us all creation, Christ all his works, the Holy Spirit all his gifts."[14]

God's act of speech to the church and the world is inseparably connected with the power of the Holy Spirit, who was actually poured out upon all flesh at Pentecost. With the gift of speech, people of every nation can understand each other. God's self-bringing to speech captures language, that is, the essence of language. This language is rooted in God's word-in-deed, that is, the Greek translation of the Hebrew notion of *Dabar* into the *Logos*.

The church is sent into the world and exists for the sake of the world, because the church as the assembly of saints is created through the Word and the sacraments in the presence of the Holy Spirit. The Holy Spirit "effects faith where and when it pleases God in those who hear the gospel . . . not on account of our own merits but on account of Christ."[15] Luther characterizes the church as a mother, saying it "begets and bears every Christian through the Word of God." The Spirit illuminates and inflames our hearts.[16]

Hermeneutic of the Gospel and Interpretation

For Luther, the Holy Spirit plays a normative role in interpretation of the Scripture. There exists a dialectical and dialogical relationship between the character of the *verbum Dei* (as spoken word) and the character of writtenness in the presence of the Holy Spirit. Insofar as gospel as the living voice of God is sung and proclaimed as an oral cry, it is a voice resounding in all

13. LW 52:45–46.
14. Large Catechism, *BC* 440.
15. Augsburg Confession, art. V, *BC* 41.
16. Large Catechism, *BC* 436.

of the world, shouted and heard in all places through the proclamation of the Word of God. Luther's chief metaphor, "what promotes Christ," plays a hermeneutical principle in establishing dialogue with the world of the entire Scripture as well as the realm of creation. This is also the criterion in judging all Scriptures in terms of whether they are in agreement with what drives Christ.[17] Thus a concept of *viva vox evangelii* implies the priority of the spoken word (God's Saying; *Dabar* in Hebrew) over the written word (the Scripture).

According to Gerhard Ebeling, the *sola scriptura* in Luther's theology is nothing else but a hermeneutical principle, because it does not reduce the source of revelation. Scripture as *sui ipsius interpres* (interpreting itself) possesses *claritas*, which has illuminating power. A clarifying light shines from it and illuminates the tradition. Luther made a distinction between the unrestricted clarity of the *res* of Scripture and a partial obscurity of its *verba*. This perspective differentiates Luther's position from the orthodox confla-tion of Scripture and the word of God, without distinction. Little attention is given to the tension between the *verbum Dei* as spoken word and its written character in the orthodox teaching.[18]

A scientific-critical investigation of Scripture retains its validity in qualifying Reformation theology as hermeneutical, critical theology for effectively communicating the meaning of the biblical narrative to people in the world. In his introduction to the Psalter (1531), Luther further states that "there [in the whole Bible] you see into the heart of all the saints."[19] The humanity of the biblical authors and their limitations are not concealed, but actually uncovered and exposed to our exegetical investigation. The authors' historical character and the sociopolitical condition in Scripture were shaped and influenced by their lives and voices, which were embedded within the socioeconomic and historical circumstances. This perspective helps us comprehend that historically conditioned documents and social connections remain influential factors in exploring and interpreting Scrip-ture in a decisively political, prophetic, and socio-critical manner. Under-standing, therefore, assumes social and political agency in interpretation of the effective involvement of God's Word in the life of world.

In light of God's communicative action, it is worth noting that Lu-ther proposes in the Smalcald Articles that the "mutual colloquium and

17. "Preface to the Epistles of St. James and St. Jude," in Dillenberger, *Martin Luther*, 36.

18. Ebeling, "Word of God and Hermeneutics," in Robinson and Cobb, *New Her-meneutic*, 86 n. 15.

19. Gollwitzer, *Introduction to Protestant Theology*, 58.

consolation of brothers and sisters"[20] is the fifth form of the gospel, which is in reference to preaching, the sacrament, and the ecclesial office. Luther's understanding of the Word of God is richer and more profound than Karl Barth's understanding in his threefold sense of the Word of God.

God's Word, understood interpersonally, may retain an authority that is located in *mutual colloquium*. Luther adds the *consolation of brothers and sisters*, explaining it as a supplementary characteristic of God's Word. Thus Luther grounds his concept of the fifth form of the gospel in Matt 18:20: "For where two or three are gathered in my name, I am there among them." God is understood as the one who is involved in public and communicative life. "The LORD is witness between you and me forever. . . . The LORD shall be between me and you, and between my descendants and your descendants, forever" (1 Sam 20:23, 42). Luther therefore articulates the presence of God in the midst of God's people—Israel and the nations together (Zech 2:10–11; Ezek 43:7; Joel 2:27).

Accordingly, Luther's hermeneutical theology in a critical and prophetic relief is in accordance with Heb 1:1, according to which "God spoke to our ancestors in many and various ways by the prophets." The word of God in Jesus Christ is indispensably connected with God's act of speech, which was undertaken throughout all the ages in their plural horizons of effect. A Hebrew way of expression remains in force, because God's word is related to a real thing or action, transcending the question of ontology. God's being is in God's word-in-deed, that is, speaking is doing, so that the word is the deed.[21] *Dabar* entails a historical understanding of the word, implying that in which a thing shows itself, thus characterizing the basic structure of the word in terms of participation, communication, and dialogue.[22] Luther is convinced of the necessity of interpretation, because Scripture is not merely the written word belonging to the past. Rather, it is the *living* voice of God, which encounters us in our midst, here and now (Heb 4:12–13; 1 Cor 1:18; Isa 55:10, 11). Luther's creative engagement with the living and prophetic word of God can be undertaken over and against a normative and authoritative interpretation as previously established and placed over Scripture.

A notion of critical, contextual theology in this regard becomes indispensable, because the living word of God is not mechanically conveying or repeating certain words or statements from Scripture to people in different times and places. Considering human life, language, and culture in

---

20. Smalcald Articles, *BC* 319.

21. Marquardt, *Das christliche Bekenntnis zu Jesus*, 1, 141–45.

22. Ebeling, "Word of God and Hermeneutics," in Robinson and Cobb, *New Hermeneutic*, 103.

the translation of biblical narrative, we observe that even the same word can be said differently to another context. Luther is a clear inspiration for advancing the relationship between God's word and interpretation through a contextual-constructive translation (or inculturation) of the biblical narrative, which remains central to the theological project of World Christianity today.[23] Gospel tied to God's act of speech, is not reduced to cultural linguistic confinement, but remains the constant in shaping and guiding different translations of the biblical narrative in an open-ended manner. This perspective becomes arbiter in radicalizing Luther's insights, when it comes to political economic responsibility, the integrity of life in creation, and recognition of the people of other cultures and faiths.

Gospel in the Midst of Political Witness

Luther's view of the gospel in the midst of political witness entails critical and prophetic potentials in critiquing and renewing the problems of social structure. As Luther argues against the corruption of the powerful,

> The princes and "big shots" find it quite tolerable that the whole world should be criticized if only they themselves are exempted from this criticism. But they must certainly be criticized too, and anyone entrusted with the office of preaching owes it to them to point out where they act unjustly and do wrong, even if they protest that such criticism of rulers will lead to rebellion.[24]

Accordingly, the political realm belongs to the political *diakonia* in faithfulness to God in terms of *parrhesia* (telling the truth in an audacious manner). For the sake of the freedom of the gospel, Luther spoke out against those who sought to ideologically misuse his theology of justification for a theology of revolution.[25] However, for Luther, the justified becomes a collaborator with God, because faith alone justifies. Once justified, we enter the active life of loving toward the neighbors.[26] Faith is active in love seeking justice and prophetic *diakonia* in the public realm, because the grace becomes, indeed, impulse and motivation for praxis and transforming activity.

23. Sanneh, *Whose Religion Is Christianity?*

24. Cited in Duchrow, *Alternatives to Global Capitalism*, 7.

25. Although his discourse—"suffering, suffering, cross, cross is the Christian's right, no other"—was attacked during the Peasants' War (1524–25), Luther's radical critique of the state's violence must not be forgotten.

26. Gollwitzer, *Krummes Holz-aufrechter Gang*, 313.

The grace of justification, which entails the living Christ in union with us in Word and sacrament, makes the grace of justification and faith dynamically related to the service of the needy in the public sphere. Luther prophetically expresses eucharistic theology in connection with our anamnestic reason standing in solidarity with people who suffer.

> Here your heart must go out in love and learn that this is a sacrament of love. As love and support are given you, you in turn must render love and support to Christ in his needy ones. You must feel with sorrow all the dishonor done to Christ in his holy Word, all the misery of Christendom, all the unjust suffering of the innocent, with which the world is everywhere filled to overflowing. You must fight [resist], work, pray, and—if you cannot do more—have heartfelt sympathy.[27]

The grace of justification, which is grounded in the sacramental dimension of God's promise and righteousness, underpins the church's responsibility in coping with the unjust suffering of the innocent in terms of resistance, labor, prayer, and heartfelt sympathy. The celebration of the Eucharist reinvigorates the church's participation in God's mission standing in solidarity with the unjust suffering of the innocent, in whom the risen Christ is present. A critical, emancipatory theology finds validity in witness to the God of justice in connection with the dangerous and subversive memory of Jesus who is in deep solidarity with *ochlos-minjung* (Luke 4:18–19).

As articulated in Luther's commentary on the Magnificat (1520–21), Mary actually became impoverished and was completely wrapped up in poverty. Without any human help, God alone may do the work.[28] Mary as an example of the grace of justification shapes and underscores the church in terms of preferential service of the subaltern-*minjung*. She addresses a challenge of God's initiative against the patriarchal culture of the powerful, their hierarchical system, and institutionalized dominance.

Luther, in a letter to Friedrich (March 7, 1522), expressed his new discovery of political theology with a theological turn. "The spiritual tyranny has become weak. That is only what I regard with my writings. Now, I see that God drives further, insofar as God works in Jerusalem and two regiments. I have learned newly that not merely spiritual, but also worldly power must obey the Gospel. . . . It shows itself clearly in the story of the Bible."[29]

27. "The Blessed Sacrament of the Holy and True Body" (1519), in Lull, *Luther's Writings*, 247.

28. LW 21:328–29.

29. WABr 2.461.61.

God and Economic Justice

Moreover, Luther's view of the economic realm marks a promising field, as seen in his critique of the system and practice of early capitalism. Until 1525, Luther was preoccupied with the question of usury. Luther regards mammon as the chief example in opposition to God, fighting for the sake of the poor and needy against the system of "devouring capital," which dominated the social reality of early capitalism in his day. Luther argues that those who think they have God and everything they need (money and property)—without care for anyone else—have a mammon-god. They set their "whole heart" on money and property: "This," he says, "is the most common idol on earth."[30]

In the Old Testament, God's grace summons us to uphold corresponding action, because faith in the God of Torah is active and effective in love and service of our fellow humans as well as care for other creatures. Economy (*oikonomia*) is the law or the management of the household which compounds *oikos* (household) and *nomos* (law or management). Since our relationship to God is influenced by economic realities, unjust economic conditions have the power to ruin the true worship of God because worship of God is replaced by worship of mammon.

Luther's understanding of the Torah becomes a catalyst in appreciating the correlation between law and gospel for the sake of economic justice. His deliberation of the unity of the Word of God maintains that word and deed are one in God and the Hebrew word *dabar* is expressed as *verbum facere* (to do the Word). Torah in the Latin term *institutio* and *doctrina* (denoting command and promise) must be comprehended in the Jewish sense of the Bible as divine instruction rather than the translation of it as law.[31]

Torah contains law/gospel, command/promise, judgment/grace, identifying the unity of the Word of God in such correlation. The Torah is more comprehensive than the accusing law, since the word of covenant and the promise of salvation are the same as revealed in Jesus Christ.[32] Luther comprehends faith in accordance with the first commandment, which implies *Deum justificare* (giving God justice). When we act on faith in God's promise and accept God's forgiveness, we give God justice, the justification of God. In other words, God justifies human beings by grace and they

---

30. Large Catechism, *BC* 387.

31. Lapide, "Stimmen jüdischer Zeitgenossen zu Martin Luther," in Kremers, *Die Juden und Martin Luther*, 172.

32. In his *Table Talk*, Luther said, "The Hebrew drinks from the spring source, but the Greek from water that flows from the source. The Latin drinks from the puddles" (WATr 525).

acknowledge God's justice in terms of confession of their sins. In this mutual event both the sinner and God is given the right. The grace of justification is the promise of an all-inclusive setting to give right on God's part. It comes to terms with the eschatological horizon of the resurrection of the dead and the creation from nothing.[33]

In faithfulness to *dabar* as God's effective word, Luther's discovery of the Torah can facilitate our understanding of the law-gospel hermeneutic in a more dynamic, living, and prophetic manner, especially in matters of church's responsibility and the economic justice. For Luther, the Old Testament entails "certain promises and words of grace, by which the holy fathers and prophets under the law were kept, like us, in the faith of Christ."[34] Luther notices "the promises and pledges of God about Christ"[35] as the best thing in Moses, in whom there is a fine order, a joy about the gospel of Christ. Moses is a well of all wisdom and understanding.[36] Here is evangelical freedom or delight in appreciating and undertaking the gospel dimension of the law (*paranesis*), that is, an evangelically conceptualized notion of the law.[37]

According to Pannenberg, Reformation teaching of the forgiveness of sin encourages us to promote the will of God freely, such that we are not anxious to strive for works righteousness. Luther perceived the connection between forgiveness of sin and God's righteous demand, because the first commandment is the quintessence of gospel, not just law. Luther was able to find traces of the gospel in the Old Testament and of the law along with the gospel in the New Testament. Luther never developed a notion of the third use of the law for the regenerate unlike Melanchthon, Calvin, and in the Formula of Concord.

In confrontation with the antinomians, Luther suggests Paul's teaching of apostolic *paraclesis* on exposition of the new being in Christ. Apostolic direction must not be described as law, or comprehended as the necessary form of the gospel. But for Luther, apostolic paranesis or paraclesis finds its uniqueness as exposition of believer's fellowship with Christ (Rom 12:1–2; Gal 5:13; Phil 2:5).[38]

33. Iwand, *Righteousness of Faith*, 21. See Moltmann, *Theology of Hope*, 207.

34. "Preface to the Old Testament" (1523, revised 1545), in Lull and Russell, *Luther's Writings*, 114.

35. Luther, "How Christians Should Regard Moses," in ibid., 129.

36. Ibid., 121. During his stay in Coburg, Luther wrote his letter to Justus Jonas (June 30, 1530), stating that the Decalogue is the dialectic of the gospel and the gospel is the rhetoric of the Decalogue. Therefore we have, in Christ, all of Moses, but in Moses, not all of Christ. Luther became a new student of the Decalogue. WABr 5.409, 26–29.

37. Iwand, *Luthers Theologie*, 203–4. For Luther, the first root of all good lies in taking delight in the law of the Lord (Ps 1).

38. Pannenberg, *Systematic Theology*, 3:87–90.

Given this, Luther takes seriously the core of the Torah, the Decalogue, for Christian faith. Luther's theological axiom of God versus mammon is elaborated in his critical analysis of economic issues in the context of the seventh commandment of the Decalogue ("You are not to steal") as discussed in his Large Catechism (1529). Luther remains a prophetic voice for God's *oikonomia* versus the political reality of mammon. The economic reality, which is stamped by misusing the market in an arbitrary, defiant, and arrogant way, causes the poor to be defrauded every day, and new burdens and higher prices are imposed upon their life.[39]

Ulrich Duchrow makes a substantial contribution in maintaining that the economic arena is no longer simply an ethical problem for Luther, but becomes a confessional problem. Confession to God and resistance against mammon is grounded in the confessional notion of *status confessionis*.[40] Luther takes issue with mammon as a system of totality in which people want to be god of the whole world through mammon and to make themselves worshipped as such.[41] The concept of greed assumes a critical arbiter in Luther's theological thought, when the greed is in contradiction to faith and truth in God's promise. Luther's sharp critique of the devouring system of capital accumulation entails a prophetic voice against the Christian character of early capitalism in reference to colonialism in America.[42]

In the practice of usury, speculation, and hoarding, Luther was keenly aware of the irrational and dangerous aspects of early capitalism in his ability to see clearly the political-economic alliance between the Catholic Church, Charles V, and the Fuggers. This perspective becomes an inspiration for the church in East Asia to challenge powers and principalities generated under the colonization of economic globalization and its tenet of possessive individualism today.

In this light, it is important to critically review Max Weber's evaluation of Luther's theology of economic justice. For Weber, Luther's concept of vocation has been interpreted as indifference to the spirit of capitalism, because the society is regarded as already produced and sanctioned by the divine order of creation. Accordingly, Luther's attack upon the great merchants of his time was not biblically nor prophetically grounded. Rather Weber contends that Luther's critique of economic injustice is ironically claimed as a part of the spirit of capitalism in the sense of economic traditionalism. Thus Weber

39. Large Catechism, *BC* 417–18.

40. Formula of Concord, *BC* 516.

41. Duchrow, *Alternatives to Global Capitalism*, 176.

42. Marx, *Capital*, 1:649–50. Luther stands in parallel with Bartolomé de Las Casas's (1484–1566) prophetic stance against Spanish mission and colonialism.

continues to argue that Luther has a lack of ethical rationalism because he was not capable of maintaining a fundamental relationship of worldly activity with religious principle.[43]

Against Weber's misunderstanding, however, Luther himself considers the importance of economic life and justice in his theological deliberation of God and Torah, when it comes to the connection between the first commandment and the seventh commandment. Luther's prophetic stance against structures of mammon, which is grounded in God's justice and economic righteousness in the Old Testament, forms a substantial impulse for the church's responsibility for economic justice. Luther's stance for God versus mammon is biblically inspired, prophetically driven, and deeply embedded within an endeavor of creating fair and just life arrangements.[44]

God's Universal Reign and *Creatio Continua*

Luther's teaching of justification can be seen in connection with God's universal reign, which acknowledges the dignity of people outside the walls of Christianity. God the Creator works all in all. God's ongoing act in the new creation (*creatio continua*) implies divine power itself, preserving the creation and being present in its innermost and outermost aspects. God's ongoing act of new creation in the world points to Luther's insightful concept of God, notably emphasizing the first function of law in reference to the gospel and also sharpening our identity as created collaborators with God, as St. Paul teaches to the Corinthians (1 Cor 3:9). St. Paul, in front of the Areopagus, bears witness to *solus Christus*, expressing his conviction that everyone lives, moves, and has his or her being in the universal reign of God (Acts 17:22, 27–28).

For Luther, God is wholly incomprehensible and inaccessible, as St. Paul exclaims (Rom 11:33).[45] Divine majesty is reserved for God's self alone, since "God must therefore be left to himself in his own majesty."[46] This means that God works life, death, and all in all, keeping God's self free over all things. The hidden God, coupled with God's universal reign, works in the world through irregular grace. This God is God the Provider of life arrangements for enhancing the integrity of life in creation in terms of political responsibility, economic justice, and recognition of the Other.

43. Weber, *Protestant Ethic*, 85.

44. Chung, *Church and Ethical Responsibility*, 38–40.

45. Rupp and Watson, *Luther and Erasmus*, 330.

46. Ibid., 201.

Theology of the cross, seen in connection with theology of creation, finds its validity in upholding theology of life in solidarity with those who are fragile, victimized, and vulnerable. This perspective characterizes theology of the cross in terms of theology in the flesh, which embraces fullness of life in the realm of creation and humanity in holistic manner.

For Luther, a lively faith goes hand in hand with praise of God's beauty and glory in creation. All creatures are tools in the service of God's working, or masks (*larva Dei*) under which God hides God's activity. God remains free in the ceaseless activity with which God works all in all. The article of creation is that of faith. Faith in God's creation is faith in the triune God. Faith and justification correlate with ecological or environmental stewardship, which is indispensable for shaping and directing theology in a linguistic, creational, and emancipatory manner transcending the limitation of Western modernity.

Luther's marvelous sense of the aesthetic dimension of creation is striking, because "the wonderful and most lovely music [comes] from the harmony of the motions that are in the celestial spheres."[47] This is a beautiful text for theology and for the church in East Asia, which is committed to keeping the aesthetic sense of creation intact for ecological stewardship and eco-justice. We are encouraged to listen attentively to the beautiful music of God coming from creation because creation is conceived of as a linguistic and salvific phenomenon. God's work takes place in faithfulness even in the realm of creation. Creation is the sphere of dialogue and communication occurring between God and the creatures. Given that creation is the communicative sphere, the world is to be understood as a text that is readable and decipherable, through which God may speak to us in a manner completely different from that of the ecclesial sphere. This perspective finds validity in the East Asian sense of the web of life and nature in a harmonious and holistic unity, which is crucial in Buddhist, Confucian, and Taoist visions of human life as interconnected with other creatures and nature as a living organism.

Mission: Invitation and Dialogue

In Luther's day, Spanish Catholics, after Columbus's so-called discovery of America, undertook mission in the unfortunate fashion of colonialism. Some scholars in the area of missiology tend to sidestep the sociohistorical situation of Luther and charge that Luther lacked a fundamental affirmation of the missionary duty of the church. However, the missionary duty of

47. LW 1:126.

the church as they understand it, a church involved in global mission, was not current in Luther's time. Rather, it developed in tandem with colonial politics.

Luther's teaching of justification is accused of being a way of paralyzing any missionary effort, because it emphasizes God's initiative and is preoccupied with human depravity. This perspective undergirds a pessimistic view of humanity as "mere pawns on a chessboard." There is nothing humans can do to change reality or save people, because it would be blasphemy.[48]

However, as we carefully investigate Luther's insight into the gospel as the living voice of God, missional church, and its responsibility and openness for the world, it is difficult to accept such a critique. Luther's recognition of the others invites them to the gospel, while acknowledging that the non-Christian leads a morally mature life on the basis of the commands written upon all human hearts. Furthermore, Luther acknowledges in Abraham's faith journey that God becomes an advocate for Hagar and Ishmael. Luther's remark about Ishmael is striking at this point: "For the expulsion does not mean that Ishmael should be utterly excluded from the kingdom of God.... The descendants of Ishmael also joined the church of Abraham and became heirs of the promise, not by reason of a right, but because of irregular grace."[49] Luther's christological idea of grace does not stand in competition with God's embrace of the Other through irregular grace.

Bonhoeffer incorporates Luther's radical understanding of the gospel into his theology of the cross from below: "the curses of the godless sometimes sound better in God's ear than the alleluias of the pious."[50] In Luther's dictum: *crede in Christum et fac quod debes,* that is, believe in Christ and do what you must. In other words, sin boldly.[51] The biblical radicalism of Luther's teaching of justification takes seriously such blasphemies more than any other hymn of praise.

Luther paves a hermeneutical way of speaking of God with an all-embracing and inclusive force, while retaining a radical and particular direction. A dialectic between the exclusive tendency and an all-inclusive comprehensiveness enables Luther's language *sola* (alone) to be closely associated with the term *simul* (at the same time). *Sola* in the sense of biblical uniqueness cannot be comprehended adequately without connection to God's universal *simul* in biblical openness toward the world. Thus gospel in the sense of *viva vox evangelii,* more than proclamation, becomes a living

48. Bosch, *Transforming Mission,* 242.

49. LW 4:42–44.

50. Bonhoeffer, *Act and Being,* 160.

51. Peters, *Sin Boldly.*

dynamism in underlying communication and translation of biblical narrative through dialogue with the world.

Luther's teaching of justification, when seen in light of God's universal reign and irregular grace, has an inclusive dimension, which becomes obvious particularly in his commentary on 1 Tim 2:4. Here the exclusive proposition is expressed in universal terms because God causes all people to be saved.[52] Accordingly, Luther boldly appreciates pagan authority as a model to show the task of secular authority. Luther was not reluctant to praise the Turkish state and exercise a critique of Christian authorities with unprecedented frankness.[53] A gentle and rich Lord, God grants a great deal of gold, silver, riches, dominions, reason, wisdom, languages, and kingdoms to those outside Christian religion.

Luther warns against misleading people of other religions through a forced conversion to Christianity by means of colonialism and dominion.[54] Instead, mission can only be effective when it is performed by a continual renewal of the church and the Christian, excluding the human purposes of dominion, cultural imperialism, and confessional rivalry. As Luther says, "It is not said, therefore, that God desires to convert everyone. St. Paul only declares of the Gospel that it is a cry, which he causes to go out over everyone. It is supposed to be pure blessing."[55]

Comprehended in hermeneutical conversation between "what urges Christ" and the world of creation, the *primus usus* is the unalterable will of God, which is designated as the natural law innate in the human heart. This coincides with the Decalogue. It does not imply the possibility of a conflict between the *lex naturae* and the Decalogue.[56] The *primus usus* is relative to and not separated from proclamation of the gospel. According to Bonhoeffer, God alone distinguishes between the law and the gospel. Here the church is not deprived of the universality of its mission. Mission keeps in view its responsibility for the world in light of the signs of the times.[57]

Luther's model of two kingdoms or strategies needs to be reinterpreted as a foundation for God's mission in the direction of prophetic dialogue with people in the world of creation. Luther's linguistic renovation, embracing the church and creation in light of God's language-event, remains a

---

52. LW 28:260. His reflection on Jesus's descent into hell runs also in this direction.

53. Ebeling, *Luther*, 189.

54. Luther, *Church Comes from All Nations*, 104–5.

55. Ibid., 29. Lutheran confessional theology states that "conversion to God is the work of God the Holy Spirit alone." Formula of Concord, *BC* 561.

56. Bonhoeffer, *Ethics*, 305.

57. Ibid., 309, 311.

driving force for upholding our missional vocation as prophetic dialogue with the world, characterizing it in terms of proclamation, interpretation, and engagement with the life of the public sphere.

God speaking in dialogue, seen from a Trinitarian perspective, provides a new hermeneutical model of God's mission in terms of the grace of justification, justice, reconciliation, and recognition of the Other in the world of creation. God's being, according to Luther, is in proclamation, creating, and reconciliation. Here we witness the hermeneutical notion of the fusion of horizons between the meaning of the gospel and God's irregular voice through the Other for a thick description of the gospel as living and emancipating Word. This aspect undergirds our engagement with people of other faiths, acknowledging their wisdom, language, and spiritual relationship with the ultimate truth. Luther's linguistic renovation and its dialectic of particular-universal becomes a driving force for upholding our public witness as prophetic dialogue within a pluralistic world of many religions in support of interreligious solidarity for justice, peace, and integrity of life.

Word of God and Eschatology

Luther's eschatology is publicly involved, arguing that a prolepsis of Christ's resurrection encompasses the redemption and consummation of all creation with us (Rom 8:21).[58] Luther's eschatology expresses the future renewal of the entire world and its perfection as God's creation underlines the church's mandate of healing and renewing God's creatures and creation, as God's reign for the unredeemed world.

In his exposition of the second petition of the Lord's Prayer in the Large Catechism, justified Christians come into the kingdom of grace and become partakers of redemption. Thus they remain in God's kingdom which has begun. God's kingdom is coming in a twofold sense: First, it comes through the Word and faith in our present time. Second, it comes in eternity, through the final revelation of Jesus Christ. Eschatological dynamism linked to the grace of justification pervades through the Word and the power of the Holy Spirit until the final eradication of sin and death.[59]

Christian eschatology begins with the Word of God, which established a covenant with Israel and the grace of justification through Christ for all. The Christian hope of God's final coming is grounded in God's grace of justification through the resurrection and reconciliation of Jesus Christ. The genuine hope in the biblical sense comes from the Word of God which is

58. Althaus, *Theology of Martin Luther*, 424.

59. Luther, Small Catechism, *BC* 447.

a flower bud of Christian hope. Christian hope is to clarify and actualize what we receive as a gift of God through Jesus Christ alongside the path of faith. God gives a sign of eternal life to our present life through word and sacrament. The biblical witness of the "presentative" eschatology of God in Jesus Christ retains its reality from the eschatological coming of God ("God will be all in all"). Conversely, our language of eschatology can be actualized and concretized in the framework of "presentative" eschatology, which has begun in Christ in reference to God's ongoing activity in the world of creation. The two forms of eschatology (presentative and future eschatological coming) are mutually attested in the biblical context.

In understanding Luther's theology of justification (*simul peccator et justus*), the issue involves the proclamation of the new existence, so that God's grace integrates the human existence into the future of God. Luther's theology of justification should be understood as a theology of God's Future in a proleptic sense. God's *promissio* comes to us in the gospel of Jesus Christ in the sense of *viva vox evangelii*, that is, at the heart of presentative eschatology in proleptic anticipation of God's final Future. This eschatological dimension impels the church to participate in God's ongoing work in the reconciled but unredeemed world, driven by hope in expectation of the coming of God's kingdom of glory while remaining *extra nos*. For Luther "God's kingdom comes on its own without prayer, but we ask in this prayer that it may also come to us."[60]

Luther was aware of the hope in the New Testament for the future renewal, restoring it to the medieval church. Luther's eschatology is not a worldless eschatology, but it includes all creation in anticipation of the future renewal of the entire world.[61] This perspective entails a dimension of place renewal in light of God's coming future. The gospel in the form of the kingdom of grace may be properly preached throughout the world and then it may also be received in faith and may work and dwell in us, so that God's kingdom may pervade among us through the word and the power of the Holy Spirit.[62]

An eschatological reframing of theology of justification paves the way toward undergirding public theology as prophetic theology on behalf of God's shalom, distributive, restorative justice, and a theology of hope in connection with life integrity.

---

60. Luther, Small Catechism, *BC* 356.
61. Althaus, *Theology of Martin Luther*, 424.
62. Luther, Large Catechism, *BC* 447.

Conclusion

In the study of Martin Luther and Reformation theology in an East Asian perspective, we have sought to reframe his insight into God as the Source of Life for postcolonial direction, that is, underscoring solidarity with those who are fragile, vulnerable, and victimized in our midst. In so doing, we cut through a Japanese imperial reading of Luther's theology of the cross, deepening Luther's recognition of the Other in a contextual and constructive framework underlying inculturation, emancipation, and integrity of life. I conclude the East Asian interpretation of Luther by summarizing arguments for the future of Reformation theology as expressed in this chapter.

First, the Christian confession of Jesus Christ in the tradition of Reformation theology emphasizes the Son of God as the eternal and incarnate Word as standing at the borderline between Israel and all nations, identifying himself with the lowest of the low among his brothers and sisters (Matt 25:31). This is characteristic of our understanding of the triune God as the Source of life and emancipation in solidarity with and recognition of the subalterized for the kingdom of God has come in Jesus Christ.

Second, Luther's theology of justification needs to be extended and renewed in different times and places, especially in light of Luther's congenial notion of the gospel as the living voice of God. God as the Subject of speaking encourages us to acknowledge and respect the world of creation in which God continues to work and address. The Reformation teaching of justification should break through its encapsulation within Western possessive individualism under the colonization of the Empire; rather it should be reclaimed as way of expressing God's deep compassion in the death of Jesus Christ for all, reinforcing interreligious dialogue.

Third, a postcolonial reading of Reformation theology in an East Asian context advances a project of inculturation in order to underpin interreligious dialogue, adopting a new departure in critique of imperialization of Reformation theology or misuse of its scholarship in the service of the powerful in the ecclesial context of East Asia. In dialogue with Reformation theology, a theological project of inculturation entails prophetic-hermeneutical reasoning in revealing and clarifying emancipatory and constructive values inherent in Asian religions and cultures. It archeologically focuses on what has been subjugated and foreclosed in the study of cultures and religions regarding the irregular side of history, society, and church. It is undertaken in terms of anamnestic reasoning in dangerous and subversive remembrance upon Jesus's socio-biography with his people.

Fourth, theology of the cross, seen in light of theology of creation, can overcome a previous tainting imagery between the cross and crusade in the colonial time. This refers to a refurbishing of the theology of the cross for theology of life (resurrection) in the proleptic sense, which accentuates God's solidarity with the *minjung* and economic justice for all (theology in the flesh). This claims a postcolonial formation of *theologia crucis* in the form of presentative eschatology as a radical critique of any cultural blending with colonial or imperial direction, in light of God's coming future. Through the reformation notion of irregular grace, the goodness of creation is fulfilled and restored in God's grace of justification through divine reconciliation and solidarity with the innocent victim and wholeness (shalom) for all creation.

Fifth, the Lutheran insight into the living and emancipatory Word entails self-criticism and self-renewal for the project of inculturation, emancipation, and integrity of life in order to deepen its prophetic-contextual horizon for political responsibility, economic justice, web of life in creation, and recognition of the Other. Law-gospel hermeneutics should be comprehended as a Torah-Gospel correlation in which there is an evangelical delight in doing Torah in connection with prophetic words and economic justice for the world. This teaching can become a hermeneutical bedrock for articulating God's universal reign by sharpening *theologia crucis* in terms of dialogue, recognition, and collaboration with people in the world. This reinvigorates interreligious dialogue in a practical direction for emancipation, inculturation, and ecological sustainability. For instance, universal compassion, social engagement, economic justice, and ecological sustainability in the Buddhist tradition needs to be appreciated in any contextualization of Reformation teaching of justification and political economic responsibility and social-ecological engagement, especially in the critical project of second Axial Age for undergirding interreligious solidarity for just relations and just peace.[63] Through the process of interreligious dialogue, a fusion of horizon in a critical-emancipatory framework transpires for generating a new meaning of the gospel through faith which is active in love and seeks understanding and justice in the public realm and on the globe.

63. Duchrow and Hinkelammert, *Transcending Greedy Money*.

2

Dietrich Bonhoeffer

Postcolonial Reading and Contextualization

Introduction

There is a strong tendency in the most universalistic framework of early modern philosophers to deal with humanity in terms of a radical dichotomy between us and them, in other words, the dichotomy of civilization versus barbarism. Colonialism or imperialism was justified as educational, bringing the possibility of liberty to those without it. John Stuart Mill spent most of his adult life working for the East India Company. In his philosophy of freedom, Mill justifies despotism as a legitimate mode of government which deals with barbarians. British rule in India is good despotism, in Mill's terms.[1]

In contrast, Edward Said's *Orientalism*[2] unearths how such a dichotomy has dominated Western thought. Given the problems of the history of colonization in Asia, Walter Benjamin is an important mentor who denounces the perspective that sees history's countless victims as nothing but stepping stones along the path of development. Nothing that has ever happened in the past should be sidestepped as lost and forgotten for history and for us.[3] In the postcolonial study of the public dimension of religion it is important to refuse any tendency of homogenizing the Other in light of his/her status of no-history and under the logic of colonialism. In order to

1. McCarthy, *Race, Empire, and the Idea*, 168, 172, 180.
2. Said, *Orientalism*.
3. Benjamin, *Illuminations*, 246–47.

move toward a fusion of horizons by listening to the tradition of the other, a study of contextualization in intercultural exchange can serve as an arbiter in the dialogue between Christian theology and other traditions of religious ethics, notably in the hybrid postcolonial context.

Our life in the current phase of globalization is beset by worldwide cultural polycentrism and hybridity, which necessarily impact theological works and deconstruct the dominion of Western monocentrism. In the context of "global dynamics and world-making,"[4] a contextual, postcolonial, and intercultural reading of Bonhoeffer helps our endeavor to develop theological-ethical reasoning as a way of deploying public theology, which seeks to transcend a neocolonial reality through thoughtful scholarly discourse.

Postcolonial theorists propose a methodology of suspicion, refusal, and deconstruction, while critically analyzing any missionary presentation and argument of the truth trapped within a discourse of hegemony and dominion. They seek to overcome the structure of the legitimation of hegemony under Empire, and advocate a prophetic tradition of the Scriptures and other prophetic voices in religion and politics.[5]

The necessity of postcolonial theory is articulated in terms of reinterpretation and contextualization. A strategy of interpolation seeks to dismantle the cultural capital of the imperial system imposed upon the colonized. The postcolonial passion for rewriting or re-presenting history calls for a new hermeneutical strategy for deciphering and excavating the foreclosed side of history through an archeological methodology. This archeological quest has nothing to do with a nostalgic journey back to the colonized past, but recovers the liberative voice of indigenous cultures. This archeological perspective guides me to contextualize and deepen the prophetic legacy of Bonhoeffer in the postcolonial context of East Asia, reclaiming his legacy especially in connection with *minjung* theology and in dialogue with Confucian ethics and its humanist-cosmological world view.

Bonhoeffer in the Midst of *Minjung* Theology

Bonhoeffer's legacy became influential in the first model of *minjung* theology and literatures, which began in the 1980s in South Korea and continues in the second model of postcolonial *minjung* theology in its irregular-anamnestic fashion.[6] In the first model of *minjung* theology, Bonhoeffer's "minjung" experience in prison contextualizes his social experiential theology

4. Schweiker, *Theological Ethics and Global Dynamics*, 4–5.

5. Ingleby, *Beyond Empire*, 29.

6. Chung, *Constructing Irregular Theology*.

in South Korea. The *minjung* theology in the initial stage was developed in South Korea to challenge the aftermath of Japanese colonialism and military dictatorship allied with Japanese politics.

Han is a substantial metaphor for engaging the social existential mentality or collective feeling of the victimized for theological imagination. Theologians articulate *minjung* as innocent victim, taking issue with what the dark side of Japanese colonialism and industrialization under military dictatorship have brought to South Korea.

In the *minjung* theological exegesis of Mark's Gospel, an emphasis is placed on the term *ochlos* (public sinners and tax collectors—*minjung* as the *massa perditionis*), which is in contrast to *laos* or *goyim*. The word *ochlos* includes people of the land (*am ha'aretz*), without property.[7] The *minjung* can be also conceptualized as the mixed crowd (*erev rav*), who are allowed to join the exodus (Exod 12:37). Such a perspective expresses God's embrace of the Other in connection with a hermeneutics from below.

The correlation between hermeneutics from below and ethical commitment to the subaltern-*minjung* continues to unfold in the second model of *minjung* theology in a distinctive and differentiated manner, when it comes to God's act of speech, analectical method, and social discourse, and archeological re-writing of the otherness of those vulnerable, fragile, and victimized.[8]

The imperial theology of God's pain in the Japanese context[9] does not entail *metanoia* from the previous colonial atrocities, such as the Nanjing massacre, comfort women, crimes against humanity, and the like, undermining the real victims. Given the history of the innocent victims under colonial historiography, a postcolonial inquiry begins with an archeological reading of what has been unproblematized and subjugated, seeking to unearth the underside of history and society.

Given the standpoint of the below and the Other, I appreciate Bonhoeffer's *theologia crucis* in a nonreligious frame of reference, contextualizing its inspiration for postcolonial public theology. Bonhoeffer asks, "What does it mean when the proletarian says, in his world of distrust: 'Jesus was a good man'?" The discourse of the working class about Jesus as a good man

---

7. Ahn, Byung-Mu, "Jesus and Ochlos," in Chung et al., *Asian Contextual Theology*, 36–37.

8. Chung, "Dietrich Bonhoeffer Seen from Asian Minjung Theology." As a postcolonial public theologian, I support the second model of *minjung* theology, sharply challenging the epistemology of the first model, which is based on a messianic consciousness of *minjung*, cultural psychological reductionism, and relativization of Jesus as moral exemplar of liberation.

9. Kitamori, *Theology of the Pain of God*.

implies, for Bonhoeffer, more than the bourgeois saying that Jesus is God.[10]
A radical horizon of the gospel entails a politics of the gospel in protest
against bourgeois self-satisfaction, or "a convenient reversal of the gospel."[11]

Furthermore, Bonhoeffer's classic notion of *status confessionis* was expressed in his resistance against the so-called Aryan clause. The church asks
the state whether its actions are legitimate or in accordance with its own
character. Then, the church must help those who are victimized by state
action, regardless of who they are. Finally, the church should not just bind
up the wounds of the victims beneath the wheel but seize the wheel itself.[12]

The notion of *status confessionis* was later developed in the church's
confession of guilt in his theology of reconciliation. "The Church confesses
that she has witnessed in silence the spoliation and exploitation of the poor
and the enrichment and corruption of the strong."[13] Christians should show
a real sympathy through political responsibility, which springs from the liberating and redeeming love of Christ for all who suffer. Christians are called
to sympathy and action for those for whom Christ suffered.[14] Grounded in
the radical horizon of the gospel, this perspective upholds a postcolonial direction in terms of a hermeneutics from below and the Other, that is, "from
the perspective of the outcast, the suspects, the maltreated, the powerless,
the oppressed, the reviled—in short, from the perspective of those who
suffer."[15]

Public Theology: Reconciliation and the Other

Bonhoeffer challenges any attempt to draw lines between "us" and "them" in
light of God's reconciliation in Christ with the world, while summoning the
church's responsibility in the public realm. An ethic of reconciliation, which
is in solidarity with the Other, is ready to acknowledge other humanist
sources of religion in faithful moral integrity. Other serious religious people
may participate in God's reconciliation and contribute to God's shalom
and dignity for humanity. Therefore, it is imperative to engage Bonhoeffer's prophetic legacy in interfaith and intercultural dialogue, to unearth the
contributions of those forgotten through colonial domination.

10. Bonhoeffer, *Christ the Center*, 35.

11. Bonhoeffer, *Ethics*, 64.

12. Bonhoeffer, "The Church and the Jewish Question," in Bonhoeffer, *Berlin,
1932–1933*, 361–70.

13. Bonhoeffer, *Ethics*, 115.

14. Bonhoeffer, *Letters and Papers from Prison*, 17.

15. Ibid., 17.

For Bonhoeffer, the world-come-of-age cannot be properly understood apart from the perspective of the underside of history. Bonhoeffer provides a theological critique of modernity through a postcolonial inquiry into the life of the subaltern-*minjung*. In Bonheoffer's theology of reconciliation, the godlessness of the world is full of promise, paradoxically even in its stance against religion and the church.[16] The world-come-of-age is more godless, and perhaps for that very reason, Bonhoeffer argues, it is nearer to God.[17]

His understanding of Jesus and the church is clearly articulated: Jesus is given for others, so "the church is the church only when it exists for others."[18] Jesus's "being there for others" stands, in effect, for the masses. The church existing for others "should give away all its property to those in need," and "take the field against the vices of *hubris*, power-worship, envy, and humbug, as the roots of all evil."[19] When "for the other" is left behind, the church remains on the defensive, not taking risks for others.[20] Here, a notion of alterity, the dignity of the Other, may break into Bonhoeffer's discourse about God in Jesus Christ, under whose trace the Other stands. Under the divine trace, the others are "the weakest and most defenseless brothers and [sisters] of Jesus Christ."[21]

Bonhoeffer offers a particular nonreligious critique of the notion of the *deus ex machina*. This is literally "god from a machine," which, in the ancient Greek drama, means seeking a solution to a problem or crisis through the intervention of a god on a stage. In contrast, for Bonhoeffer, only the suffering God can help. He offers a critique of modernist notions of God according to onto-theo-logy, because "there is no God who 'is there.'"[22] God cannot be conceived according to an analogy of human ontology, but according to an analogy of relationship through God's initiative in Jesus Christ for us. God allows God's self to be driven out of the world onto the cross. We must live in the world as if there is no God.[23] Thus, "the Crucified, the man who lives out of the transcendent,"[24] lives as if there is no God.

---

16. Bonhoeffer, *Ethics*, 104.

17. Bonhoeffer, *Letters and Papers from Prison*, 362.

18. Ibid., 382.

19. Ibid., 383.

20. Ibid., 381.

21. Bonhoeffer, *Ethics*, 114.

22. Bonhoeffer, *Act and Being*, 115.

23. Bonhoeffer, *Letters and Papers from Prison*, 360.

24. Ibid., 382.

I therefore utilize Bonhoeffer's insight into reconciliation and the Other to undergird public theology in postcolonial relief. Bonhoeffer explores a creative way of translating and appropriating the biblical narrative in the cultural and political realms, hermeneutically mediating the biblical narrative with contextual integrity. Pubic theology can be comprehended in view of Bonhoeffer's insight into theology after Shoah, as driven in light of God's act of speech through the otherness of the Other in the reconciled world. Because God speaks through the otherness of the Other, it is essential for the church to engage in dialogue with traditions outside of its experience, to discover the ways that God is speaking through the religious tradition of the other.

The theological subject of reconciliation in Bonhoeffer's fashion fuels a prophetic correlation between "responsibility for" and "commitment to" those who are suffering, while also paving the way toward configuring an ethics of recognition in a multicultural society. This implies hermeneutical reorientation by postcolonial contextualization for the faith journey. Encounter with the Other, especially the Jewish community is inevitable for postcolonial (or post-Shoah) theology. For Bonhoeffer, "Western history is, by God's will, indissolubly linked with the people of Israel, not only genetically but also in a genuine uninterrupted encounter."[25]

Biblical Israel remains an inspiration for Bonhoeffer to trace the mystery of God in the experience of the Other. This can be a threshold toward unfolding a postcolonial hermeneutic, which aims at unearthing the suffering history of those who are buried under colonial hegemony and authority.

Investigating the deepest meaning and moral importance for the sake of the integrity of life and its enhancement therefore leads to the apprehension of a multidimensional theory of moral value in light of God's reconciliation in Christ with the world. Ethical themes, such as responsibility, freedom, and the integrity of life, cannot be deployed or reduced to any single metaphor. In promotion of the moral space of life, it is important to consider a pluralistic idea of freedom, responsibility, or integrity of life in rich religious traditions. When a theological notion of reconciliation encounters ethical and religious pluralism, it promotes many metaphors already existing in a moral lexicon. One form of thought or just one master metaphor should not exhaust or wear out many different metaphors. Public theology requires a range of metaphors about freedom, responsibility, and rectification and moral reasoning in the globalized world, and therefore insists upon the ethical contribution of diverse traditions to the reconciled world.[26]

25. Bonhoeffer, *Ethics*, 90.
26. Schweiker, *Theological Ethics and Global Dynamics*, 214.

Contextualization and Prophetic Dialogue

In Bonhoeffer's thought, there is a correlation between the gospel and the world, by taking seriously the Jewish "No" to Jesus Christ. Ethical maturity of humanistic atheism or moral wisdoms of other religions may find their place and dignity in hermeneutics of recognition, which discerns the mystery of the God of Israel under whose trace stand suffering people in the world. Thus, the Jewish "No" to Jesus Christ can be understood as the faithfulness of the Jews to the Torah,[27] which is central to Jesus's life (Mark 12:29–30, 34; cf. Deut 6:4–5). This perspective further establishes "a new hermeneutical culture: the culture of the recognition of others in their otherness."[28]

Furthermore, Bonhoeffer's dictum is pertinent: "God would rather hear the curses of the ungodly than the alleluia of the pious."[29] God listens and responds to the outcry of those fragile, vulnerable, and victims outside the walls of the Christian church, because Jesus exists for and in solidarity with them. *Theologia crucis* may be comprehended in relating God's act of speech to their life, outcry, and social discourse, in which the word of God in an analectical and social sense is materially embodied, transcending the scholastic-hierarchal sense of analogical language. God is in relation with humanity and the world in terms of *verbum relationis*.

The church keeps in view its responsibility for the world in light of the signs of the times. Thus the transcendental is not infinite and unattainable, because God's transcendence comes to us through the otherness of our neighbor within reach. The Crucified, therefore, the man for others, lives out of the transcendent within reach and under any given situation.

A reading of Bonhoeffer in this direction helps me to undertake dialogue with Confucian ethics of rectification and its humanist-cosmological orientation. As the voice of God is heard in the otherness of the Other, we must enter into authentic and thoughtful dialogue with religious others. In the *minjung* contextualization of Bonhoeffer it is essential to engage Bonhoeffer's ethics of reconciliation with Confucian ethics of rectification, therefore deepening the purpose of *viva vox evangelii* for a gospel of reconciliation in a diverse context. Our study shifts to engaging the challenges of *minjung* theology with the specific ethical contributions of Confucian humanism, listening carefully for the *viva vox evangelii* in the otherness of the Other.

27. Marquardt, *Theological Audacities*, 19, 29.

28. Metz, "1492—Through the Eyes of a European Theologian," in Metz and Moltmann, *Faith and the Future*, 70.

29. Bonhoeffer, *Ethics*, 104.

Confucian Ethics and Rectification

Currently, the Chinese government has adopted a market economy, remarkably changing the socialist critique of religion as an opiate of the people. Religion is rather appreciated as an instrument of mediating and consolidating the individual, community, and society.[30] Bonhoeffer's works find a renewed interest in Christian-Confucian dialogue in East Asia. In a recent study titled *Dietrich Bonhoeffer and Sino-Theology*,[31] Chinese scholars in Taiwan and Hong Kong have initiated a dialogue with Bonhoeffer, contextualizing his theology in a Confucian context.[32]

A retrieval of Confucian philosophy calls for a daunting hermeneutical task and praxis that aims at actualizing and contextualizing insightful observations about the Confucian living tradition and its modern relevance and renewal.[33] Confucians historically have generated a way of life profoundly concerned with all aspects of human life in terms of deeply shared cultural orientations, sensibilities, and achievements, which are still alive and influential today in personal, social and public life in China, South Korea, Japan, and Vietnam.[34]

No individual in history has so profoundly influenced the life and thought of the Chinese people as has Confucius (551–479 BCE). He shaped the Chinese mind and character as "a transmitter, teacher and creative interpreter of the ancient culture and literature."[35] The stages of Confucian evolution have demonstrated formation, adaptation, transformation, and renovation, undergoing creative and interpretive periods.[36]

The two terms *ren* ("goodness" in Waley's translation) and *li* ("ritual" in Waley's translation) are pivotal in characterizing the Confucian teaching. *Ren* is the highest virtue because it includes all the other virtues, while it does not lose its mysterious and cosmological quality. *Ren* as benevolence is deemed appropriate as the primary translation only from the time of Mencius.[37] A translation of *ren* as humanness may capture the element of religious, ethical aspiration for an ideal related with Heaven. *Li* (ritual/

---

30. Lin, *Ethical Reorientation for Christianity*, 23, 44.

31. Green and Tseng, *Dietrich Bonhoeffer and Sino-Theology*.

32. Tang Sui-Keung, "An Ethical Case of 'The Son Concealing the Misconduct of the Father,'" in Green and Tseng, *Dietrich Bonhoeffer and Sino-Theology*, 365–93.

33. Chung, *Hermeneutical Self and Ethical Difference*, 17–18.

34. Berthrong and Berthrong, *Confucianism*, 1–5.

35. De Bary and Bloom, *Sources of Chinese Tradition*, 15.

36. Yao, *Introduction to Confucianism*, 7–9.

37. Graham, *Disputers of the Tao*, 112–13.

propriety) is generalized as a way of relating to the world and fellow humans. All the while, it is expressed with the same ethical depth as *ren*.[38]

Confucius lamented that society and public life are out of joint. It was beset in a period of rapid growth demographically, economically, and militarily as well as being in the midst of political turmoil. Confucius criticized the reality of moral evil driving the rampant pursuit of wealth, power, fame, dominion, sensual passion, and greed.[39] His task was to set them right, rectifying reality in accordance with its name, which was later radicalized in Mencius's teaching of rectification.

Mencius (dates uncertain, but usually given as 390–310 BCE, or more likely 372–289 BCE)—in Chinese, Mengzi—took Confucius as his ideal, developing the Confucian doctrine in a religious ethical direction and with an idealistic flavor. His context, the period of the Warring States (475–221 BCE), imprinted its social and political conditions into his work. These conditions were much worse than in the time of Confucius. Mencius takes humanness and justice/righteousness as essential ingredients of true humanity. He develops his theory of four germinations, or beginnings, in terms of the four basic human feelings, or dispositions: commiseration, shame and dislike, deference and compliance, and right and wrong.

The feeling of commiseration, which is the transcendental ground for morality, implies the actualization of humanism. Insofar as human moral practices are driven by the universal condition of the feeling of commiseration, the four germinations refer to the distinctive uniqueness of human beings based on the universal yet transcendental morality in difference from other animals. This perspective supports humanism in the Confucian fashion.[40]

Furthermore, Mencius's self-cultivation based on the theory of four beginnings cannot be adequately comprehended apart from his ethical consideration of people's rights. In this light, Mencius provides an insight to overcome limitations of virtue ethics, while emphasizing an ethical relationship between the moral character and social life of the people on the margins.

Mencius advocates the rights of people by radicalizing the ethics of Confucius based on the rectification of names. For Mencius, the relationship between the ruler and the ruled is based on the cooperative division of labor in respect of Heaven's mandate. Heaven's mandate, though unfathomable

38. Confucius, *Analects* (Waley), 11.

39. Bellah, *Religion in Human Revolution*, 422.

40. Tang, "Interpreting Dietrich Bonhoeffer's Theology of Sociality through the Lens of Confucianism," in Frick, *Bonhoeffer and Interpretive Theory*, 145–46.

and incomprehensible, is known through the lives of people. As Mencius maintains, "the people are the most important element (in a state); the spirits of the land and grain . . . are secondary; and the sovereign is the least. Therefore to gain the peasantry is the way to become Emperor . . . ."[41]

Mencius maintains that the Confucian doctrine of the rectification of names is central in striking rebellious ministers and villainous sons with terror. Governmental office is the highest of all positions, filled by persons of the greatest virtue. The Emperor must follow the will of the people, because the mandate of Heaven comes through their face and voice. Mencius attacked the rapacious ruler who had brought the life of people to poverty-stricken misery, because *vox populi* is *vox dei*. "Heaven sees with the eyes of the people. Heaven hears with the ears of the people."[42]

Emphasizing the service of authority in the direction of serving the lives of people, Mencius states,

> Do not take away the time proper for the cultivation of a farm of one hundred acres, and its family of several mouths will not suffer from hunger. . . . There has never been a case of one who did not become a (real) king when (under his rule), persons of seventy wore silk and ate meat, and the common people suffered neither from hunger nor cold.[43]

By emphasizing the import of *vox populi*, Mencius' ethics becomes a fulcrum for upholding the rights of people. The Confucian ethic of rectification of names indicates there should be no blindly loyal relationship between the ruler and the officials. When the ruler violates and does not rectify the name as the benevolent ruler, tyrannicide becomes necessary.

The Confucian vision is social and communal such that Mencius provides a classic formulation: there should be affection between parent and child, rightness between ruler and minister, gender distinctions between husband and wife, an order of precedence between older and younger siblings, and trustworthiness between friends.[44]

Confucian ethics itself did not create a hierarchical system or patriarchy, rather it offers an important insight into the taking of people's lives and rights—the most important factors in a society.[45] Actually, the Mencian vi-

---

41. *Mencius* VIIb, 14; quoted in Fung, *History of Chinese Philosophy*, 1:113.

42. *Mencius* (Lau), 5A5, 144. See Bellah, *Religion in Human Evolution*, 464.

43. *Mencius*, Ia, 3, cited in Fung, *History of Chinese Philosophy*, 1:118.

44. *Mencius* 3A:4.

45. Bell, *Confucian Political Ethics*, 8. The so-called doctrine of the three bonds (concerning the relationship between the ruler/minister, father/son, and husband/wife) cannot be found in the Confucian classics. Rather, such doctrine was codified later in first-century CE Han texts, when Confucianism became the ideology of the imperial state.

sion of mutuality grounded on the teaching of rectification is best regarded as the authentic expression of Confucianism, further underscoring that correlation between *vox populi* and *vox dei* is the heart of the Mencian vision.

Given this, Weber contends that Mencius puts forth a charismatic leadership and that in his work people become representatives of God's mandate, which "leads to a revolutionary reevaluation of everything and a sovereign break with all traditional or rational norms."[46] Furthermore, Fung Yu-lan insists that Mencius's economic position retains democratic-socialist implications, giving the existing social system a new interpretation in the Confucian sense of transmitting.[47]

In Bellah's account, the hallmark of Confucian utopianism is based on the rule of virtue by ritual, moral example, and rectification in emphatic listening to the voice of the people in the public sphere. It replaces the rule of war and punishment by establishing and promoting peaceful unification in the world.[48] Certainly, Confucian scholars as public intellectuals have contributed to revitalizing the moral order, the communal spirit and purifying the ethos—for example, their commitment to social renewal and change through public duty and political engagement. Confucian insight in a living tradition becomes a dialogue partner for Christian religion in East Asia, as driven together in pursuit to articulate their common, but unique horizon and commitment to good society.

Interreligious Dialogue and Ethical Reorientation

Many Chinese Christians do not repudiate the Confucian moral teaching, but rather acknowledge the Confucian value. In the recent context, dialogue between New Confucianism and Christianity proceeds to expand horizons as both groups learn some of the other's values and incorporate wisdom and experience for mutual benefit and renewal. Confucianism's living tradition needs to be reinterpreted for our century to promote moral responsibility, transmission of moral values, and people-oriented democracy and to shape Confucian ethics as the ethics of rectification from below, that is, ethical reorientation toward solidarity and humanism. This perspective reinforces the Sino-Christian theological endeavor to promote ethical reorientation in terms of the Confucian contribution to social and moral construction,

---

46. Weber, "The Nature of Charismatic Domination," in Weber, *Max Weber: Selections*, 230.

47. Fung, *History of Chinese Philosophy*, 1:118–19.

48. Bellah, *Religion in Human Evolution*, 587, 476, 576.

especially in collaboration with Chinese collectivism for the individual-community-society relation.[49]

Through unfolding ethical reorientation in interreligious dialogue, I retrieve the marginalized domain of Bonhoeffer's thought in reference to the religious other. Certainly, Bonhoefer took an interest in Gandhi and the Buddhist world, an interest he showed in a letter written in February 1928. Gandhi's importance for Bonhoeffer lies in his interest in the origin of Christianity in the East. Bonhoeffer took interest in Gandhi's pacifistic method of nonviolent struggle. In another letter (May 22, 1934), Bonhoeffer argued that more Christianity exists in the world of the "heathens" than in the whole state church of Germany.[50] This said, Bonhoeffer's nonreligious inquiry must not be comprehended as an exclusive critique of other religions. Rather, it paradoxically paves a way toward interreligious exchange, which is grounded in the universal horizon of the gospel and reconciliation.

In the study of contextualization in the interreligious context, I have endeavored to advance Bonhoeffer's theology of reconciliation in encounter with Confucian ethics of rectification. In God's act of speech through the Other, human language acquires a new horizon of meaning in the event of encounter, argument, critique, and mutual learning. The hermeneutical self is driven in responsibility to God and in acknowledgement of the ethical difference of otherness. The theology of speech-event cannot be fully understood apart from God's reconciliation in which God's ongoing activity of speech and address can be heard in the social discourse and outcry in the life of margins.

A concept of archeological hermeneutics in this regard seeks to decipher and unravel the history for the margins and from them. This requires the hermeneutical audacity to reinterpret the traditional story or texts for engendering a new, fresh, extraordinary meaning for the sake of a fusion of horizons, which aims at reconstructing the project of the present in expectation of God's Future.

Given this, I seek to project Bonhoeffer's insight in my reading strategy of Mencius. Confucian ethics of rectification entails a social-ethical orientation toward the dignity of people's lives. An archeological inquiry challenges us to undertake a thick description by deeply reading the Confucian moral and philosophical assumptions underlying East Asian civilization laden with ethical, social-critical, and religious implications. Mencius' ethic of rectification remains an inspiration for undergirding a notion of Confucian democracy and social justice in opposition to political despotism, social

49. Lin, *Ethical Reorientation for Christianity*, 28–32.
50. Bethge, *Dietrich Bonhoeffer*, 138, 184, 379.

oppression, and violence, because the mandate or voice of Heaven can be heard and discerned in the life of downtrodden people, the most important factor of a society. Tao (mandate of Heaven) as speech-event in the sense of *vox populi* as *vox dei* continues to challenge the powerful in government and society to care for those who are fragile, vulnerable, and poverty-stricken.

It is important for public theology in postcolonial formation to analyze how a dominant social discourse has played a formative role in establishing and legitimizing the hidden relation between knowledge, information, power, labor and capital. This configuration facilitates a new reading of Confucian ethics of rectification in encounter with Bonhoeffer's prophetic-ethical insight into learning to see the great events of world history from the standpoint of those who are subalterized. It also incorporates Mencius's rectifying reasoning into the transformation of the social structure beset by mechanisms of injustice and violence.

Creation and Eco-justice in a Christian-Confucian Context

Confucianism cannot be properly understood apart from its anthropological-cosmic dimension embedded within the "unity of Heaven and humanity," which embraces Earth. The human is embedded in the naturalistic-cosmic process and order, because the unity of Heaven, Earth, and humanity is identified and affirmed in a comprehensive manner. The Confucian worldview, rooted in earth, body, family, and community, is not adjustment to the world or to the status quo. Rather, it is dictated by an ethic of responsibility and rectification informed and guided by the mandate of Heaven in connection with the right of people. For us as collaborators of Heaven, a cosmological decree or mandate is not merely ethically oriented, but also embodied in the web of life.

The famous "eight steps," as seen in the first chapter of the *Great Learning*, provide a holistic vision of Confucian self-cultivation for illuminating the illuminating virtue to all under Heaven through personal life, family, and the state. Then peace is under Heaven.[51] This holistic vision of a peaceful world based on self-cultivation includes the natural world and the larger cosmos. The human in the Confucian worldview is an active participant in the cosmic process, having the responsibility of care for life in the environment. Human participation in cosmic processes constitutes unity with Heaven and Earth, standing in solidarity and empathy with all living creatures. Confucian ethics promotes respect for the Earth and life in all its

51. Confucius, *Confucian Analects*, 356–57.

diversity, in care for the community of life with compassion and empathy and in commitment to securing present and future generations. Human beings emerge as an integral part of nature, coming out of the primordial forces of production and reproduction (yin and yang in an interplay of material elements), which generates mountains, rivers, and the whole of the planet. They occupy a distinctive place as moral beings in the evolutionary-cosmological drama.

For instance, Zhang Zai (1020–77), considered the father of Neo-Confucianism, was inspired by the *Book of Changes*. He articulated the cosmic-pneumatic vision of all lives in terms of *qi* for the sake of the unity of all creation. Qi as the source of the universe is both the Supreme Ultimate and the driving force of endless change; Zhang Zai argues that both yin and yang and the five elements as generative forces are basically expressions of material force (qi). The primordial qi without form (which is called the Great Void) contracted and consolidated to generate Heaven (yang) and Earth (yin). In the interaction between the qi of Heaven and the qi of Earth, different forms and things have come to existence. Unity of Heaven and Earth including humanity and the myriad things becomes the cosmological family. The principle is one but its manifestations are many (*Ji yi fenshu*). Every daily activity under Heaven and Earth is in unity with the principle of the universe.[52]

As Zhang Zai states,

> Heaven is my father and Earth is my mother, and even such a small creature as I finds an intimate place in their midst. That which fills the universe I regard as my body and that which directs the universe I consider as my nature. All people are my brothers and sisters, and all things are my companions.[53]

An eco-friendly ethics can be reformulated in a Confucian moral-cosmic worldview to support a more comprehensive global ethic for sustainable community, social justice, and peace. Humanity as an emergent part of a vast evolving universe is alive with a community of planetary life. We live in connection within an ever-emerging web of the fecundity and creativity of nature. Given the idea of the unity of Heaven and humanity embedded within inseparable dimensions of self, community, nature, and Heaven, a harmoniously sustainable relationship between the human species and nature provides a practical guide for nature, the role of humanity, and environmental ethics.[54]

52. Lin, *Ethical Reorientation for Christianity*, 92.

53. Chan, *Source Book in Chinese Philosophy*, 497.

54. Tucker and Berthrong, *Confucianism and Ecology*, xxxv–xxxviii.

Confucian humanism informed by an anthropological and cosmic vision may become a dialogue partner for Bonhoeffer's theology of creation and reconciliation. Bonhoeffer articulates an insight into the correlation between creation and reconciliation which can be comprehended in an evolutionary-ecological direction. Bonhoeffer's consistent orientation toward earth characterizes him as an ecological theologian who affirms Christian this-worldliness.[55]

For him, Jesus Christ is a cosmic Christ at the center of nature, humanity, and history. The cosmic Christ is the incarnate God who is crucified. The bodily way of Christ (bodiliness or corporeality) refers to the end of God's own way.[56] There is continuity between God and God's work through God's word, such that God's word as command relates God to what is created. This divine word is the spoken word, thereby, what it designates. God's word is in deed, because "with God the imperative is the indicative."[57]

Anyone who evades the earth does not find God. Anyone who loves God loves God as Lord of the earth. Bonhoeffer contends that Darwin and Feuerbach could not use stronger language than Genesis regarding the fact that we are a piece of earth. The human being is taken from God's earth.[58] It is not by the process of evolution, that is, by some cruel fate in the earthly world. But by way of God's command, humankind is summoned out of the earth, since God's living word and breath creates that which lives out of what is dead. God calls a mere piece of earth into human life.[59]

The earth becomes the mother of the living and God has handed over to living creatures the work of upholding and maintaining.[60] The power of the day makes the physical day into the natural dialectic of creation. The biblical thinking transcends the question whether the creation occurred in deep time, thereby rhythms of millions of years or in single days.[61] A notion of evolution may be incorporated into God's act of creation. The nature would provide for itself, and the fixed nature of law and the fecundity of living things entail the powers upholding the world together. Such rhythm and power in the planetary world is driven only in the freedom of God's word and steered in God's sustaining and upholding activity.[62]

---

55. Rasmussen, "Bonhoeffer: Ecological Theologian."

56. Bonhoeffer, *Creation and Fall*, 121.

57. Ibid., 42.

58. Ibid., 76.

59. Ibid., 77.

60. Ibid., 57–58.

61. Ibid., 49.

62. Ibid., 58.

A human being is body and soul. We must take seriously that our existence is in bond with mother earth.[63] People who reject their bodies reject their existence before God the Creator. Humanity is the image of God precisely in its bodily nature, in which human bodies are related to the earth and to other bodies in dependence upon each other.[64] A notion of *imago dei* refers to *imago relationis*, in social, biological relationship with others. But humankind as God's new, free work is placed in connection with the animal world, though it has nothing to do with the Darwinian notion of natural selection.[65] God allows us to be free for the Creator such that freedom takes place through the other. Being free means being-free-for-the-other. I am free only because I am bound to the other.[66]

In Michelangelo's painting of the creation in the Sistine Chapel, Bonhoeffer acknowledges that the human being in the deep sleep of creation experiences life through the finger of God. God's hand no longer holds the human being in its grip, because God has established the human being as a free creature. With the creative power of God's hand, God expresses a yearning love to humanity.[67] We do not rule, but the world rules humankind. Technology seizes the earth and molds it, but we lose the ground. We become estranged from the earth. The dominion of the earth is an illusion, since "God, the brother and sister, and the earth belong together."[68]

An eco-theological understanding of humanity is of Christological character, because Genesis must be seen in light of the new creation of Jesus Christ underlying *creatio ex nihilo*. "The world exists from the beginning in the sign of the resurrection of Christ from the dead."[69] This implies God's act of liberation, wrestling out of nonbeing, that is, from the Babylonian primeval sea, the *tehom*.[70] The protology is already set within eschatology, because resurrection and new creation in Christ is the fulcrum for the life of humanity rooted in the earth. *Creatio continua* is justified only in connection with *creatio ex nihilo* through God's act of resurrection and new creation in Jesus Christ.[71] It is justified upon the ground of God's order of

63. Ibid., 77.
64. Ibid., 79.
65. Ibid., 62.
66. Ibid., 63.
67. Ibid., 78.
68. Ibid., 67.
69. Ibid., 34–35.
70. Ibid., 37, 47.
71. Ibid., 46–47.

preservation, which is counter to the idea of order of creation, distorted and perverted in Nazi nature romanticism.[72]

Entering into God's creation, God creates freedom. God in Christ attests to God's being for humankind, which refers to *analogia relationis* (analogy of relationship), which includes the realm of creation in the sense of the first function of the law. Bonhoffer's notion of *analogia relationis* is different from Barth's notion of *analogia relationis* in a Christocentric framework, which discards a place of the first function of the law as the penultimate in regard to the ultimate.[73] Bonhoeffer's theology of nature in a Christological sense is grounded in Luther's notion of *finitum capax infinitum* (the finite bears the infinite). In short, we belong wholly to this world, because it bears, nurtures, and holds us.[74]

Public theology in Bonhoeffer's sense takes seriously the church's responsibility in stewardship of all living creatures. This is the public witness of the church to serve God's life in the planetary web of life and its integrity in sustainable community. Therefore, Bonhoeffer's legacy can enter into dialogue with the Confucian notion of human beings in unity with Heaven and Earth in order to contribute to ethical engagement with the ongoing threat of global climate crisis.

Public Theology and Telling the Truth

In the postcolonial endeavor to contextualize Bonhoeffer's insight in East Asia, I have reinterpreted Bonhoeffer's deliberation of reconciliation, theology of the cross, and creation in dealing with *minjung* theology and Confucian ethics and its humanist-cosmological orientation. A postcolonial character of public theology has come to the fore by refining contextualization in an interreligious framework of archeological inquiry and anamnestic reasoning.

In conclusion, I find a hermeneutical retrieval of Bonhoeffer's truthful discourse to be of special significance. For the truthful discourse of God and the Other, Bonhoeffer asks, "What is meant by 'telling the truth'?"[75] "Tell-

72. Ibid., 140.

73. Ibid., 65. The editors here tend to miss the difference between Bonhoeffer and Barth regarding the notion of *analogia relationis*, because Barth eradicates the dimension of the first function of the law for the sake of christocentrism. Rather, Barth provides a space for the realm of creation in light of God's act of speech in the reconciled world, unlike Bonhoeffer, who affirms a hermeneutical connection, or correlation between the gospel and the world of creation.

74. Ibid., 66.

75. Bonhoeffer, *Ethics*, 358. Bonhoeffer's essay "What Is Meant by 'Telling the

ing the truth" implies a context-sensitive horizon because it is something different at each particular time and situation. Trustful speech is indebted to God, because the living God has set us within this living context. *Parrhesia* is the truthful speech of God and in solidarity with the Other, and is therefore set against a metaphysical notion of God as *deus ex machina*, but entails a prophetic hermeneutical dimension.

I evaluate Bonhoeffer's notion of resistant *parrhesia* against the cultivation and adoration of biological and nationalistic life in the context of Nazism, which utilized religious categories from biblical texts and made Hitler into a messianic figure in order to cajole and persuade his audience. A religious discourse was politically manipulated and political life was sacralized, as in this excerpt of a speech by Hitler:

> Once you heard the voice of a man, and it spoke to your hearts, it awakened you, and you followed that voice. [John 3:4] Year in and year out you followed it, without even having seen the speaker; you only heard a voice and followed it. [John 20:19–31]. . . . Not every one of you can see me and I do not see each one of you. But I feel you and you feel me! It is faith in our nation that has made us little people great, that has made us poor people rich, that has made us wavering, fearful, timid people brave and confident; that has made us erring wanderers clear-sighted and has brought us together! [John 16:16–17; Luke 7:22]. . . . Now we are together, we are with him and he is with us, and now we are Germany! [John 14:3][76]

Challenging the falsification of biblical language, Bonhoeffer embodies a notion of telling the truth against God as a general principle or metaphysical idol, because the living God entered into the world through Jesus Christ. Satan is called the father of the lie (John 8:44). The lie contradicts that which God has spoken in Christ. It is "a matter of correct appreciation of real situations and of serious reflection upon them."[77] For Bonhoeffer, the cynic claims to speak the truth but he demonstrates only a lifeless image of the truth. Telling truth in a destructive way, the cynic betrays the community and laughs arrogantly at human weakness. The cynic feels like a god

---

Truth'?" is now part of vol. 16 of Dietrich Bonhoeffer's Works (2006), because it was written when Bonhoeffer was already in prison (during the interrogations of 1943). See Bonhoeffer, *Conspiracy and Imprisonment, 1940–1945*, 601–8.

76. Stern, *Hitler*, 90–91.

77. Bonhoeffer, *Ethics*, 359.

above these feeble creatures.[78] In contrast, the Christian notion of telling the truth refers to "God's living reality in Jesus Christ."

The living truth is dangerous, and the trustful speech as *parrhesia* is raised when the truth can be adapted to each particular situation, in which the idea of truth is destroyed and the gap between truth and falsehood is narrowed. As Bonhoeffer argues,

> She [the church] has failed to speak the right word in the right way and at the right time. . . . She has brought upon herself the guilt of the godlessness of the masses. . . . The Church confesses that she has witnessed the lawless application of brutal force, the physical and spiritual suffering of countless innocent people . . . and that she has not raised her voice on behalf of the victims.[79]

A notion of *parrhesia* becomes indispensable for deploying public theology as a discourse ethic and emphasizing discipleship by speaking the truth audaciously for the silenced and marginalized. The word of the cross can be assumed as a discursive form of *parrhesia*, "as much alive as life itself."[80] It challenges us to radicalize God, seen from the standpoint of the subjugated and victimized. The exposed flesh of the crucified Christ allows us to see God's exposure in the face of Christ and his suffering people. "God's truth has become flesh in the world and is alive in the real. . . . The concept of living truth is dangerous."[81]

A discourse of *parrhesia* is an audacious and even dangerous form of Christian witness and discipleship for God's shalom and solidarity in addressing the reality of powers and principalities in terms of the naked Christ on the cross. According to Proverbs 31: 8, "Speak out for those who cannot speak, for the rights of all the destitute."[82]

Jesus's discourse of *parrhesia* (Mark 8:32) is undertaken in his vocation of forgiveness and reconciliation for God's sake and the world. A discourse of *parrhesia* demonstrates a spirit of resistance, questioning how the institutionalized authority is connected with the religious and political spheres. *Parrhesia* entails political-religious meaning for the sake of the marginalized, the victim, and the voiceless.[83]

---

78. Ibid., 360–61.

79. Ibid., 113–14.

80. Ibid., 360.

81. Ibid., 361.

82. Bonhoeffer to Erwin Sutz, September 11, 1934, in Bonhoeffer, *London, 1933–1935*, 217.

83. Foucault, *Fearless Speech*.

In the new deliberation of *theologia crucis* in terms of *parrhesia*, a public theology in postcolonial relief takes issue with the symbol of *theologia crucis* that is blurred and tainted with colonial images of assimilation, crusade, *tabula rasa*, and hegemony during the time of colonialism. According to James Cone, the cross that is placed alongside the lynching tree can help people to see Jesus in a new light in terms of the crucified *minjung* in history and society.[84]

When *theologia crucis* connects with the discourse of *parrhesia* and with the life of the subalterized, public theology has a task to contextualize meaning of the biblical narrative to become more pertinent to people of other cultures. It must recognize and appreciate their religious, moral reasoning and their contribution to ethics of responsibility, compassion, and rectification. If faith seeks moral understanding[85] in light of reconciliation, faith and moral reasoning are grounded in the living Word of God (*viva vox evangelii*), which can be heard in the church and through the world, especially in the life and outcry of those who suffer.

Our praxis for public discipleship in speaking the truth of the gospel does not separate itself from our discipleship in conformity to the life and ministry of Jesus for the kingdom of God. According to Bonhoeffer, God has spoken "Yes" and "Amen" in Jesus Christ to all, underlying the church's discipleship and responbility for the public sphere. The unbiblical idea of meaning is a version of the biblical notion of promise. God's *pro-missio* underlines the life-giving meaning for all, welcoming people to the glad tidings of God's grace of justification and reconciliation.

A postcolonial reading of Bonhoeffer in East Asia does not necessarily mean imposing Bonhoeffer upon the Asian church that they should emulate his theology without reservation. Rather, it must be sought critically and constructively in engagement with his thought and insight for a new horizon of theological meaning through intercultural exchange and enrichment. It grants a space for Bonhoeffer to speak himself in a different manner, making his theology meaningful and relevant to people of other cultures. Likewise, the church is enriched by an encounter with the *viva vox evangelii* in the otherness of the Other in conversation with Confucian religion. For public theology in a postcolonial age, dialogue must take place between diverse perspectives in order to gain necessary insights into ethical responses to the worlds pressing issues such as globalization and global climate crisis.

---

84. Cone, *Cross and the Lynching Tree*, xix.
85. Schweiker, *Responsibility and Christian Ethics*, 5.

3

Karl Barth

Analogical Hermeneutics, Divine Action, and Public Witness

B arth is regarded by contemporary scholarship as the chief representative of neo-orthodox theology, having no interest in religions, cultural issues, and scientific communities because of his excessive emphasis on the revelation from above and in his harsh rejection of natural theology. His theology has generally been regarded as inappropriate for pubic theology, natural science, and recognition of the Other in the postcolonial context of World Christianity.

However, my concern in this chapter is to clear out such misunderstandings, evaluating his contribution to public theology, science-religion dialogue, and recognition of the Other in a pluralist context. My analysis will be given to his theological hermeneutics linked to analogical theology, while examining his deliberation of the universal effectiveness of the Word of God in the public sphere. Driven by analogical hermeneutics, I shall deal with several theological themes such as natural science, divine action, creation, God's eternity and time, eschatology, and the like. In conclusion, I shall articulate the relevance of his theology for postcolonial theology.

Analogical Imagination and Public Witness

In a tension between the word of God and hermeneutical problems, we see that the passion for the word of God tends toward disparagement of the hermeneutical question. All the while, the interest in the hermeneutical question appears to run the risk of suppressing what is said of the word of God. Aware of this tension, Barth never surrendered his initial hermeneutical impulse on to the path of his *Church Dogmatics*, presenting an implicit answer to the hermeneutical problem in light of the Word of God.[1]

For Barth, Scripture consists of the canon as it imposes itself upon the church, by virtue of its content, that is, God's revelation. Basically, critical-scientific study of Scripture can be accepted in terms of theological subject matter. The demand for a historical understanding of Scripture indicates that the Scripture was written "in the human speech uttered by specific men at specific times, in a specific situation, in a specific language and with a specific intention."[2]

Insofar as the subject matter is grounded in the freedom and mystery of God in Christ, our interpretation of Scripture is in approximation of God's truth, transpiring in an open-ended and eschatological direction.[3] For this reason Barth endorses the biblical-exegetical position in terms of Luther's principle: *veritas scripturae ipsius* (the truth of the Scripture itself) in reference to the internal testimony of the Spirit within the Bible.[4] Accordingly, Barth comments on Luther that the gospel should be proclaimed and put in a living voice (*viva vox evangelii*). It must sound forth and be proclaimed and heard everywhere in the world.[5]

For Barth, many evangelical passages, which are embedded within the passion narrative, entail the proleptic dimension, because they acquire their proper sense only through the message of the resurrection.[6] The Word of God is proleptic because God cannot be mastered. Rather God inspires and controls human interpretation of the Word of God.

Barth brings out the unity of hermeneutics by applying the dictation of Scripture upon the general validity for the hermeneutic. For a linguistic interpretation of Scripture about the reality of the mystery of God, Barth advances his epistemology—God is known by God—in terms of analogical

1. Ebeling, "Word of God and Hermeneutics," in Robinson and Cobb, *New Hermeneutic*, 84.

2. Barth, *Church Dogmatics* I/2, 464. Hereafter cited as *CD*.

3. Gadamer, *Truth and Method*, 521. Barth does not undermine linguistically oriented hermeneutics, since Barth's way for special hermeneutics is informed and prescribed by, and concerned with the subject matter of Scripture.

4. *CD* I/2, 494, 536.

5. *CD* I/1, 122–23.

6. *CD* I/2, 487. In Barth's account Luther's statement—all Scripture has its light from the resurrection—restores the doctrine of the inspiration of Scripture as the doctrine of a divine mystery, true and redemptive. *CD* I/2, 521.

imagination. He does not abrogate, abolish, or alter human cognition, rather human understanding is fulfilled in concepts and imagery. In the act of the knowing of God, we are active as the receivers of images and creators of counter-images, becoming capable of receiving images of the divine.[7] Our knowledge of God is self-critical, because it consists only in approximation, always remaining incomplete and open-ended. It is in need of correction at every point.[8]

In deliberation of the veracity of human knowledge of God, Barth avoids the terms *parity* and *disparity*. The word *parity* implies that God has ceased to be God and become merely creature. The term *disparity* implies that *de facto*, we do not know God at all. There is no veracity of human knowledge of God under the rubric of a simple disparity. This perspective leads Barth to adopt a theology of analogy. Analogy means a partial correspondence and agreement, which is helpful in investigating God's truth in revelation as it forms the basis of the veracity of human knowledge of God. In the revelation of God coming to us, we, with the word of similarity, participate in the comprehensible similarity that is posited in God's revelation.[9]

Barth considers a circle in the understanding of faith: human participation, God's adaptation to analogy, and analogy in relation to revelation. Barth's thesis—God is known by God—develops an analogical hermeneutic in light of the *circulus veritatis Dei* (circle of verity of God). A linguistic concept of similarity, analogy, and partial correspondence and agreement become foundational for Barth's theological hermeneutics.[10]

For Barth, the analogy in an attribution is sought in the relationship of an *analogans* with an *analogatum*. The *analogia* is *analogans* (one who makes the analogy) in the first, while it is *analogatum* (that which is analogized) in the second. This teaching refers to the similarity between God and the creature. This analogy is undertaken as *analogia relationis* in which the Creator-creature relationship is established by the Creator. The humanity of Jesus, his fellow-humanity, his being for human beings, indicates, attests, and reveals the correspondence and similarity between the creator and the creature.[11]

---

7. *CD* II/1, 182.

8. Ibid., 202. In matters of the relationship between the Word of God and human experience, God is involved in the human experience of the Word of God. The human being experiences the Word of God in a particular social and historical context. *CD* I/1, 200.

9. *CD* II/1, 232.

10. Ibid., 231–32.

11. *CD* III/2, 220. Barth engages in a critical dialogue with Quenstedt, who expounds the Lutheran teaching of analogy in terms of *analogia attributionis*.

In Eberhard Jüngel's judgment, the analogy of attribution is hermeneutically constituted by an *analogans* on which the *analogatum* depends.
The relation of dependence in the fashion of Scholasticism is translated into
the ontological context.[12]

More than that, Barth's theology of analogy entails a horizon of nat-
ural-material and socio-political life. This is seen notably in the political
correspondence between God's kingdom as *analogans* and the democratic-
social option as *analogatum*.[13]

The Word of God in Universal Effectiveness

Barth advances his analogical theology in connection with the universal effectiveness of the word of God in his inquiry of secular parables about the
various truth claims in a pluralist society. Barth accepts secular parables
as free communications of Jesus Christ,[14] which underscores his doctrine
of true words *extra muros ecclesiae*.[15] God cannot abandon and withdraw
God's control from any secular sphere in the world, "even where from the
human standpoint it seems to approximate most dangerously to the pure
and absolute form of utter godlessness."[16]

As a theist, Barth is convinced that God is present and active in other
religions and even ungodly culture. Profane words and lights are extraordinary ways and free communications, which analogically may bear witness to God's reconciliation in Christ. The church has the task of examining
closely that these profane words and lights are in agreement with Scripture,
church tradition, or dogma, and whether the fruits of these words outside
Christianity are good and their effect in the community is positive. Barth
calls this inquiry a "supplementary and auxiliary" criterion, referring to "the
fruits which such true words have borne and seem to bear in the outside

---

12. Jüngel, *God as the Mystery,* 272. According to Aristotle, analogous speech is in
the middle between equivocity and univocity. In the analogy of attribution, B, C, and
D all relate in varying ways to A. The many things are all related to that one common
thing in a relationship of dependence.

13. In his 1946 article "The Christian Community and the Civil Community," Barth
justifies the civil community or the civil society as the parable (corresponding and analogy), in relation to the kingdom of God for the sake of more democracy and more
social justice. Chung, *Karl Barth,* 188.

14. *CD* IV/3.1, 130.

15. Ibid., 122.

16. Ibid., 119.

world." "They have their more or less strange and puzzling origin, i.e., in the secular world surrounding the community."[17]

According to Barth, the languages, however alien their forms may be, are the language of parables of the kingdom of Heaven. He transforms the dimension of natural theology in its traditional, ontological form, socially, materially, and culturally through divine action in the world. For him,

> We may think of the peace of creation, or its very puzzling nature, and the consequent summons to gratitude. . . . We may think of the lack of fear in face of death which Christians to their shame often display far less readily than non-Christians near and far. . . . Especially we may think of a humanity . . . in which we find a simple solidarity with them and unreservedly take up their case.[18]

Barth incorporates the secular parables, whether in natural scientific, atheistic, or secular pluralist form, into the universal horizon of the Word of God for the sake of public witness to the grace of God.

Scientific Theology and Natural Science

Barth defines revelation in terms of *Dei loquentis persona* (God speaking in person). God comes to us as speech event which is of a remarkably hermeneutical character and significance. Barth has managed to open a universal dimension of God's act of speech in the sphere of creation. Creation is the external basis of the covenant, which is the internal basis of creation. In Barth's thought, there is a hermeneutical conversation between creation and covenant. In God's faithfulness to creation, the language of the self-witness of the creaturely world is discovered, integrated, and instituted in terms of God's self-interpretation in Christ. God's self-interpretation and communication in Christ makes the self-witness of the world into a parable of the kingdom of Heaven, that is, *ministerium verbi divini* (service to the Word of God).[19] A Christian understanding of God and creation does not preclude a hermeneutical horizon of human language of analogy and metaphor.

In the school of theology of nature, critical realists such as Ian Barbour find it very useful to articulate metaphorical discourse concerning the relation between theology and science. Linguistic discourse such as imagination, analogies, and metaphors in critical realism can be used to express the

17. Ibid., 127.
18. Ibid., 125.
19. Ibid., 164.

correspondence between theory and observational data since criteria such as agreement with empirical data, coherence, scope, and fertility play a constructive part in critically and realistically embodying the truth principle in correspondence.[20]

In the school of theology of nature, Barth's assertion concerning natural science has been regarded as an independent model or two-language theory.[21] Natural science has to retain a free and independent realm compared to theological inquiry. Theological inquiry also has to be free from natural science, rather than bound to scientific observation.

In dealing with creation, Barth combines the knowledge of God with creation rather than scientific assertion. Apart from Christian faith in God the Creator and also without divine revelation, cosmological or natural scientific inquiry does not give a full account of the meaning of creation. However, Barth's distinction of theology from natural science does not necessitate a two-language viewpoint, that is, two independent and non-overlapping realms.

To what extent does Barth formulate and conceptualize a relation between theology and natural science? First of all, Barth secures the theological area from other disciplines, but he does not intend to isolate theology from human sciences, which easily leads to theological arrogance or self-glorification. As Barth maintains,

> Within the sphere of the Church philosophy, history, sociology, psychology, or pedagogics, whether individually or in conjunction, might well take up the task of measuring the Church's talk about God by its being as the Church, thus making a special theology superfluous. . . . All sciences might ultimately be theology. . . . The separate existence of theology signifies an emergency measure on which the Church has had to resolve in view of the actual refusal of the other sciences in this respect.[22]

Barth's theology does not mean a reversion to the inner sphere of the church "in view of the actual refusal of the other sciences."

Barth interprets creation in terms of a faith-article and grounds his thought on the linguistic form of saga which does not exclude a scientific question of cosmology or evolution. This linguistic form takes in earnest natural scientific insights and findings, because the scientific language serves to explicate the interrelation between God and the universe. By exploring

20. Barbour, *Religion and Science*, 106–15.

21. *CD* III/1, ix–x.

22. *CD* I/1, 5–7.

God's reality in the creaturely world through scientific language, the church can deepen its discourse of God as the Creator.

In Barthian fashion, "scientific theology is active engagement in that cognitive relation to God in obedience to the demands of His reality and self-giving."[23] As a science, theological inquiry is guided by this objectivity of God, rather than imposing upon theological reality a religious a priori or an idealistic-metaphysical framework. However, the objectivity of God does not exclude the natural realm per se, but makes it serve as a parable of the theater of God's glory:

> So it is with natural theology: brought within the embrace of positive theology and developed as a complex of rational structures arising in our actual knowledge of God it becomes "natural" in a new way, natural to its proper object, God in self-revealing interaction with us in space and time. Natural theology then constitutes the epistemological "geometry," as it were, within the fabric of "revealed theology."[24]

Barth grants a new locus of *theologia naturalis* within his revealed theology (*theologia revelata*). The truth of the divine creation is included in the reality of divine grace. In this regard Barth concurs with Thomas's dictum that "grace does not destroy nature but completes it."[25]

Goodness of Creation, Its Luminosity, and Theodicy

From the beginning, God's eternity is inclusive, universal, and open, but realizes itself in the present by challenging the nothingness of powers and principalities in the world. God preserves the existence of the world, preventing it from falling back into nonbeing. Even more, Barth emphasizes God's ongoing activity within time and space as a free act of God, conserving the world against the threat of dissolution or menace by chaos (Gen 1:2). This act of preservation is an overflowing of God's free love and incomprehensibility.[26] In the election of God's grace God's overflowing goodness preserves the life of the creature.

The goodness of creation implies that God has made it serviceable for the rule of God's free and omnipotent grace and for the lordship of Jesus

---

23. Torrance, *Theological Science*, v.

24. Torrance, *Reality and Scientific Theology*, 39.

25. Barth, "Church and Culture," in Barth, *Theology and Church*, 342.

26. *CD* III/3, 60, 68.

Christ, kingdom of his dear Son (Col 1:13). Creation is not glorious in itself, but it can become so only in the right hand of the living God. Barth uses the *analogia fidei sive revelationis* in the description of creaturely occurrence as a mirror and likeness.[27]

Barth emphasizes the independence of creaturely realms in the doctrine of reconciliation. There are words of creatures which have their own lights and truths, languages and words.[28] Expressions such as "creation revelation" or "primal revelation" are accepted in a clear and positive sense. They are valued as independent frameworks of creaturely being, namely constant or continuity of cosmos.[29] The self-shining lights of the creaturely world embrace the law of the natural world and intellectual world, the empirical science, and yes, even technology.

As Barth argues,

> the so-called exact sciences built on empirical observation and investigation on the one side and mathematical logic on the other, are constituted in virtue of the knowability and in the knowledge of laws. And human technics in the narrower modern sense consists in the application of laws. . . . We live not only, but also by such science and technology, namely there are—as obviously relatively durable and useable working hypothesis— such partially, formally, innerworldly valid formula as indication of relative necessity.[30]

For Barth, natural science and technology can be an indication that God is the Creator of the world and Lord of all natural laws.[31] The creaturely world, the cosmos, the nature of this sphere, has its own lights and truths and therefore its own speech and words.[32] Thanks to the faithfulness of God the Creator, the persistence, self-witness and lights are not extinguished by the corruption of the relationship between God and humans. The divine work of reconciliation does not negate the divine work of creation, nor deprive it of meaning, so that it does not take from it its lights and language,

27. Ibid., 51.

28. *CD* IV/3.1, 157.

29. Ibid., 155.

30. Ibid., 147–66.

31. In his volume of posthumous work, Barth says, "God's name, then, is already holy in the world that he created good long before Christianity began to pray for its hallowing or to be zealous for the honor of God. Is not his name holy in every blade of grass and every snowflake?" Barth, *Christian Life*, 121.

32. *CD* IV/3.1, 139.

nor tear asunder the original connection between creaturely *esse* and creature *nosse*.[33]

In clarification of created lights in the cosmos, Barth speaks of them as the luminosity of the creaturely world with which Barth speaks positively of the persistent luminosity of the world. In the *theatrum gloriae Dei* there is a luminosity of the creaturely world which means lights of its own words and truths. The created world is also a text which may be read and understood, and at the same time its own reader and expositor. Lights of the world bring illumination, preventing the world from being merely dark or being plunged into absolute gloom by the sin of human beings.[34]

For this reason, it would be foolish and absurd to despise, ignore, and deny them, because we cannot live without them. The intelligibility and intelligence of the divine created world and cosmos makes itself known to humans and actually come to know and to be known in humans to the extent that it addresses its reason to the grasping of these lines, continuities, and constraints. The objective and the subjective reason of the cosmos assumes multiple forms including the many, the particular, the change, the alteration and the diversity rather than reduced and exhausted into mathematical or other rational patterns or laws. There is "the peace immanent to the world as such in and in spite of every contradiction and conflict."[35]

Barth now characterizes the existence of the cosmos as the existence for one another, that is, the basic form of what is lasting, persistent and constant in the creaturely world. The existence for one another in the intelligible and the intelligent cosmos is not a static but a dynamic reality "impregnable, unalterable and indestructible" within its limits. The multiform cosmos has a definite rhythm involving constant repetition, the recurrence of the encounter, the continual resumption of converse. In the persistent and constant endurance of the creaturely world and cosmos there is "always beginning, cessation and new beginning," "constant discovery, concealment and rediscovery, continual coming and going, no becoming without perishing, but no perishing without new beginning."[36]

God does not take away freedom and movement, and process of evolutionary-ecological existence in one another and for one another in the realm of creation. In the natural and cosmic existence of interrelationship "the general divides off into the particular and the particular is subordinated to the general. The whole is only in the part, yet the part, too, is only

33. Ibid.
34. *CD* IV/3.1, 141.
35. Ibid., 143.
36. Ibid., 144.

in the whole."[37] Barth's idea of a whole-part system in the interrelationship of intelligible and intelligent cosmos points to the biblical idea of dynamic rhythm "in the course of an unbroken and never-ceasing cycle" (Gen 8:22).

In the posthumous ethics of reconciliation, Barth reflects on the known and unknown God and posits that God is known and at the same time unknown for us all. God is not absent in God's hiddenness, but present, not concealed, but revealed. God has a holy name, so becomes known. The Christian petition on "hallowed be thy name" calls for God's glory in the world, in the church first and above all in the heart and life of the Christian. At this juncture, Barth discusses an objective knowledge of God in God's creaturely world in its entirety. We discern the glory of God in the universe in its animated and non-animated movement.[38]

What is at issue here is not only the appearance of the new humankind, but also the coming of the new Heaven and the new Earth. The objective knowledge of God in the natural world, world history, and human nature is not based on the inherent human capacity of knowing God. Rather the objective knowledge of God comes from God's free grace. The reason for human failure to recognize God fully and adequately in nature is due to the sin of the human who is at fault.

In conscription to service of God's glory, the lights in creation can be true words in speaking of the goodness of original creation. Barth could hear such lights in creation from the music of Wolfgang Amadeus Mozart. That is to say, the peace of creation or, conversely, its profound enigmatic character and the call for the thankfulness proceed from the peace of creation and in face of its enigmatic character. This perspective characterizes Barth's approach to theodicy.

From 1756 to 1791 God was under attack for the Lisbon earthquake. In the face of theodicy Mozart was able to hear the harmony of creation, a part of which is the shadow, but the shadow is not darkness. In the life of creation deficiency is not defeat, sadness cannot become despair. Trouble cannot degenerate into tragedy. Mozart had the peace of God, because the light shines, breaking forth from the shadow, and even the dead of Lisbon. The whole world of creation is enveloped by this light. In the symphony in G-minor of 1788 he heard the negative only in and with the positive, because he heard creation with no resentment and impartiality. He produced the music of creation in regard to the twofold and yet harmonious praise of God. Creation praises its master and is therefore perfect.[39]

37. Ibid.
38. Barth, *Christian Life*, 121.
39. *CD* III/3, 298–99.

Barth interprets the meaning of the music of Mozart in the context of creation and eschatology, encouraging us to attentively and constantly listen to them in the creaturely sphere and look for them in every direction. The character of creaturely lights cannot be reduced to a single form, but the voices uttered and heard in creation take manifold form.[40]

In the power of God's integration, the words and truths in the creaturely realms are instituted, installed, and ordained to the *ministerium verbi divini*. As the service to the Word of God, they reflect the eternal light of God and correspond to God's truth. In speaking of a relation between the Word of Jesus Christ and created lights, Barth's reflection of scientific theology stands for, beyond limitation of *theologia naturalis*, a new model of theology of nature, when it comes to creation and evolution, intelligibility and contingency in cosmology.

Barth and Divine Action in the Midst of Creation

For Barth, even the eternal God does not live without time. God's eternity is authentic temporality, therefore becoming the source of all time. In God's eternity, past, present, and future are not successive, but simultaneous.[41] The eternity of the living God is not understood as "a uniform gray sea before, above, and after time," but as a perichoresis of the past, present, and future of God's eternity.[42]

In the Augustinian tradition, time is created out of God's timeless eternity. God is before all things in the past and transcends all things in the future. Augustine's notion of the creation of time or creation *with* time, contrasts with creation *in* time. Thus, eternity is timelessness. However, the Augustinian thesis—the world was created with time (*creatio mundi cum tempore*)—has a consequence that time is transferred only on the side of the creature whereas eternity is on the side of the divine. In so doing, Augustine approximates a timeless beginning.

For Barth, however, creation of the world with time (*cum tempore*) means creation in God's uncreated time. His grounding thesis reads: *mundus factus cum tempore, ergo in tempore*.[43] God created the world in God's uncreated time. *Creatio ex nihilo*[44] does not mean the beginning of creation

40. *CD* IV/3.1, 158.

41. *CD* III/2, 437.

42. *CD* II/1, 639.

43. *CD* III/1, 71.

44. *Creatio ex nihilo* is not formulated in Gen 1 and 2. The idea is literally found in 2 Macc 7:28 in connection with the narrative of the martyr. The youngest among seven

in the past, but as divine action with sovereignty from which the world and humanity receive life and temporality. Creation is not an event done once and for all in the past; rather, creation lifts up history and orients it toward the goal—the resurrection of Jesus Christ. The *creatio ex nihilo* points to God's act of resurrection of Jesus Christ from the dead, which implies God's new creation at the final time, thereby from God's eschatology.

For Barth, it would be impossible to give a real answer to the enigma of *creatio ex nihilo* without connection to eschatology. The chaos (*Das Nichtige*) speaks of the old, which is radically past in light of the death and resurrection of Jesus Christ (2 Cor 5:17). God's *creatio ex nihilo* foresees God as all in all (1 Cor 15:28), namely in divine zeal of new creation. Since the creation in the past gains meaning from God's Future and is open to God's *novum*, God's sovereignty is not abandoned, nor is a natural or process panentheistic theology smuggled into Christian thought.

God as the source of time is identical with the future of God. God's eternity as the locus of time is defined as the freedom of God in regard to created time. Here we are liberated from Babylonian captivity of abstract contradiction into the time concept.[45] True eternity includes the potentiality of time, taking time to itself, ready for time.[46]

God, therefore, is free to hand over God's self to the evolution of created time. Nature and history, creation and evolution cease to contradict each other. The creation is God's work, which praises its master in waiting for divine use and care. God sustains the creation and preserves it. God does not cease; rather, God stands as creator for the whole of the world and remains active as the creator within it.[47]

God's providential relevance to the world is a relevance of time such that God is actually present in the evolutionary and ecological process of creaturely life. In referring to God's gracious covenant with all living creatures, Barth states that the covenant of grace is prepared in natural life. Making comments on Psalm 8:7, Barth does not take this passage to endorse expansion of human dominion over the animal world. In the context of Dan 7:1, Barth counters the idea that God has actually given the earth to humans, not to animals, and that the human stands in kingly superiority to

---

martyred brothers is charged by his mother to recall the death of his brothers. "Behold heaven and earth and all, what is inside there: This all God has made from nothing! The gracious God makes together with your brothers again living." Link, *Schöpfung*, 1:515.

45. *CD* II/1, 611.

46. Ibid., 617–19.

47. *CD* III/1, 223.

the animal.[48] All living creatures, human and animal, are invited and welcomed to the table of the Lord.

Barth's ecological concern and deliberation on living creatures moves in a transition from evolutionary history of nature toward the history of covenant and thus paves the way of the actual grace of God toward all living creatures. The creaturely living place on earth becomes obvious as an unshakably erected sign of the real grace of God turning to creature. Indeed, Barth does not regard the biblical idea of *dominum terrae* (Gen 1:26) as the authentic definition granted to humans. Barth rejects an unlimited mastery of human technology over the earth. What is more important in a biblical account of dominion over the earth is not human mastery of nature, nor "the whole program of the cultural history of the human race."[49]

Furthermore, Barth interprets providence as a *continuatio creationis*, which points to the biblical text of eschatological indwelling that God will be all in all (1 Cor 15:28). God in the final revelation will come to divine zeal within creatures, without ceasing to be God the creator.[50] This eschatological indwelling and rest with God's people and all creatures is already projected in the protological sense of God's Sabbath.

Given this, the Sabbath is the crown of the work of creation in which God identifies God's self with the world and humanity, "willing to be fully immanent even in His transcendence."[51] The fulfillment of creation does not consist in the creation of the Sabbath. God does not create the seventh day. Divine cessation is the divine perfection of creation. On the Sabbath, God celebrates ascending to the throne against the created world. As inauguration of divine rule over it, the Sabbath belongs to the essence and continued existence of creatures and hence to the creation of the world, implying the *creatio continua*.[52]

A notion of Sabbath in interaction between transcendence and immanence refers to God's freedom in dynamic love, which challenges any notion of deism. The notion of deism compares God to a great clock maker, suppressing the biblical notion of God's covenantal relationship with the world and humanity.[53] For Barth, "God is never absent, passive, non-responsible

48. Ibid., 205.

49. Ibid.

50. *CD* III/3, 86.

51. Ibid., 8.

52. *CD* III/1, 220. Barth appreciates Luther's fine phrase of creation as the masks of God, because the history of God's glory takes place in, with, and under that of creation. *CD* III/3, 19.

53. *CD* III/3, 12.

or impotent, but always present, active, responsible and omnipotent,"[54] because God is always living and always concerned. When God permits, God is always holding the initiative. God is always doing something new and disclosing something new, including miracles.[55]

God's *menuha* (God's final rest) consists rather in God's being, thus it is not created. In this self-revelation of God's true deity is displayed in genuine freedom and love of the Creator. Uniting God's self with the world, the Sabbath completes and crowns all creation. After God creates the world and humans, God becomes worldly immanent and human in Jesus Christ.[56] The Sabbath is God's world immanence, an event of anticipation of revelation in Jesus Christ—thereby the crown of creation. The Sabbath of God from the beginning presupposes the Sabbath of the final rest, which is promised in Heb 4:9–10. The Sabbath of God stands in messianic hope, and what is toward the future promise of God in Jesus Christ is not the law, but the gospel from the beginning.

Primary Cause and the Secondary Cause

In dealing with the relationship between primary cause and secondary cause, Barth argues, concurrent with the activities of creatures, *concursus* does not obviate the independence of creaturely activity. God accompanies the creature, working simultaneously in it. The *concursus divinus* is a *concursus simultaneus.*[57] Barth uses the concept God's accompanying with the creature in reference to the concept of *concursus.*[58]

The omnipotent operation of God does not destroy or suppress the activity of the creature, but it continually makes the activity of the creature free. God does not play the part of a tyrant toward the creature. The creature is not subject to God like a puppet or dead matter. God's power is expressed as the grace, and divine grace makes human freedom possible. God loves the creature in accepting solidarity with it.[59]

By the grace of God the events of nature and history are qualified to co-operate with God.[60] God's eternal love operates in relation with the creature, and in the overflowing of this love God loves the creature. Barth builds

54. Ibid., 13.
55. Ibid., 161.
56. *CD* III/1, 216.
57. *CD* III/3, 132.
58. Ibid., 94.
59. Ibid., 93–94.
60. Ibid., 110.

up the doctrine of *concursus* in terms of God's free and gracious love, which allows for freedom, autonomy, and collaboration on the part of the creature. However, the activity of the creature does not impose any condition upon or restrain the activity of God.[61] There is no withdrawal on the part of God, because God does not retire when the creature has attained its end and goal.[62]

There is no contradiction between the sovereignty of God and the freedom of the creature. God limited the freedom of creaturely activity by law and necessity while God created it free. In the divine permission the creaturely freedom encounters the divine freedom. God's lordship does not do violence to any creature in its particularity (*CD* III/3, 166, 168). Given this, Barth's theology of *concursus* is different from the theory of a freewill defense which conceptualizes God's self-limitation for creaturely freedom in the context of divine action. In the free will defense it is presumed that divine power and creaturely freedom are intertwined at the same level.[63]

Barth appreciates the Lutheran teaching of the *concursus* as *particula veri* in terms of "the relative autonomy of creaturely activity."[64] The divine activity in *concursus* with that of creature cannot mean an abrogation of the activity of the creature or of its manifold individuality.[65] Furthermore, Barth considers the relation between *causa prima* and the *causae secondae* in the context of *concursus*, because God alone is unequivocally *causa prima*. God is eternal love, preceding and accompanying and following the *causae secundae*. In the biblical context there is no difference between salvation history and world history in general.[66]

The primary cause, seen in light of God's loving and free activity, cannot be identified with a secondary natural cause as understood by scientific observation. There is a similarity, a correspondence, and an analogy of relation (*analogia relationis*) in matters of the relation between the primary cause and the secondary cause. The divine cause is self-grounded, self-positing, self-conditioning and self-causing, in distinction from the creaturely.[67] God is present and active in all laws of the creaturely world and this necessity is the necessity of God's love, acting according to God's good pleasure revealed in God's freedom.[68] God is the One who loves in freedom.

61. Ibid., 113.
62. Ibid., 152.
63. Peters and Hewlett, *Evolution from Creation*, 130.
64. *CD* III/3, 97.
65. Ibid., 145.
66. Ibid., 133.
67. Ibid., 103.
68. Ibid., 110.

Barth's critique of Aristotle and Thomas lies in the fact that they tend to not safeguard the absolute unlikeness between God as the primary causation and the creaturely life as the secondary causation.[69] Thomas Aquinas held the doctrine of the *concursus* in an appeal to Isa 26:12. The activity of God is sufficient as primary agent, but this does not make redundant the activity of the secondary agent as such. In Thomas's thought, the latter has a legitimate place for itself to be side by side with the former. However, Barth does not take the path chosen by Thomas, but for Barth, the notion of *concursus*, the simultaneous activity of God and the creature, must be grounded in the Word of God.[70]

Furthermore, there is a lack of eschatological thinking in the Thomist framework of the primary-secondary causation. It is not yet the new creation that is taken up into unity with the Creator in Jesus Christ, because a new creation (Gal 6:15; 2 Cor 5:17) is not the repetition of the first creation.[71]

God's Eternity, Time, and Eschatology

The priority of Jesus Christ in the doctrine of election constitutes the fundamental-hermeneutical principle in dealing with who God is and how God acts in relation to the world. God's time is pre-temporal, because God in Jesus Christ created all things and was before all things. The eternal covenant becomes the internal basis for creation itself. Pre-temporality is related to supra-temporality, including all epochs prior to Jesus Christ. This is because God's eternity is not in a timeless eternity, but in every epoch, every lifetime, and every passing hour: "All in eternity is like a child in the arm of its mother."[72] God's eternity, including past and present, is also post-temporal because Jesus has a future, whose glory is both promised and not yet to come in light of resurrection and *parousia*.

God's Future is not meant to be *futurum* (what will be), which refers to the future as the cumulative result of causative forces of the past or the actualization of existing potential stemming from the past. Rather, God's Future is the *adventus* (what is coming), based on God's in-breaking action into history by bringing about something radically new. Barth does not develop the concept of creation unilaterally from the standpoint of the beginning.

Barth focuses three forms of the temporality of God (*CD* II/1) on the threefold time of Jesus Christ and the threefold *parousia* of Christ (*CD*

69. Ibid., 103.
70. Ibid., 133.
71. Ibid., 6.
72. *CD* II/1, 623.

IV/3). The eschatological kingdom of God is proleptically present in the event of Jesus Christ and can be seen in the sense of pre-temporality, supra-temporality, and post-temporality. The resurrection of Jesus and his presence in the Spirit are not the completion of history, but the foundation for the future. The resurrection is the *parousia*, but only in its first and not its final and conclusive form. Easter, the first form of the new coming of Jesus Christ in the impartation of the Holy Spirit, is a matter of participating in God's present in anticipation of the eternal and everlasting kingdom. The new creation has taken place in the resurrection of Jesus Christ.[73]

In Jesus Christ, the future arrives ahead of time without being exhausted into the present time. Barth does not comprehend time in terms of eternalizing time, but God's eternity in the threefold sense is eschatologically conceptualized in light of the coming kingdom of God, without suppressing God's past and present.

Barth sharpens the notion of divine action—preservation, conservation, *concursus* and governance—by qualifying this theological discourse in light of transforming *adventus* of God's Future. He promotes the time of creature as the participation in God's present in transition from the death-determined past to God's Future, which comes at Easter ahead of time as the final *parousia*. God's eschatological future as the restoration of the whole of time is the ground of creatures in coexistence with God's present. God will be all in all (1 Cor 15:28) does not mean that the creature will cease to be distinct from God's self. Rather, the creature will see God in the final revelation to have attained God's ultimate goal in all things with the creature.[74]

Barth thinks theistically of the triune God as the source of time. Yet, the Word became flesh, becoming time. God's time is defined for us in christocentric as well as eschatological terms. As a result, the present and the future of salvation are grounded in the coming of One, who has already come. God's being is becoming in the coming of God's Future. Barth's definition of God as the all-encompassing, changing, and transforming reality (qualifying and sharpening *totaliter aliter* as *der ganz ändernde*—[the Wholly Changer]—thereby *alles in allem real verändernde Tatsache dass Gott ist* [God's existence as the reality changing and transforming all in all]) makes theological statements hypothetical, scientific, and self-critical. All theological thinking and speech is of an eschatological character in regard to God, out from God and toward God. In other words, prolepsis in a Barthian sense means the in-breaking reality of God's kingdom in our midst with the signs of liberation, making even scientific community, social

73. *CD* IV/3.1, 300.
74. *CD* III/3, 86.

movement, and other humanistic endeavors into parables witnessing to the kingdom of God.

For Barth, governance (*gubernatio*) indicates that God works with goal or aim. Barth articulates God's *telos*, provocatively claiming God's Future as "coup d'etat" or "God's revolution," which comes "as the overcoming and dissolution of the past by the future, not as an equilibrium."[75] This aspect entails a critical transcendence in view of the status quo, a hermeneutic of suspicion, which calls into question the ideological bias of the science-power relation within the scientific community, as often controlled and manipulated in the service of the powerful in society.

Karl Barth toward Postcolonial Theology

Barth's theology of God *totaliter aliter* has gained attention in the circle of postcolonial theologians. In her book *The Touch of Transcendence*,[76] Mayra Rivera redefines the notion of divine transcendence in terms of irreducibly Other, beyond our grip but not beyond our touch.[77] Rivera's postcolonial theology of God is based on the touch of transcendence. This is a relational transcendence, which provides a vision of divine transcendence within creation and between creatures.

Rivera acknowledges that the idea of transcendence is associated with Karl Barth's notion of the Wholly Other (*totaliter aliter*), expressing her affinity to Barth's critique of liberal theology in light of God the Wholly Other. For Barth, Jesus intersects the plane of created existence, "vertically, from above." The Holy Spirit touches the old world of the flesh as a tangent touches a circle, without touching it.[78]

Concurring with Rivera's appropriation of Barth, I contend that Barth's notion of the Wholly Other in early stages cannot be adequately understood without Barth's socialist activity in solidarity with economic others, which underlines his theological critique of liberalism and the imperialism of World War I.

Barth underscores the radical political notion of God the *totalier aliter* as the revolution of God in the first edition of *Romans* (1911), then incorporating it into Kierkegaardian negative dialectics of qualitative difference between God and humanity in the considerably revised second edition of *Romans* (1922). In his debate with Erik Peterson in the 1920s,

75. *CD* II/1, 544.

76. Rivera, *Touch of Transcendence*.

77. Ibid., 2.

78. Ibid., 4–5.

Barth acknowledges the limitations of dialectical theology and turned to the importance of analogical theology. His dialectical-analogical theology grounded in God the *toaliter aliter* cannot be comprehended adequately without consideration of his socialistic activity in his early phase.[79] In *Church Dogmatics*, Barth further comprehends the living God as *totaliter aliter* in terms of *Dei loquentis persona* (God speaking in person) in connection with *viva vox evangelii*.

A postcolonial reflection of *totaliter aliter* in the Barthian sense of *viva vox evangelii* addresses us and the church through the otherness of the world. God may speak to us through a pagan or an atheist. This implies postcolonial insight into the freedom or mystery of God's act of speech,[80] which finds parallel with Levinas's distinction between saying and said.

For Barth, Jesus Christ as "partisan of the poor" is in solidarity with those who belong to the party of the godless assailed by the Pharisees, as visible in Jesus's table fellowship with publicans and sinners.[81] Jesus Christ announces God *totaliter aliter* as "the One whose will is that [God's people] should be totally changed and renewed."[82] He stands in God's "corresponding partisanship of those who are lowly in this world."[83] Barth's theology moves in the direction of a theology from and for the margins in light of God the *totaliter aliter*, which upholds postcolonial politics of solidarity with the subaltern.

At any rate, Rivera takes into account Homi Babha's postcolonial notion of "beyond," which expresses more than a disillusionment toward contemporary culture, while implying its hope to break through its shortcomings. She argues that, in terms of God-talk, Derrida analyzes carefully how texts and systems of knowledge produce all-encompassing foundations. These deny that there is anything beyond.[84] Derrida's critique is related to the Western theological and philosophical tradition of onto-theo-logy, in which God is comprehended and expressed according to being. Rivera acknowledges that there is a certain affinity between Derrida's deconstruction and negative theology. In Derrida's challenge to onto-theo-logy Rivera argues that Derrida's texts still remain haunted by reference to the Wholly Other, alterity, and the beyond.[85]

---

79. Chung, *Karl Barth*, 8–14.

80. *CD* I/1, §5.4.

81. *CD* IV/3.2, 586.

82. *CD* IV/2, 180.

83. Ibid., 248–49.

84. Rivera, *Touch of Transcendence*, 11.

85. Ibid.

Barth might share Derrida's critique of onto-theo-logy in his rejection of liberal theology for *totaliter aliter*. Nonetheless, Barth's dialectical-analogical method remains crucial in shaping his understanding of the word of God according to an analogy of faith. This provides an insight into integrating social political discourse to the gospel about the kingdom of God.

Nonetheless, a question can be posed whether Barth offers enough to overcome his scholastic notion of analogy and correspondence theory for the embodied dimension of human language, that is, social discourse imbued with power relations and economic material formation. In my judgment, God's relationship with us and the world must not be merely comprehended in scholastic-analogical fashion, which tends to perpetuate a hierarchical notion of imitation, copy, and correspondence. What appears is mere appearance, a deficiency concerning the relation of the ideal and the real. The copy never equals its prototype.

Drawing upon a correspondence theory of truth, Barth takes a path of analogy in seeking to break through the ontological difference between God and creatures through revelation from above. When he considers God's word-act in a universal horizon through the others, he requires the church to examine closely whether the profane words and lights are in agreement with the Scripture, church tradition or dogma.

However, this perspective is unilaterally oriented toward a Christian dogmatic tradition, sidestepping an emic standpoint which articulates the unique understanding of those who receive the gospel in non-Western culture. Cultures, through which God continues to speak, are internally diverse, always in flux and impacted by social stratification and power relations. Granted that our understanding of the revelation is refracted and prejudiced in the plurality and difference of the world, a hermeneutical deepening seeks to understand that which is different, particular, and local.

God does not work and liberate our life in terms of analogy and dialectics, but God's own power of the Word and promise in terms of self-showing in our midst. "For my thoughts are not your thoughts, nor are your ways my ways, says the LORD" (Isa 55:8). "So shall my word be that goes out from my mouth; it shall not return to me empty, but it shall accomplish that which I purpose, and succeed in the thing for which I sent it" (Isa 55:11). Prophetic language, which awakens us to a divine promised future, breaks through the scholastic and hierarchical language of analogy and its negative dialectics.

Despite his major contribution to the theology of divine action, political theology, and theology of nature, I sense that Barth's analogical theology embedded within Kierkegardian negative dialectics tends to undertake pan-analogical encapsulation of the freedom, transcendence, and future of God grounded in divine promise and love in our midst.

Excessively indebted to the scholastic-analogical method, Barth does not pay attention to critical analysis of language as social discourse imbued with the mutual dependence between knowledge, interest, dominion, and power. Language includes ethnic stratification, social inequalities, and sociopolitical representation

Given language and culture in mutual interaction concerning change, context, and power, I argue that a theological understanding of revelation is also influenced, circumscribed, and refracted under historical effectiveness and within social location. A dynamic interaction between the gospel, God's ongoing activity in many worlds, and human expressions of ultimate reality, must be taken through a threefold practice: appreciation, critical distance, and reconstruction in terms of approximation and the open-ended step in attention to the Other. This critical-constructive epistemology facilitates a critical renewal of the hermeneutical malnutrition in Barth's theology. A critique of Barth should be understood as the theological audacity to break through his theology for shaping postcolonial public theology, respecting his provocative charge to his students: Don't become Barthians!

PART II

Public Theology and Scientific Rationality

4

Postcolonial Imagination, Postmodernity, and Recognition of the Other

Postcolonial theory marks a challenge to the Western theory of rationality by critically analyzing the neocolonial or neoimperial reality in the colonial aftermath. Although "post-" denotes "having gone through," or "after" in a temporal, successive sense, postcolonial theory takes into account events in constant flux ensuing from the domination of empire. Postcolonial theory entails a project of recovering histories in order to subvert Western hegemony and heal colonized narratives.[1] The "once colonized world" is replete with hybridity and liminality as postcolonial people navigate the mixed and in-between nature of lives in the aftermath of empire.

Michel Foucault is a central mentor, together with Jacque Derrida, inspiring postcolonial critics to engage in colonist discourse of Orientalism for the deconstruction of the Western dominion system. Edward Said, deeply influenced by Foucault, undertakes groundbreaking work to uncover the discourse of Orientalism. Said's study of Orientalism, namely a Western style of domination of non-West, establishes the watershed of postcolonial theory, analyzing the ideological dominion of the West over the Orient.[2]

Given the postcolonial imagination in our postmodern condition, I seek to configure postcolonial public theology in a critical-hermeneutical manner. By way of analectical epistemology and social discourse, I seek to

1. Gandhi, *Postcolonial Theory*, 8. See further Westhelle, *After Heresy*, xvi.
2. Said, *Orientalism*.

refine a theological or philosophical notion of God's speech event or Saying by the otherness of the Other. This project is driven by archeological hermeneutics, recognizing the locus of the Other. Its ethical responsibility is formulated in commitment to making the world a better place in light of the coming kingdom of God.

A project for the future becomes possible first of all from the act of *metanoia* from wrong steps and fatal mistakes in the previous colonial time. It is substantial to unfold postdevelopment rationality in transcending the limitations of modernity and public ethics by recognizing and rethinking the dignity of the Other from the standpoint of those fragile, broken, and victimized and through whose faces God continues to address.

The Enlightenment, Its Unfinished Project, and Postmodern Critique

Postmodern resistance wages war on totality, universality, and the metaphysical grand-story raised by modernity. For Lyotard, postmodernity is "incredulity toward metanarratives."[3] Under the dominion of the metanarrative, the specific, different, and unique narratives are reduced into a metaphysic of universal story, such that the voice of the Other is unnoticed, marginalized, and suppressed.

According to Jürgen Habermas, the project of modernity, as formulated in the eighteenth century, undergirds "the relentless development of the objectivating sciences, of the universalistic foundations of morality and law, and of autonomous art." This project also results in "[encouraging] the rational organization of social relations."[4] For Habermas, modernity's project is not yet finished, despite its shortcoming and setbacks.

Philosophically, the Cartesian principle of *cogito ergo sum* (I think, therefore I am) set the agenda for the centrality of the human mind in subsequent centuries. Matter is only knowable in reference to what is known by the mind. In the narcissism of self-consciousness, *cogito ergo sum* reduces the diversity, plurality, and multiplicity of the world to the contents and rationality of our mind and that which can be deduced by mathematical demonstration.[5]

The Cartesian principle of the certainty of the "thinking I" culminates in Kant's critical philosophy. In his essay "What is Enlightenment?" Kant

3. Lyotard, *Postmodern Condition*, xxiv.

4. Habermas, "Modernity: An Unfinished Project," in d'Entrèves and Benhabib, *Habermas and the Unfinished Project of Modernity*, 45.

5. Gandhi, *Postcolonial Theory*, 36.

quotes Horace's *Sapere aude!* (dare to know), insisting that the free exercise of human reason is fundamental to the distinctiveness of the Enlightenment.[6] Kant characterizes Enlightenment as the way out of immaturity, "man's exit from his self-incurred minority."[7] The Enlightenment has a motto, an instruction, and a heraldic device: *Sapere aude*, encouraging one to use one's own intelligence through the audacity to know. Since dogmatism and heteronomy are the illegitimate uses of reason, the modern attitude is seen as "an escape from self-caused immaturity"[8] through a critical consciousness in discontinuity with tradition, promoting a will to idealize the present. This implies a myth of progress that supports a colonial logic of white supremacy and burden in connection with the non-West.

According to Robert McCarthy, the Kantian historical-developmental perspective justifies slavery as one of the evils which contributed to the advance of the human race through the diffusion of European culture. Innocent victims in history and society may serve as stepping boards providentially toward the kingdom of ends. In short, the end justifies the means.[9] On the other hand, the name of Darwin linked to social Darwinism and the eugenics movement had incorporated the "white man's burden" (Kipling) into the developmental model of laissez-faire capitalism and racism, which found its apex in Hitler's anti-Semitism and the horrors of the Holocaust.[10]

In critical view of the historical and social ramifications of Western modernity, Frantz Fanon maintains that the modern civilization of Europe has been built upon the burden of the sweat and dead bodies of Negroes, Arabs, Indians, and the yellow race.[11] The colonial discourse reveals the often neglected suffering, victimization, and subalternization of the non-Western world. Foucault argues that the Enlightenment project constitutes the self as autonomous subject, and upheld human self-invention for elevating the present as a formative stage for modern humanity. In exclusion of the non-Western other, he refers to the Enlightenment legacy as the "blackmail of the Enlightenment,"[12] as visible in the historical examples of colonialism, slavery, and exclusion of the Other.

As Thomas McCarthy contends, postcolonial neoimperialism, together with post-biological neoracism, continue to operate after the eventual

6. Kant, "What Is Enlightenment?" (1784), in *Basic Writings of Kant*, 135.

7. Ibid.

8. Ibid., 140.

9. McCarthy, *Race, Empire, and the Idea*, 65.

10. Peters and Hewlett, *Evolution from Creation*, 52–58.

11. Fanon, *Wretched of the Earth*, 102.

12. Foucault, "What Is Enlightenment?," in Foucault, *Essential Foucault*, 51.

demise of formal colonies and scientific racism. The shift to neoimperialism and neoracism is mediated by power relations.[13] Such cultural pathologies remain hidden in all-inclusive conceptions of progress, modernization, developmentalism, and cosmopolitan universalism. It is necessary to undertake a multiple study of modernities in order to transcend such a defect and pathology. I find a multiple study of modernities helpful to conceptualize an integral transmodernity as one of the alternatives to the shortcomings of the Enlightenment project in the postcolonial world.

Postmodern Deconstruction and Hermeneutical Reorientation

Derrida's theory of deconstruction is applied to denounce the colonial discourse of representation which survives the death of colonialism. The development paradigm is driven inherently by the dialectics of domination according to a unitary process with a uniform future. Alterity and ambivalence are the effects of deconstruction, which ineluctably inhibits Western thinking about the Other. Decolonizing the historical and social imaginaries between ex-colonizers and ex-colonized is an ongoing process of deconstruction of the white myth of progress and development linked to the Western value of justice, dignity, and democracy. Derrida rejects colonial and neocolonial discourse as an attempt to construct a totality through exclusion or homogenization of the Other. Unlike Derrida's deconstructive orientation, Thomas McCarthy offers a reconstructive undertaking of postcolonial theory in his endeavor to articulate a critical theory of global development.[14]

In the undertaking of postmodern hermeneutics, David Tracy argues that both the Enlightenment model of rationality and the traditionalist model of heteronomy are inclined to destroy our capacity of interpreting the claims of the classics in a creative and refreshing manner.[15] In the philosophical tradition, Husserl's phenomenology begins its return to the thing itself by challenging modernist mathematization of the world, in which the world has become captive to technology. To salvage the world from its technization, Husserl introduces a phenomenological concept of lifeworld. In protest against scientific technization of the world, Husserl argues that the lifeworld is pregiven in every connection with others. The lifeworld was always there prior to science and objective critical thinking. It deals

13. McCarthy, *Race, Empire, and the Idea,* 7.

14. Ibid., 184.

15. Tracy, *Analogical Imagination,* 196

a powerful blow to Cartesian epistemology, because Descartes privileged mathematics as the cognitive method. To think of the world mathematically, that is, *mathesis*, Descartes argues that all things need to be mastered by calculation.[16] However, mathematization of the lifeworld leads inevitably to its colonization. We must be emancipated from the bondage of mathematization of the world.

The world horizons of human beings are different, since Europeans, Africans, and the Chinese have their truth and fixed facts, yet all in radically different manners. Despite all relativity, the lifeworld constitutes a universal structure beyond the relative condition. Human consciousness is affected and conditioned in the historical horizon of lifeworld and social location of cultural life. In my judgment, Husserl provides an insight into shifting consciousness of intentionality to historical effectiveness and social cultural location. Knowledge of what is taken for granted must be put in brackets, because it is socially constructed.

Along this path, Heidegger and Gadamer take steps further in seeking an ontological, linguistic hermeneutics, challenging the methodical spirit of science and technology. Interpretation, as seen in light of a history of effect, inheres in human life in the public sphere because of the use of language in daily communication. Being historical implies that one's knowledge can never be complete and exhausting.[17]

Heidegger's concept of *Da-sein* (being-in, or being there), that is fundamentally being-in-the-world, marks the most telling critique of Descartes and Kant. The human being as a being-in-the-world is enmeshed in personal, social, and linguistic networks. Language as the house of being brings the human world into existence. Inspired by Heidegger's insight, Gadamer further refurbishes the notion of the history of effect or influence upon the individual life and understanding. The human relation to the world is thoroughly linguistic, hence intelligible and understandable. Given this, interpretation experienced as a fusion of horizons is of a dynamic and open-ended character in hermeneutical circle, breaking through the Cartesian-Kantian autonomous self.[18]

Following in the footsteps of Heideggar and Gadamer, Vattimo presents a constructive philosophy for the postmodern, hermeneutical condition. For Vattimo, Heidegger's notion of a *Verwindung* of metaphysics aims at weakening Being through the destruction of ontology.[19] A constructive

---

16. Gandhi, *Postcolonial Theory*, 36.
17. Gadamer, *Truth and Method*, 302.
18. Heidegger, "The Way to Language," in Heidegger, *Basic Writings*, 397–426.
19. Vattimo, *End of Modernity*, 11.

philosophy in hermeneutical reorientation seeks to incorporate a moment of deconstructive critique into a renewed meaning.

Sociological Analysis of Rationality, the Reality of the
Iron Cage, Divine Transcendence

In sociological analysis of the process of Western rationalization, Max Weber advances a notion of the selective affinity between the Protestant ethic and spirit of capitalism. Weber saw the paradox of social rationalization in the development and institutional embodiment of formal, purpose rationality tied to Calvinist innerworldly ascetic of life, which finally has led to an "iron cage" transpiring in the process of the disenchantment of the world.[20] The legacy of the Enlightenment is an emphasis on the autonomy of human reason, human rights, and the struggle for a just society. This legacy has brought technological marvels and advancements in the twenty-first century, while it has also unleashed the exercise of instrumental reason that has resulted in human domination over the natural world and ecological devastation.[21]

In an analysis of the Western process of modernization, Max Weber introduces and examines the concept of purpose rationality. The rise of purpose rationality leads to the disenchantment of the world. This process of disenchantment has gradually led Western people to rely on the technological control of nature and society as well as a loss of meaning. In Weber's diagnosis, Western civilization, unfettered by the disenchantment of the world, has unleashed the one-sided development of human purpose rationality. Through human mastery over the external world, the Western form of reason has become instrumentalized, resulting in the state of the iron cage.[22]

Foucault shares Weber's diagnosis of Western civilization captive to the iron cage in his analysis of the panopticon that assures the automatic functioning of power. The panopticon is a machine in the center through which one sees everything without ever being seen. It produces the homogenizing effects of power, presenting itself as "a cruel, ingenious cage" and defining power relations in terms of human everyday life in a society.[23] It is

20. Weber, *Protestant Ethic*, 181.
21. Lakeland, *Postmodernity*, 13.
22. For the term "iron cage," see Weber, *Protestant Ethic*, 182.
23. Foucault, *Discipline and Punish*, 205.

a new political anatomy, a technology in terms of the relations of discipline and mechanism.

Foucault argues that we live in this architectural apparatus, invested by its effects of power, bringing ourselves to a part of its mechanism. Both the docility and the utility of all the elements of the system are increased in political, economic, educational, military, industrial or medical spheres. Thus the accumulation of people and the accumulation of capital have come together because the techniques enabling the cumulative multiplicity of useful and amenable people accelerate the accumulation of capital. The technological mutations of the apparatus of production, the division of labor and the elaboration of disciplinary techniques retain very close relations. Consequently, the human body is reduced to a political force and maximized as a useful force.[24]

Enlightenment that discovered the liberties of human life also invented the disciplines. Foucault debunks the dominant discourse in the structured and networked interplay between power and knowledge in the religious institution, the political structure, ideological legitimation, and institutionalization. The correlative constitution of power and knowledge determines the forms and the possible domains of human knowledge in a given society.[25] Thus language or *episteme* constitutes the human self, rather than becoming the ultimate source and ground for language.[26]

Those who adopt Foucault's genealogy of knowledge and power as a critical frame of reference find a neocolonial regime of power/knowledge in a theory of development or modernization in the aftermath of colonialism. A theory of modernization is a central strategy of modern power rather than a path to emancipation from such power.[27] The Western notion of universal reason is internally linked to relations of power. What is rational is right and true for everyone to follow. Disciplinary strategies are embedded in power relations, which are driven to subjugating, normalizing, and dominating non-Western peoples. Local traditions and their indigenous and practical knowledge are disqualified in the development paradigm. A need is required for outside assistance from already developed societies whose agencies, officials, and experts are vested with power/knowledge. A top-down authority and knowledge system is inherently structured to propel development; hegemony of reason is exercised and secured by the power structure. Foucault's genealogical strategy is to debunk and subvert the

24. Ibid., 221.
25. Ibid., 27–28.
26. Foucault, *Order of Things*, 386–87.
27. Escobar, *Encountering Development*.

constitutive Eurocentrism of discourse like development, modernization, or progress. Such metadiscourse entails complicity with technologies of neoimperial power.[28]

In *Dialectic of Enlightenment*, Horkheimer and Adorno analyze the historical process tied to the domination of instrumental reason, arguing that it brought humankind into a new kind of barbarism.[29] They name Christianity, idealism, and materialism as accountable for the barbaric acts that have been perpetrated in their names in matters of power, self-interest, and dominion. The dominance of nature through scientific progress is the basis of the philosophy of Enlightenment. According to Francis Bacon, scientific knowledge is instrumental in mastering the world of nature. Nature is disenchanted through the rule of computation and utility for the sake of the ideal of Enlightenment.[30]

Performing a totalistic critique of instrumental reason, Horkheimer's suspicion of Western reason leads him to a search for the transcendent God as the hope for humanity and the world dominated by instrumental reason. Religious and moral longing for the transcendence of God finds its impetus in Horkheimer's critique of human reason for the sake of God's radical alterity. Divine transcendence implies God's Future as the hope of preventing human reason from being instrumentalized and even captive to the iron cage.

Given this, proleptic theology, which is driven in hermeneutical frame of reference and postmodern holism, deserves attention. Ted Peters presents this hermeneutical task as a theological response imbued with the project of reinterpreting the original meaning of biblical narratives and symbols, making them meaningfully relevant for the new situation. To advance a postcritical hermeneutic, Peters considers the reconstruction type of wholeness in contrast to the deconstruction type of postmodernity. Implying that the whole is greater than the sum of the parts, a holistic understanding of human reasoning or imagination includes both thinking and feeling, comprehending the human being in a context of meaning.[31] This epistemology endorses the epigenetic-evolutionary view, according to which the sum of reality, in the synthesis of the new with the old materials, is creating a new emergent in the course of evolution.[32]

28. McCarthy, *Race, Empire, and the Idea*, 181–82.

29. Horkheimer and Adorno, *Dialectic of Enlightenment*, xi.

30. Ibid., 6.

31. Peters, *God—the World's Future*, 15–20.

32. Smuts, *Holism and Evolution*, 89.

The new wholes are the center and creative source of reality. This holistic perspective helps us cultivate an eschatological consciousness of the yet to be consummated whole of future. God's radical transcendence must be sought in a proleptic-messianic notion of God's coming future as the source of the whole, awakening our consciousness in longing for the future. God's determined whole has been revealed ahead of time in the life, death, and resurrection of Jesus. Peters' approach to postmodern holism aims at recovering meaning, inspiring our longing for God's transcendence as God's coming Future. In the act of belief in the transcendent God, our life is reoriented in this world toward the divine Future, redeeming the world from the iron cage.

Given this, I undertake a revisionist interpretation of the postcolonial world in terms of a new critical method in seeking non-colonial or transmodern resources in the past and the present and also challenging the neocolonial reality in light of God's coming Future.

Archeological Hermeneutics, Social Discourse, and Meaning-Event

In an attempt to undertake a dialectic of decolonization, "archeological" is a technical term which implies unearthing the past materials, religious classics, wisdom, and life of people marginalized and voiceless by Western tradition and history. "Hermeneutics" means one's interpretive engagement with tradition, history, and texts, as well as social discourse in one's contemporary location through sharing, conversation, and empathy.

Foucault defines discourse in terms of a group of statements or a group of conditions of existence.[33] The statement is the basic unit of discourse, making proposition, utterance, or speech acts meaningful. Discursive formation shapes the background knowledge and every understanding of meaning. In discourse analysis Foucault's "outside" position assumes an anti-humanist and structuralist form. Foucault runs short of excavating a deeper meaning underneath discourse in terms of one's preunderstanding, which is influenced and shaped by one's history, ethos, and social location.

Foucault's concern is how to show the principles of meaning production emerging during various epochs (the Renaissance, the Age of Enlightenment, and the twentieth century). This posture allows Foucault to focus on the role of discursive practices. However, unlike Foucault, the discourse statement (*episteme*) as such does not unilaterally generate the condition for meaning. Rather meaning takes place as event in the interaction of the

33. Foucault, *Archeology of Knowledge*, 117.

interpreter's horizon with the *episteme* and also in the critical analysis and investigation of the life connection with others. Given this, I maintain that discourse as structure should not necessarily be accepted as the epistemic origin or as essentially fixed, independently of socio-cultural reality as well as their economic-material basis.

I call this discourse-meaning connection a hermeneutical clearing-out of Foucault's archeological genealogy based on anti-humanism. An archeological hermeneutics incorporates Foucault's notion of discourse and power in critical hermeneutical frame of reference, with anamestic passion for *metanoia* from colonial and neocolonial wrong steps and driven through anticipatory power in light of the irruption of the kingdom of God in our midst.

This hermeneutical position runs in contrast to technological objectivity or colonization of lifeworld which overwrites Foucault's archeological genealogy of the totality of power. Discourse analysis can be justified on a hermeneutical circle, because every understanding comes from one's own preunderstanding within the spectrum of historical effectiveness and social location.[34]

If hermeneutics in the sense of Heidegger and Gadamer is oriented to tradition, history, and language in a historical sense, Foucault's genealogy is a form of synchronic interpretation with an eye to the strategic analysis of the interrelation of power, knowledge, and truth in the form of social discourse. For Foucault, the effective history, unlike Gadamer's concept of the history of effect, seeks to put everything in historical motion, dissolving an illusion of identity and continuity, with passion for refusal through the weapon of counter-hegemony against the metadiscourse of metaphysics. It is important for me to incorporate Foucault's effective history into the irregular notion of history as the otherness in my constructive hermeneutics of archeology.

Gadamer tends to minimize critical reasoning within the confinement of the history of effect while Foucault tends to maximize power structures outside the history of effect. Thus, Gadamer sidesteps the irregularity of history, while Foucault undermines the power coming from the history of effect. Nonetheless, at the archeological level, Foucault endorses the important locus of history as effect. For him, "History gives place to analogical organic structures." It is "the depths from which all beings emerge into their precarious, glittering existence." History is "the mode of being of all that is

---

34. Kögler, *Power of Dialogue*, 201.

given us in experience." "History has become the unavoidable element in our thought."[35]

In this regard I find that Foucault's archeological epistemology does not necessarily counter a hermeneutical understanding of history as effect, conceptualizing the human being as linguistic being in the world. Although this archeological inquiry discards all the chimeras of the new humanism, it still retains language, discourse, and history, which shape and condition human life in the world. A history of effect, although often standing in tension with the discrepancy and irregularity of different and diverse histories, still influences one's own subjecthood.

The experience of language belongs to the archeological network, because language sets the task of restoring an absolutely primal discourse, expressing the discourse in approximation to it. Knowledge and language are interwoven in social discourse.[36] Thus, human being becomes being of discourse, which does not escape the historical, social circle of labor, language, and life. Through this, I critically revise Foucault's archeological genealogy through a hermeneutical reorientation toward God's act of speech through the Other and its domain of subjugated irregularity in anticipatory power of meaning. I thus attempt to clear-out of Foucault through a hermeneutical frame of God's speech event imbued with an anamestic passion of metanoia from a neocolonial reality.

Public Theology: Analectical Method and Speech Event

For postcolonial public theology, I take up Levinas's distinction between "saying" (living discourse) and "said" (written text) to develop postcolonial hermeneutics of intertextuality concerning God's saying in the otherness of the Other. *Dabar* in Hebrew means to speak, dialogue, and revealing related to the God of promise, transcendence, hope, and future. A hermeneutical reflection of God as the infinite horizon of speech-event comprehends a textual world of intertexuality embracing intratextual narratives and extrabiblical narratives of the social world through a dynamic process of the fusion of multiple horizons. It seeks to propel a critical and emancipatory ethic of social discourse in the context of power relations, employing a standpoint from, through, and for margins—thereby *massa perditionis / minjung*-subaltern.

---

35. Foucault, *Order of Things*, 219.
36. Ibid., 41, 43.

The analectical method begins with ana-logy, because *dabar* in a Hebrew manner entails ana-logy, which assumes an attitude of trust in the obedience of a disciple toward the Other.[37] The language of analogy finds its effectiveness in terms of approximation, tentativeness, and open-endedness. It provides linguistic imagination for interpreting the relation between God, humanity, and the world through a play of resemblance, which is driven by an endless and incomplete task of knowing and understanding what is similar. However, in endless quest for similitude, our experience of analogy could become deceptive, if its signifying function is confined only to a play of resemblance, undermining the language of social discourse.

Against this trend, the analectical perspective pays attention to the communicative dimension of God involved in our social discourse. In the Hebrew Bible, God is also understood as the One who is involved in the life of the public sphere. "The LORD is witness between you and me forever. . . . The LORD shall be between me and you, and between my descendants and your descendants, forever" (1 Sam 20:23, 42). The biblical witness speaks of the presence of God in the midst of God's people and in the inclusion of the nations. God will dwell in their midst—Israel and the nations together (Zech 2:10–11; cf. Ezek 43:7; Joel 2:27). God's living discourse in Jesus Christ for all is to be seen in light of God's universal-particular reign, in which God's multiple acts of speech become significant throughout all the ages in their plural horizons driven by the universal-particular horizon of the Holy Spirit.

Thus, the analectical method is connected with God's speech event involved in the life of the public sphere and its dimension of social discourse. The integrative model between the analectical method and social discourse, driven in light of the hermeneutics of intertextuaity, entails an ethos of liberation and seeks to rewrite a history in privileging the standpoint of history's forgotten Other. To the degree that the dimension of living discourse is embedded within the analectical method, the Word of God can be received even by those who can misuse the word. God's Word and God's promise of presence are vulnerable. Despite this vulnerability, "the word of the LORD is truthful, and what he promises, he certainly keeps" (Ps 33:4). The Word as promise and future event poses the problem of understanding in spite of the limitations and vulnerability of human language in understanding the Word of God in light of God's Future.

The analectical method, framed within the relation between similarity and dissimilarity, is grounded in a dialectical interaction between appropriation, a critical or deconstructive critique, and reconstruction, while

37. Barber, *Ethical Hermeneutics*, 51.

recognizing the Other in reference to the interplay between power, knowledge, self-interest, and dominion. Analogy and dialectic in an analectical fashion sharpens and strengthens the hermeneutical spiral and its historical effectiveness to be embedded within the Other's social location.

This perspective incorporates the social discourse of the *dissimilarity* and *irregularity* in the life of those who are colonized and victimized. When we see our current history and society in light of similarity, we must comprehend its other side of difference and dissimilarity in an archeological-anamestic reasoning of the marginalized history and society in anticipatory meaning from the in-breaking reality of God's coming in our midst.

Inculturation and Recognition of the Other

Public theology in the aftermath of colonialism entails a socio-critical and hermeneutical reflection on colonial discourse and its hegemonic structure set within the religiously institutionalized framework. It sees colonial discourse not only of the past but also of the current dominating discourse *critically* in light of God, the infinite horizon of discourse-event. If faith seeks understanding, it should be contextualized in deep conversation not only with its own tradition but also with other traditions, which undergirds a hermeneutical reading of correlation between scriptural reasoning and other religious texts. Faith, understanding, and acquired meaning in a hermeneutical open-ended circle belong to a semantic of God's narrative and symbols supporting the ethics of discipleship.

Human life is suspended in webs of significance. Within such webs of significance, culture is interpretive; in search of meaning in social, cultural, and anthropological locations.[38] In a hermeneutical conversation with others, a new meaning emerges, helping dialogue partners to better understand their own traditions. A project of inculturation of biblical narrative seeks fresh theological insights that learn from the newly encountered traditions and the home tradition in light of the coalescence of multiple horizons.

In the biblical context God is revealed as the One who speaks. God's speaking in person is identical with God's action in self-manifestation. Insofar as the Scriptures witness to the living Jesus Christ, who transcends the written words and law, historical, scientific, and postcolonial criticism is accepted on these hermeneutical grounds.[39]

If faith seeks understanding, it implies that the language of faith reinforces dialogue and communication in the experience and recognition of

---

38. Geertz, *Interpretation of Culture*, 5.

39. Ebeling, "Word of God and Hermeneutics," in Ebeling, *Word and Faith*, 318.

the world and in renewal of it in terms of proclamation, communicative action, and inculturation. Understanding and investigating the human words in the Scriptures can be done in light of the theological subject matter of the living and emancipating gospel about the kingdom of God. This perspective characterizes public theology as a form of hermeneutical activity which is engaged in the living word of God in connection with cultural life. In comprehending and contextualizing the word of God, we are not in a position to escape from history, society and culture as sites of effect, because it is out of the question to take an outside-hermeneutical position in light of the viewpoint of God's eye. Our understanding of God, revelation, biblical narrative, symbols, or doctrines is socially constructed, culturally conditioned, and linguistically expressed.

The concept of thick description (Clifford Geertz) is helpful in this regard. Culture is a context within which cultural linguistic systems of construable signs and symbols work together. It can be understandably, meaningfully, and intelligibly interpreted, that is, thickly described. Understanding a people's culture exposes their normalness without reducing their particularity and it engages multiple meanings of human behavior, gesture, and expression in different contexts.[40]

For the sake of thick description of the Word of God and Christian symbols, it is important to consider that all human behavior, language, and understanding are interconnected within history. All our words are, to some degree, polysemic, so that human discourse is undertaken in a diverse and different sense and accomplished within a context. Polysemy is the pivot and culmination of semantics, referring to the fact that a word has the character of an event, because it produces multiple meanings. For Paul Ricoeur, in the case of symbolic analogy or metaphor, a word is a cumulative entity, capable of engendering and acquiring new dimensions of meaning in different times and places.[41] This semantics integrates the context-sensitive skill of thick description into the hermeneutical ever-renewing process and circulation.

Coupled with its public ethical implication, the hermeneutical perspective of fusion of multiple horizons in the process of translation undergirds steps of interpretation: that is, appropriation of traditional and indigenous meaning for biblical narrative, critical distance from the alien and oppressive element and the backwardness of the tradition, and creatively self-renewed construction of biblical translation in an open-ended manner in terms of appreciation, deconstructive critique, and self-exposure, and

---

40. Geertz, *Interpretation of Culture*, 14.

41. Ricoeur, "Structure, Word, Event," in Ricoeur, *Conflict of Interpretations*, 93.

self-renewal in dialogue with the biblical text and the other culture. The domain of untranslatability affirms translation as a process built on analectical similarity-in-difference. This hermeneutical long route keeps translation from any notion of translation reductionism or indigenous syncretism as seen in the postcolonial method of interpolation.

In the act of the covenant in the Genesis narrative, blessing is a key term testifying to God's work as the creator. God's election of Abraham does not exclude God's goodness to "nonchosen" people. Coupled with the blessing, promise is the most basic category that moves beyond what the creation provides. God makes promises even to Hagar and Ishmael (Gen 16:10–11; 17:20; 21:13, 18), becoming the advocate for their life and dignity in the wilderness.[42] Foreigners are expected and allowed to come to the temple to worship (1 Kgs 8:42–43). Concern for the poor and the widow and hospitality for the foreigner are indispensable parts of understanding the prophetic character of the biblical narrative.

In the Lucan account, Paul recognizes in Athens a religious concern, a reverence and awe, especially in their veneration of "the unknown God." Bearing witness to *solus Christus* in light of God's reconciliation in Christ, Paul is convinced that everybody lives, moves, and has her being in the universal reign of God (Acts 17:22, 27b, 28). Here we observe Paul's striking quotation of pagan writers: "For 'in him we live and move and have our being'; as even some of your own poets have said, 'For we too are his offspring'" (Acts 17:28). Paul's concept of God's reconciliation with the world (Col 1:20; Phil 2:10; 1 Cor 15:22, 25, 28; Rom 5:18; 11:32; Rev 21:5, etc.) provides an insight for undertaking inculturation of the biblical narrative in the recognition of the Other.

In the narrative of the Samaritan woman (John 4:7–26) Jesus's radical openness to religious outsiders is displayed as he breaks down the barrier between Jews and Samaritans. God's love and compassion is obvious and manifest in Jesus's eagerness to welcome the signs of faith among people outside the house of Israel. Culture and cultural diversity will be redeemed and blessed for eternity rather than destroyed or wiped away (Rev 21:24).

42. Fretheim, *Abraham*, 10.

5

Faith, Scientific Rationality, and Evolution

Faith seeks understanding in the science-religion dialogue. While constructing a theology of nature, this chapter expands faith's understanding by incorporating knowledge of nature gained from the natural sciences—especially evolutionary theory and global ecology—as well as other religious perspectives on the sciences. Special attention will be given to Buddhist contributions to an evolutionary and ecological view of life. With such an interdisciplinary interaction, this chapter attempts to refine and enhance a classic Christian epistemology.

Faith Seeking Understanding

The phrase given to us by Anselm, *fides quaerens intellectum* (faith seeking understanding) can enhance the dialogue between science and religion. For Anselm, faith seeking understanding characterizes theology as rational science. He boldly maintains that the unbeliever's quest for the truth should be treated as identical with the quest of the believer. A concept of God as mystery remains central in Anselm's approach to God as insuperable (*id quo maius cogitari nequit*—such that nothing greater can be conceived). His theistic perspective places all things in reality in relationship to the one God, paving the way for the theologian to incorporate knowledge of the things in this world gained through the research of the natural scientist. The scientist reveals nature to us, while the theologian constructs a theology of nature based upon faith in God.

Anselm's argument has received attention from two important theologians in the twentieth century, Karl Barth and Charles Hartshorne. Barth takes his notion of *analogia fidei* from Anselm's epistemology, which incorporates *analogia entis* and natural theology into his theological framework. This analogical epistemology remains central in shaping his theology in *Church Dogmatics*.[1] Unlike Barth, Charles Hartshorne reworks Anselm's ontological argument for God's existence. Hartshorne criticizes classical theism because classical Christian theism has held to a self-contradictory notion of perfection. Anselm accepted the equivalence of completeness and insuperability. In Greek metaphysics, the perfect cannot change at all. Only in God's effects upon creatures is God compassionate, while not in God's own reality. God remains quite unmoved, indifferent to whatever happens to any creature.[2] Taking issue with this classical theism espoused with Greek metaphysics, Hartshorne presents neoclassical theism for a God of love (God's passibility). God is capable of surpassing God's self. God is passable so that God may receive value from and be relative to the world, knowing and loving it. God is active, free yet wholly necessary, rather than immutable.[3]

Given Barth's approach to God as mystery or Hartshorne's approach to God's relationality, I want to develop an approach to the relation between God's freedom and relationality in terms of analogical hermeneutics for upholding dialogue with science and interreligious dialogue, especially regarding Buddhist contributions to an evolutionary-ecological view of reality. David Tracy articulates an alternative vocabulary to a univocal language (where all is the same) or an equivocal language (where all is different). This analogical imagination within the framework of similarity in difference prepares one to risk all present self-understanding, in the face of the claims of the other, including scientific challenges.[4]

Limit Question in Religion and Science

There is no universally agreed upon single definition for the human phenomenon called religion. In theological circles, the tradition initiated by Schleiermacher (a feeling of absolute dependence) has been developed both by Rudolf Otto's phenomenological description of the holy as *mysterium*

1. Chung, *Karl Barth*, 330–44.

2. Hartshorne, *Anselm's Discovery*, 39.

3. Ibid., 302. David Tracy appreciates Hartshorne's critical interpretation of Anselm's ontological argument. Tracy, *Blessed Rage for Order*, 174.

4. Tracy, *Blessed Rage for Order*, 32.

fascinans et tremendum. Paul Tillich furthers his ontological analysis of the Schleiermacher-Otto-Troeltsch tradition in his famous analysis of ultimate concern underlying the religious dimension of our experience. On the other hand, social science has also developed its own approaches to religion, as classically formulated in the works of Max Weber and Emile Durkheim. Phenomenologists in the context of sociology of knowledge such as Luckmann and Peter Berger articulate the social functions of religion in terms of social constructs for reality.

Given the definition of religion, there is a conflict of interpretation within the context of religious studies. Such complex perspectives can facilitate our understanding of a broader horizon of religion rather than contradicting each other. Our existence is bound to history, tradition, and language, because a human being is defined as a historical being. Such limitation points also to our existence beyond tradition through our critical distance or creativity for the sake of reconstructing a new meaning in a fusion of horizons. We can also raise questions about scientific values and ethics as well as the ramifications of scientific progress and technology related to ecological crisis. The scientific question can also be described as a religion-as-limit question, since limit questions about the world cannot be entirely answered by science.[5]

Social Dimension of Darwinism as Limit Question

We may see such an example of a limit-question within the scientific context of evolutionary theory in social Darwinism and Sociobiology. Charles Darwin (1809–82) presented a theory of speciation governed by the interaction of variation in inheritance and natural selection. Variants in inheritance are acted upon by natural selection, leading gradually over long periods of time to new species with new traits. The notion of descent with modification is an essential feature of Darwin's theory. All human characteristics might be accounted for in terms of the gradual modification of anthropoid ancestors by the process of natural selection, the result of which comes from the brutal working of blind chance and indifference to life and humanity.[6] Random variation in inherited traits along with the struggle for survival upholds natural selection as the impersonal and directionless force of the evolutionary process.

Darwin became a major figure in opposition to the natural theology of William Paley, an Anglican priest (1743–1805), who provided us with the

5. Ibid., 98.
6. Greene, *Darwin and the Modern World View,* 44.

design argument for God's existence. Paley introduced the analogy of the watch and watchmaker concerning the relation between the Creator and the universe for his argument from design. For Paley, the watch must have had a maker, because an artificer designed and constructed it for use.[7] Nature is like the watch, said Paley; it needs a designer.

Darwin disagreed with Paley, replacing the designing God with natural selection. Darwin received the idea of natural selection from political economist Thomas Malthus and his *Essay on Population*. According to Malthus, the rate at which populations increase is greater than the rate at which resources can be provided. This brings individuals into competition with one another. Unlimited self-interest is the driving force for survival in competition. Because the population is too large for the environment to support it, many people die. The weak or unfit die, while the strong (the fit) live on to pass their traits to subsequent generations.

Darwin's evolutionary biology provided a naturalist foundation for three influential ideologies: Thomas Huxley's agnosticism; Herbert Spencer's social Darwinism; and Francis Galton's eugenics. Of particular interest to us here is social Darwinism.[8] Hebert Spencer (1820–1903) supports Darwin's model of natural selection for the sake of the survival of the fittest in economics, culture, and politics.[9] In the evolutionary struggle, Spencer argues that economic competition must be free from government regulation. Competition therefore fosters human welfare, becoming a driving force for the evolution of society. According to Spencer, the poor among us are unfit; but the rich among us are fit. The poor should die away while the rich should survive and pass their traits to future generations. Our biological nature, as Darwin describes it, provides a naturalist foundation for human ethics. "The whole effort of nature is to get rid of such [poor or unproductive people], to clear the world of them and to make room for better. . . . It is best that they should die."[10]

Darwin, who maintained that Spencer's deductive manner is wholly opposed to Darwin's own framework, did not accept Spencer's "developmental hypothesis."[11] However, Spencer's survival of the fittest in the framework of the developmental hypothesis yielded to natural blood, "red in tooth and claw" (from Alfred Tennyson's poem of 1850, "In Memoriam").

7. Paley, *Natural Theology*, 1.

8. Depew and Weber, *Darwinism Evolving*, 78–82.

9. The term "survival of the fittest" appears in the first volume of Spencer's *Principles of Biology* (1864). Peters and Hewlett, *Evolution from Creation*, 53.

10. Spencer, *Social Statics*, 414–15.

11. Depew and Weber, *Darwinism Evolving*, 158.

Furthermore, Francis Galton (1822–1911) championed Darwin's idea of evolution for the sake of eugenics. His eugenic standards are based on his own racial identity and culture. Western European civilization must be the pinnacle of evolutionary achievement. His plea for eugenics policy politically upheld the civilizing influence of Britain on the world. Galton's eugenics program to speed up human evolution by limiting new births to intelligent, prosperous, and wealthy white people led to widespread programs of sterilization of the mentally disabled, physically disabled, diseased, and poor persons in Britain, the United States, and Germany. Adolf Hitler adopted the Darwin inspired eugenics program for the Nazi "racial hygiene" program, establishing gas chambers for handicapped children and, later, the Jewish victims of the holocaust. Only healthy members of the Aryan race were fit to survive, according to the Nazi doctrine of eugenics. In the colonial context, Rudyard Kipling's phrase "white man's burden" is incorporated into the Darwinian model for natural selection and survival of the fittest.[12]

Against the tradition of social Darwinism and eugenics, however, we may mention Theodosius Dobzhansky in our discussion of evolution and the scientific question as limit-question. He supported the idea of mutual aid—that changes in gene frequencies take place in a volatile ecological theater. For Dobzhanski, diversity is good for populations and provides the basis for a pluralist society and even democracy. He refuted eugenics not only as a blot on the Darwinian tradition but also on American democracy. As he states, "Equality is necessary if a society wishes to maximize the benefits of genetic diversity among its members."[13] Dobzhanski's genetic pluralism and ethic of toleration offers a radical alternative to social Darwinism. It also anticipates a movement arriving on the scene in the late twentieth century, sociobiology, and its child, evolutionary psychology.

Sociobiology and Its Critics

In the twentieth century, genetics and evolutionary theory were brought together in a systematic neo-Darwinian framework called "the modern synthesis" (Julian Huxley). The modern synthesis seeks to incorporate genetics and molecular biology into the Darwinian model. Darwin had observed variation in inheritance, but he could not explain it. By adding genetics, neo-Darwinists now could explain variation in traits due to genetic mutation. In the history of science, few theories have proven themselves as fertile

---

12. Peters and Hewlett, *Evolution from Creation*, 56.
13. Depew and Weber, *Darwinism Evolving*, 297.

for new research as Darwinian biology. However, society seems to want to make more of Darwinian theory than just biology.

Darwinian evolution as a science has been used to justify the philosophical stance of naturalism, ontological materialism, and even atheism. This perspective is developed in Richard Dawkins's book *The Blind Watchmaker*, which maintains that Darwin made it possible to be an intellectually fulfilled atheist.[14] Dawkins's argument entails a radical critique of Paley's natural theology, which necessitates an intelligent designer like the watchmaker for nature's fine organization.

Similarly, Edward O. Wilson in his *Sociobiology* argues that a doctrine of genetic reductionism and genetic determinism must be the foundation for explaining all human behaviors. Wilson's method is to study social behavior in nonhuman animals—behavior such as aggression, sexual habits, and reciprocal altruism. Submissive behaviors as seen in every wolf pack or group of monkeys are comparatively expressed in human deference to charismatic leadership and religious authority, especially to a male God as the hyper-dominant. A religious epic must be fulfilled by the true evolutionary epic.[15]

Sociobiologists such as Dawkins and Wilson rely upon a fundamental doctrine they have proffered, namely, the selfish gene. According to this apparently scientific doctrine, all of evolutionary history has been directed by one principle: the desire on the part of DNA sequences (genes) to replicate themselves through reproduction. Reproductive fitness becomes here the criterion for measuring the survival of the fittest. It is genetic determinism in the form of the selfish gene that drives evolution forward, according to this school of thought.

However, several scholars challenge a notion of genetic determinism based on the Darwinian model of evolution. Stephen Jay Gould is critical of sociobiologists who seek to ground philosophical, theological, or ethical conclusions on the science of biological evolution.[16] Gould, together with Niles Eldredge, presents a theory of punctuated equilibrium, maintaining that the majestic unfolding of the evolutionary process did not proceed through continuous gradual changes over time, which is caused by long sequences of successive mutations. Throughout evolutionary history there have been long periods of stability, or stasis, punctuated by sudden and

14. Dawkins, *Blind Watchmaker*, 6.

15. Wilson, *Consilience*, 265. Wilson seeks to place the unity of knowledge within science—consilience. Genetic explanation is responsible for a wide variety of phenomena and human culture, because the genes hold culture on a leash, on all of human culture, morality, and religion.

16. Gould, *Rocks of Ages*, 6.

dramatic transitions and major structural changes. Speciation could occur rapidly without much genetic variation, therefore critiquing the Darwinian model of evolution as incomplete in accounting for speciation. This demonstrates that the sudden transitions were caused mechanisms, which are quite different from the random mutations of neo-Darwinist theory. Although the neo-Darwinian synthesis incorporates the idea of punctuated equilibrium within its framework, it represents a holistic view in the unfolding of a speciation rather than mutations in single genes.[17]

Furthermore, a dissipative structure (Ilya Prigogine) as an open system articulates interconnection between structure, flow, and change; and the spontaneous emergence of new forms of order could occur at a bifurcation point, a point of instability. Living organisms can maintain their life process under condition of nonequilibrium. The system far from equilibrium is described by nonlineqar equations such that dissipative structure based on "far from equilibrium" and "nonlinearity" played a major role in the study of self-organization. This implies that order emerges spontaneously at states far from thermodynamic equilibrium, that is, at the edge of chaos—complex patterns arising out of turbulence.[18] Dissipative structures in open systems become a source of order, maintaining themselves in a stable state far from equilibrium. But they may even evolve, because the instabilities and jumps to new forms of organization are the result of fluctuation, which are amplified by positive feedback loops.

The dissipative structure challenges the Darwinian evolution which contends that in the course of evolutionary change organisms will gradually adapt to their environment under the pressure of natural selection until they are fit enough for survival and reproduction.

Now, evolutionary change must be seen as the result of life's inherent tendency to create novelty, whether it may or may not be accompanied by adaptation to environmental conditions.

Thus, Stuart Kauffmann insists that we must rethink evolutionary biology: "Much of the order we see in organisms may be the direct result not of natural selection but of the natural order selection was privileged to act on. . . . Evolution is not just a tinkering. . . . It is emergent order honored and honed by selection."[19]

On the other hand, it is argued that in the reproduction of a cell, genes can only function embedded in the epigenetic network rather than merely

---

17. Barbour, *When Science Meets Religion*, 92.

18. Prigogine and Stengers, *Order Out of Chaos*, 142. See Haught, *Science and Religion*, 143.

19. Kaufmann, *Origins of Order*, 408, 644.

determined by a genetic blueprint. The complex dynamics emerge as the epigenetic network encounters the whole cellular network—membranes, enzymes, organelles. The cell needs to use a continual flow of energy from its environment to stay alive. Creativity in the generation of new forms becomes a key property of all living systems as open systems evolve. The rate of mutation is regulated by the cell's epigenetic network rather than a matter of pure chance. Continually, life reaches out into novelty in the emergence of self-organization.[20]

According to the emerging new theory, the driving force of evolution challenges the neo-Darwinian theory, which argues that it is seated in the chance events of random mutations. Gene mutation is caused by a chance error in the self-replication of DNA. Against this, the emerging new theory argues that the driving force of the evolution lies in life's inherent tendency to created novelty, that is, the spontaneous emergence of increasing complexity and order.

In her study of genetics, Lynn Margulis became aware that other genetic systems with different inheritance patterns exist. Generally, the genes are believed to be in the nucleus, thus the nucleus is the control of the cell. However, all the unruly genes belong to distinct living organism, which are living small cells residing inside the larger cell. According to Margulis and Dorion Sagan, symbiosis, which refers to the tendency of different organisms to live in close association with one another, often inside one another, helps us to understand long-term symbioses which continue to lead to new forms of life. Here, the theory, known as symbiogenesis, maintains that new forms of life are created through permanent symbiotic arrangements which are the principal avenue of evolution for all higher organisms. "Life did not take over the globe by combat, but by networking."[21]

In the theory of symbiogenesis, emphasis is given to the formation of new composite entities through the symbiosis of formerly independent organisms, because it has been a more powerful and more important evolutionary force.[22] This perspective helps to recognize the vital importance of cooperation in the evolutionary process in contrast to Social Darwinism which prioritizes competition in nature, "red in tooth and claw." But now we

---

20. Capra, *Hidden Connections*, 12–13.

21. Margulis and Sagan, *Microcosmos*, 15, 17. Margulis presents the so-called mitochondria, the powerhouses inside most nucleated cells, as the most striking evidence for evolution through symbiosis. The mitochondria were originally free-floating bacteria that invaded other microorganisms in ancient times, taking up permanent residence inside them. Here a symbiotic alliance becomes permanent. See Capra, *Web of Life*, 231.

22. Margulis, *Symbiosis in Cell Evolution*, 164.

begin to see continual cooperation and mutual dependence among all life forms as the central aspect of evolution.

More than that, those who retain the perspective of cultural evolution argue that transmission of cultural symbolic information and evolution of morality take place through language, tradition, education, and social institutions rather than biological evolution based on selfish genes and altruism.[23]

Evolution and Christian Faith in Mutual Recognition

Does evolution really nullify all world views that depend upon the spiritual? For Gould, each domain entails its respective questions, rules, and criteria of judgment. Overlapping between two entities is not desired, because science covers the empirical realm while religion extends over questions of ultimate meaning and moral value.[24]

More than Gould, the author of widely used textbooks in biology, Kenneth R. Miller presents an independent relation between science and religion. Miller believes in God because evolution is right. Darwinian evolution does not preclude the existence of God, rather it is consistent with religion. For Miller, evolution is not inherently hostile to religious belief. Evolution does not deny the biblical account, but rather completes it. Darwin himself said that agnostic would be the most correct description. But on the other hand, he is open to being called a theist.[25] The Western God stands back from God's creation to allow God's people true freedom. Miller defends Darwin's God by quoting from the final sentence of the *Origin of Species*. For Darwin, there is grandeur in this view of life, having been originally breathed by the Creator into a few forms or into one. From a simple beginning endless forms most wonderful and most beautiful have been and are being evolved.[26]

Miller's scientific method contends that everything in nature can be reduced to material determinism. Yet, Miller believes in God, and the deistic form of belief is inadequate for him. According to quantum theory, the probalistic activities of electrons and photons and other particles contradict the machine-like behavior of nature. Electrons and photons do not behave like machines, but behave individually in unpredictable ways. At the quantum,

23. Nolan and Lenski, *Human Societies*, 15.

24. Gould, *Rocks of Ages*, 6.

25. Miller, *Finding Darwin's God*, 287.

26. Ibid., 292.

or atomic level, the indeterminacy of the natural world remains. For Miller, unpredictable quantum activity is responsible for unpredictable genetic mutations. Quantum physics helps us to see the unpredictable behavior of the subatomic particles in our cells. In replication of DNA, no intermediate chemical process can be detected. For Miller, God is the architect of sub-atomic indeterminacy. Indeterminacy is a key feature of the mind of God.[27]

God did not completely abandon creation after God designed it. A spiritual reality surpasses the physical reality of nature. The big bang made the first cause real. The big bang casts a theological light on the origin of the universe. The physical constants of the universe were set up in a way that made our existence possible, referring to an anthropic principle.[28] Miller's position is characteristic of classical, biblical theism with openness to God's activity in the evolutionary world.

We cannot expect today's evolutionary biologists to incorporate a con-cept of God into their research science. As scientists, they are looking for *natural explanations* of nature's phenomena. They are not looking for divine design, as Paley might have. Nevertheless, theologians can incorporate into a faith-informed worldview all that we learn from biological science. Healthy science leads to a healthy theology of nature. However, the theologian must be wary of ideological superimpositions piled on top of the science such as atheism, social Darwinism, eugenics, or sociobiology. In seeking under-standing, faith must absorb science but absorb it only critically.

Metaphorical Language and Critical Realism

In our examination of the Darwinian model of evolution, we have discov-ered that Darwinism is still evolving. This scientific unfolding helps us to construct scientific epistemology in a revised understanding of evolution in linguistic-metaphorical expression, which critical realists uphold. This articulates a hermeneutical horizon in scientific enterprise, which also re-considers a theological epistemology (faith seeking understanding) in light of this hermeneutical circle. Science itself is an enterprise of interpretation set within the scientific structure of revolution.[29]

Faith seeking understanding does not necessarily mean one sided fide-ism, but expression of interaction between faith and reason. This perspec-tive helps us to pursue a post-Cartesian version of St. Anselm's definition of theology as faith seeking understanding. As Ted Peters states, "Once we

27. Ibid., 213.
28. Ibid., 228.
29. Kuhn, *The Structure of Scientific Revolution*.

have entered the belief-understanding circle, the process of interpreting Christian symbols begins to illuminate our own life and makes it understandable in relation to the divine reality."[30]

Both science and theology are engaged in this enterprise of interpretation. Just like the theologian who cannot see God yet interprets evidence for God, so also the scientist cannot (in all cases) see the object of his or her research. Electrons are as invisible as angels. In order to see what is invisible, scientists construct theories that point to what cannot be empirically assessed. The epistemological framework at work here is *Critical Realism*, or CR. In the words of theologian Ted Peters and physicist Carl Peterson, "as a form of realism, it [CR] includes a methodological set of assumptions presupposing that an objective world actually exists and that we can know it through inquiry. As critical, it presupposes that human subjective analysis and construction contributes to what we deem to be knowledge."[31]

Scientific rationality incorporates the relativity of constructive knowing, and the language of scientific discourse makes it subject to critical analysis by the theologian.

To study language as discourse is to discover plurality, difference, and ambiguity, because a discourse analysis demonstrates interplay between knowledge and power which shapes the discourse as a truth. Scientific discourse cannot evade its analogical language and its embeddedness with the power-relation complex within a specific social cultural context. This entails a critique of the foundational metanarrative which legitimates modernity, science, and technology for the sake of a post-foundational shaping of rationality in light of a fusion of horizons between evolutionary epistemology and hermeneutical concern.[32] We already perceived the social, political, and cultural implications of social Darwinism and sociobiology in connection with its critics.

In science, language inevitably influences our understanding of both data and facts, truth and reality. Arthur Peacocke emphasizes that science depicts the realities of the natural world in metaphorical language to answer the question "why."[33] A scientific theory constructs a proper analogy provided by a model which drives our metaphorical and theoretical ideas. Theoretical models originate in a combination of analogy to the familiar and creative imagination in constructing the new. Metaphor is intrinsically open ended in its application, extensible and suggestive of new hypotheses. Such

30. Ibid., 30.

31. Peters and Peterson, "Higgs Boson," 192–93.

32. Van Huyssteen, *Shaping of Rationality*, 33.

33. Peacocke, *Theology for a Scientific Age*, 87.

models are taken seriously analogically, metaphorically but not literally. They are partial and inadequate ways of describing what is not observable.[34]

Ian Barbour's model of critical realism has a distinctively hermeneutical-metaphorical character. Science does not lead to certainty and its conclusions are always incomplete, tentative, and subject to revision. A critical realist does not claim for the attainment of absolute truth, but endeavors to construct better maps of physical reality.[35] Theories influence observational data in many ways through scientific imagination, using language of analogies and establishing models. Because reality (for instance, quantum reality of indeterminacy) is not completely accessible to us, the criteria of truth, which corresponds with reality, must include all four criteria: agreement with data, coherence, scope, and fertility.

As an expansion of critical realism, Barbour endorses process theology as the best metaphysical scheme for conceptualizing a theology of nature. A theology of nature necessitates epistemology by developing the perspective of what we are learning about nature and contemporary science. Based on religious experience and historical revelation, it seeks to reformulate and revise traditional doctrines in light of current scientific claims.[36] Nature is today understood to be a dynamic, interdependent, ecological, and multi-leveled evolutionary process. The world we know by faith to be created by the God of grace is now understood according to evolutionary discourse. Nevertheless, critical realists tend to sidestep, for the representational theory of correspondence of truth, the factor of historical effectiveness and social, material formation correlated with knowledge-power interplay and political economic life connection, which shapes and influences scientific rationality and knowledge systems.[37]

Hermeneutical Theory of Process and Neurophenomenology

At any rate, Barbour characterizes Whitehead's metaphysics in terms of an ecological view of reality, because the biological world is a web of mutual dependencies. Whitehead's philosophy of organism maintains that every event (an actual occasion) occurs in connection with the prehensive phase

---

34. Barbour, *Myths, Models, and Paradigms*, 47–48. See further McFague, *Metaphorical Theology*, 79.

35. Polkinghorne, *Scientists as Theologians*, 17.

36. Cobb and Griffin, *Process Theology*, 63–79.

37. For this postcolonial epistemology, see Chung, *Church and Ethical Responsibility*, 6.

and then its concrescent phase, that is, in a context which affects it. This entails a social view of reality. To prehend means roughly to feel, like experience. The notion of prehension expresses that nonconscious experience is universal, while conscious experience is highly specialized. Conscious experience is composed of countless nonconscious experiences. When we touch a stone, the chain of reaction along the arm requires the experiential interaction of many billion of cells and atoms, which are beyond the reach of consciousness.[38]

Thus, an actual entity or activity affects its own concretion of other things. Concrescence is the growing together, making of a concrete or atomic actual reality. The expansion of the universe in regard to actual things shapes the first meaning of process, and the universe in any stage of its expansion refers to the first meaning of organism.[39] A process of concrescence is a creative advance into novelty. Creativity is the principle of novelty when it comes to any novel expansion so that we may regard every being as a potential for becoming, which refers to a creative advance into novelty.[40] The ultimate metaphysical principle implies that the advance from disjunction to conjunction creates a novel entity other than the entities given in disjunction.[41]

Reality consists of an interacting network of individual moments of experience. The influence of the past on the present can be viewed externally as efficient causality. An element of self-creation or self-causation is a way of appropriating its past, relating itself to various possibilities and producing a novel synthesis. However, Barbour questions whether process philosophy grants a space for "the radical diversity among levels of activity in the world and the emergence of genuine novelty at all stages of evolutionary history."[42]

The process perspective facilitates an attempt to conceptualize a hermeneutical methodology in a social-ecological framework. A hermeneutical methodology takes into account a relativistic notion of process, since the relativistic theory of $E = mc^2$ acknowledges that mass is a form of energy at the subatomic level. Energy associated with activity, or process is intrinsically dynamic and interconnected, such that it may qualify a quantum theory of indeterminacy in terms of complementarity, which implies a hermeneutical circularity or connection in comprehending the relation between the part and the whole.

38. Whitehead, *Process and Reality*, 120.

39. Ibid., 215.

40. Ibid., 21, 28.

41. Ibid., 21.

42. Barbour, *Religion in an Age of Science*, 227.

As we have previously seen, creativity emerges in the process of self-organization, resulting in the creation of novelty. In the nature of an emergent phenomenon, consciousness and experience can be seen as a process, involved in bringing forth a world through the process of living and interconnection. This refers to neurophenomenology,[43] which seeks to comprehend conscious experience in the emergence from complex neural activities. A phenomenological way of leading back to the source is performed in understanding consciousness as a process in reference to an irreducible emergent phenomenon. This perspective can be further articulated and unfolded in the hermeneutical theory of interconnection, which offers a radical alternative to the Cartesian philosophy of consciousness (*cogito ergo sum*).[44]

Given this, I seek to revise the historical-ontological hermeneutics of Hans-Georg Gadamer by way of a methodological frame of reference. We are beings of dialogue, a discourse which is influenced by the historical effectiveness of tradition and language. The history as effect is compared to Whitehead's notion of efficient causality. We appropriate, understand, and interpret the past through the language of our present life, which articulates a hermeneutical notion of self-creativity in terms of appropriation and critical distance. Human experience is not merely confined to historical effectiveness, but relates the self to dialogue with the other in society for producing a novel synthesis or reconstruction. A notion of fusion of horizons occurs vertically as well as horizontally, in other word words, historically as well as socially. This hermeneutical circularity underpins a holism, which sees the tendency in nature to form wholes that are more than the sum of their parts. This hermeneutical holism suggests that our knowledge of truth is undertaken in an open-ended manner, rather than a fixed and static claim to the truth. This perspective becomes an undercurrent in conceptualizing a theology of creation, or planetary life within an evolutionary-ecological framework in connection with a theology of God's eschatological future, a new Heaven and a new Earth.

43. See Varela, "Neurophenomenology." Phenomenology, founded by Edmund Husserl, entails a hermeneutical dimension of relating human experience (through phenomenological reduction under the bracketing of natural and naïve beliefs—epoche) to the horizon of lifeworld. See Gadamer, *Truth and Method*, 246.

44. The legacy of Cartesians makes the fundamental division between the realm of mind (*res cogitans*—thinking thing) and that of matter (*res extensa*—the extended thing).

Evolution, Ecology, and Eco-theology

Our discussion of hermeneutical and holistic circularity imbued with the in-breaking reality of God's Future leads us to examine the life of evolution within the ecological frame of reference.

The sciences, especially ecology and evolutionary biology, offer a new view of the place of humanity in nature and our interdependence with other forms of life. Ecology has also led to a new understanding of our dependence on our environments. The term ecology was coined in 1866 by the German biologist and social Darwinist Ernst Haeckel (1834–1919). It derives from two Greek words, *oikos* (household), which means house or home, and logos, meaning reflection or study. Ecology means the study of the conditions and relations that make up the habitat (the house) of each and every person and indeed every organism in nature. The word economy is also derived from the same root, *oikos*. Originally, *oikonomia* refers to the small-scale economics of the household. According to Haeckel's definition, "Ecology is the study of the interdependence and interaction of living organisms (animals and plants) and their environment (inanimate matter)."[45]

The work of Alfred Lotka provided the foundation for ecological theory. He emphasized the complex interactions among animals, plants, minerals, and the physical environment and considered them involved in an interconnected and integrated process. Lotka was keenly aware that biological systems are not thermodynamically isolated. Although the earth as a whole can be considered approximately closed, it only receives energy from the sun. The second law of thermodynamics provides a boundary condition for biological activity,[46] because the earth can be understood as an open system in interaction with its environments. According to the second law of thermodynamics, the universe, or the present state of order seems to cool down or break down as the slopes of entropy lead toward abyss. Nonetheless, more various and complex forms of order toward creativity and novelty emerge out of the edge of chaos, at states far from the thermodynamic equilibrium.

The science of chaos and complexity emphasizes that a small change in the initial condition, a local action, has caused an influence on a global scale, an enormous change in the final result.[47] Considering the enormous transformation from a simple order to surprisingly rich forms of unpredictable

---

45. Boff, *Ecology and Liberation*, 9.

46. Depew and Weber, *Darwinism Evolving*, 408–9.

47. According to the "butterfly effect," the trajectory of a hurricane may be influenced and even determined by an insignificant flapping of a butterfly's wing as initial physical conditions.

order, the evolutionary emergence of life is contingent upon the initial environmental conditions and constants. The self-organizing pattern of complexity in the evolutionary progression does not follow the Darwinian model of natural selection; rather it paradoxically points to creativity and novelty of emergent, adaptive self-organizing organisms.[48] The science of chaos and complexity maintains that a universe is still in the making, always open to a freshness and novelty for a new creation, new order, and new life.

A theological notion of *creatio continua*, seen in light of the science of chaos and complexity, can uphold a theology of ecology. Evolutionary life and the universe as an open system seem to be guided more by tenderness, God's gentile and persuasive power toward its fulfilling in the eschatological comprehensive renewal of nature, rather than brute force.[49] Evolution occurs within an ecological theater, while the theater itself changes by way of the autonomous dynamics of self-organizing systems. Ecology reaffirms the interdependence of beings, interprets all hierarchies as a matter of function, and repudiates the so-called right of the strongest. All creatures manifest and possess their own relative and intrinsic autonomy. This aspect helps us affirm God's solidarity with and promise for nature as imparted by God at the final consummation.

Given God's promised future, I find it meaningful to comprehend the Gaia hypothesis in a qualified sense in terms of the life of holism and open system by recognizing the global functions of local and regional ecosystems. James Lovelock presents the idea that the planet Earth as a whole is a living, self-organizing system. Earth's atmosphere is an open system, far from equilibrium, which is characterized by a constant flow of energy and matter. The process of self-regulation in Earth's life is an alternative to the conventional science that sees Earth as a dead planet. His hypothesis of Earth as a self-regulating system argues that all of life is tightly coupled with all of its environment, forming a self-regulating entity.[50] Lovelock's idea represents a powerful ancient myth, called the Gaia hypothesis, in honor of the Greek goddess.[51]

The evolution of the first living organisms becomes possible in connection with the change of the planetary surface from an inorganic environment to a self-regulating biosphere. James Lovelock, later in collaboration with Lynn Margulis, identified a complex network of feedback loops as the

---

48. Trinh, *Chaos and Harmony*, 67–68, 283.

49. Haught, *Science and Religion*, 156,

50. Lovestock, *Healing Gaia*, 12.

51. A strong resistance is given to the Gaia hypothesis, because the scientific establishment has little to do with the irrational evocation of the powerful archetypal myth.

one that brings about the self-regulation of the planetary system, linking together living and nonliving systems. In the words of Lynn Margulis, the Gaia hypothesis says that the earth is really part of life: "Life actually makes and forms and changes the environment to which it adapts. Then that 'environment' feeds back on the life that is changing and acting and growing in it. There are constant cyclical interactions."[52]

The Gaia theory helps some ecologically oriented theologians to advance a theology of planetary life, because integrated knowledge in the investigation of wider connections and cohesion in the system of earth must be guided by the concern for shared life and survival, by way of planetary life in co-operation and symbiosis. The survival of planetary life in the future will only be possible in symbiosis, coordination and concurrence with the total organism of the earth.[53]

Theology in the Flesh, *Creatio Continua*, and Divine Future

The construction of this theology of nature places us on the doorstep of *theistic evolution*. The key commitment of the theistic evolutionist is the incorporation of the neo-Darwinian view into the theologian's theory of divine action in the natural world. "Although some theistic evolutionists deny miracles while others affirm them," write Ted Peters and Martinez Hewlett, "overall this group prefers a *noninterventionist divine action* position. They want to affirm both divine action as well as a divine-hands-off understanding of the dialectic between law and chance in natural selection."[54]

It will be my task in what follows to incorporate an evolutionary-ecological perspective into a future-oriented view of God's creativity, a step to take by faith seeking further understanding.

The evolutionary-ecological perspective helps us to advance a notion of God's relationality with the world in a reciprocal manner. Systematic theology speaks of the triune God as the Creator in regard to *creatio ex nihilo* which implies the ontological sense of dependence of the world upon God. God is also the continuing Creator, who, together with nature, bringing about what science describes as the biological foundation of life on earth (*creatio continua*). We may think of God as acting, in the hidden working of the Spirit Life-Giver, in all quantum events in the course of biological evolution until the appearance of organisms capable of even primitive levels

52. Margulis, "Gaia: The Living Earth," cited in Capra, *Web of Life*, 106.

53. Moltmann, *God for a Secular Society*, 109–10; Ruether, *Gaia and God*.

54. Peters and Hewlett, *Evolution from Creation*, 30.

of consciousness. From then on, God allows the developing levels of consciousness to act out their intention somatically.[55] While not undermining a top-down approach, this refers to a bottom-up approach, which attempts "to move from the particularities of experiences to the generalities of understanding," searching for interpretation and motivated belief.[56]

According to John Haught, reflection on the Darwinian world leads us to contemplate the mystery of God as manifest in the story of life's long and often tormented journey. Its epitome lies for Christians in the crucifixion of Jesus, in whom God is the one in kenotic love yet with the power of a future. In divine presence and solidarity in, with, and under the creaturely life, God calls us to participate in God's unfinished universe and in God's continuing work. God lures us in a non-coercive manner, collaborating with us toward increased beauty, justice, and perfection. The Whiteheadian notion of God's affection through the event is incorporated into an evolutionary-eschatological framework, into more comprehensive wholes of meaning and future. Faith is nurtured by divine invitation to look for signs of future promise, because faith seeks the promise of divine future.[57]

According to Whitehead, the primordial nature of God[58] refers to God who is the ordering and the gift of potentiality. Viewed as primordial, God is with all creation rather than before all creation, because God is the unlimited conceptual realization of the absolute wealth of potentiality.[59] The primordial side of God's nature is infinite, free, complete, and eternal,[60] which expresses the primordial nature of God. More than that, God is also consequent.[61] The consequent nature of God is the physical prehension by God of the actualities of the evolving universe in which divine potentialities are actualized. God shares the actual world with every new creation. The world of creative advance enters into the life and reality of God's consequent nature, which is the fluent world. The fluent world has become everlasting by its objective immortality in God.[62] It is substantial to revise and qualify Whiteheadian metaphysics in reference to God's promised Future in the comprehensive renewal of creation.

55. Ibid., 154.

56. Polkinghorne, *Scientists as Theologians*, 9.

57. Haught, *Science and Religion*, 154–55.

58. Whitehead, *Process and Reality*, 32.

59. Ibid., 343.

60. Ibid., 345.

61. Ibid.

62. Ibid., 347.

God exerts a top-down causality on the world from the future, which is conceptualized in an eschatologically oriented notion of time. Divine action in the prehensive phase of every event seeks to lure its outcome in a favorable direction. The initiating of the concrescent phase brings about a specific outcome which lies with the actual occasion itself. This process metaphysics presents a very qualified form of panentheism, which does not necessarily undermine a metaphysic of God's Future. According to David Griffin, the reverse side of panentheism refers to our existence in the consequent nature of God, portraying God as the truly supreme power of the universe, and also as a basis for hope in the ultimate victory of good over evil.[63]

The present form of *creatio continua* finds its validity in reference to a metaphysic of future grounded in eschatological panentheism (*creatio nova*), revealing a comprehensive renewal of creation: God will be all in all (1 Cor 15). The metaphysics of future accounts for the three cosmic qualities—chance, lawfulness, and temporality—providing the raw stuff of biological evolution. Future is in a dynamic interaction with the present. The paradoxical hiddenness of God's power in a self-effacing persuasive love allows creation to come about and to unfold freely and indeterminately in evolution.[64] The role of chance in this regard does not remove the possibility of meaning, because God's self-limitation in the act of allowing for creatures to evolve and exist accompanies evolutionary history. Living systems have already organized themselves spontaneously in a pre-packaged form and creativity in evolution occurs primarily in the self-organization prior to natural selection. Natural selection is not sufficient to account for all creativity and novelty in evolution.[65] Evolutionary process operates in a suitably finely tuned natural environment in which God is not indifferent to blind alleys, extinction, and the pains of creatures.

In light of God's ongoing creation, I seek to revise a notion of *creatio ex nihilo* which is not expressed in Gen 1 and 2. This idea is only literally found in 2 Macc 7:28 in connection with the narrative of the martyr.[66] This perspective helps us seek the meaning of *creatio ex nihilo* in a metaphorical-historical-eschatological framework, that is, in light of God in the eschatological act of the resurrection of Jesus Christ. *Creatio ex nihilo* refers to *creatio ex verbis, Dabar*, embracing the *logos*, looking forward to God's

---

63. Griffin, *Religion and Scientific Naturalism*, 97–98.

64. Haught, *God after Darwin*, 97.

65. Kauffmann, *Origins of Order*, 15–26.

66. Link, *Schöpfung*, 1:515. In this story the youngest among seven martyred brothers is encouraged by his mother to the final resurrection of his brothers through the act of the gracious God.

future consummation as the crowning conclusion of creation, God's Final Rest to which God's Rest in the first act of creation refers.

More importantly, the biblical story of creation (Gen 1) implies Israel's experience of God's emancipation in the period of Persian Babylonian captivity. It refers to the subordination of mythical powers under God's liberative rule. Creation is historically structured, entailing the illuminating light and emancipation out of historical darkness in the Babylonian captivity.[67] This approach helps us to advance an integrative model between creation and redemption in hermeneutical reference to God's eschatology, by which to qualify the combination between a proleptic creation with proleptic *adventus*. A thesis of God's creation from the future[68] finds its meaning in proleptic *adventus* in solidarity with *massa perditionis* in history and victims in the evolutionary history.

Having said this, a notion of *creatio continua* in nature and history maintains that God the Great Companion in the suffering of the world integrates many blind alleys, extinct species, much waste, and pains into the divine life through the universal reconciliation which is brought about by the Cosmic Christ (Col 1:20). Grace does not destroy, but prepares, integrates, and perfects nature in light of the kingdom of God.[69] A theology of the cross refers to theology in the flesh which maintains that what God revealed in the cross of Jesus is God participating with us in suffering and death, while paradoxically bringing healing and life. God's self-emptying love (*kenosis*) and humility is ground for a self-organizing universe to come into being. *Theologia crucis* in the form of presentative eschatology does not replace the coming of God's Future, which qualifies *theologia crusis* in terms of the in-breaking reality of God in solidarity with those marginalized and foreclosed in the reality of natural selection. This perspective does not necessarily generate a logic of schizoid combination embedded with theology of the free-will defense, regarding the paradoxical relationship between God's self-limitation in allowance for natural self-organization and God's ongoing engagement with suffering, evil, and death in the physical world.[70] A doctrine of God's self-limitation must not be presented on behalf of the evolutionary logic of natural selection, justifying a picture of God as sanctioning the injustice, violence, and death of the weaker for the stronger in an ideological-colonialist framework.

67. Marquardt, *Eia wärn Wir da*, 310.
68. Peters, *God—the World's Future*, 142.
69. Moltmann, *God in Creation*, 7.
70. Peters and Hewlett, *Evolution from Creation*, 156.

Faith seeking understanding emphasizes that faith is inseparably con-nected with our discipleship of love following God's in-breaking solidarity with *massa perditionis* in the world as well as hope in anticipation of divine eschatological and comprehensive new creation from above toward the be-low. It cannot be adequately comprehended apart from God's participation in the suffering reality of the world and also our discipleship in commit-ment to justice, peace, and sustainability in the web of life.

A traditional concept of the God of the gaps or *deus ex machina* is deeply challenged, such that "faith seeking understanding" is reshaped by participation in God's solidarity with the unfit, fragile, and vulnerable in the world. Theology of the cross as theology in the flesh characterizes us as created collaborators,[71] encouraging us to take part in God's ongoing creative work in light of God's eschatological act of new creation. That is God's final solution of theodicy through a new Heaven and a new Earth in the transformation of evolutionary history as well as in divine indwell-ing with God's people, wiping every tear from their eyes. "Death will be no more; mourning and crying and pain will be no more for the first things have passed away" (Rev 21:4). This God is the Trinitarian God, the Lord God the Almighty and the Lamb in the shining glory of the Holy Spirit (Rev 21:22). A theology of the cross is eschatologically oriented, while emphasizing God's in-breaking solidarity with those victimized in the evo-lutionary world. But the world is also reconciled by God in Christ, who inspires the church, the community of the created collaborators, to renew and change the status quo of the reality of powers and principalities in light of the future of the final emancipation. The trinitarian God is the source and driving force for the evolution of life to finally fulfill its meaning as God's creation in the eschatological promise of a new Heaven and a new Earth.

This trinitarian perspective challenges an idea of providence in the traditional metaphysics of classical theism, which tends to justify the life of innocent victims as stepping stones toward more development and prog-ress. This is affirmed in Luther's saying, as interpreted in Bonhoeffer: "God would rather hear the curses of the ungodly than the alleluia of the pious."[72]

---

71. The theology in the flesh related to created collaborators may qualify a notion of God's created co-creator. Human freedom grounded in the grace of Christ's recon-ciliation places human freedom at the intersection of eschatological realism, without presupposing an idea of co-creation between God and human beings. Hefner, *Human Factor*, 121.

72. Bonhoeffer, *Ethics*, 104.

Buddhist Contribution to Ecological Sustainability

Social-ecological epistemology and theology of God's vulnerability is consonant with the Buddhist understanding of Buddha nature in the evolutionary-planetary process and its ethics of compassion. The Buddhist teaching of dependent co-arising is established as the Middle Way (Sunyata) in the context of Madhyamika as represented by Nagarjuna (150–250 CE). Sunyata is not even a permanent and absolute substance, so that cause and effect are in interrelationship and complementarity. This challenges an essential unity between atman (self) and Brahman (ultimate reality), reducing the Upanishadic equation to the Buddhist Sunyata and Enlightenment upon which the Four Noble Truths are based. All life in suffering through change (*dukkha*)—the first Noble Truth—implies that all things are subject to impermanence, change, and vulnerability in the world of the endlessly cycled wheel of unsatisfactory lives (*samsara*).

The Buddhist idea of ultimate truth is beyond linguistic comprehension and definition. Nonetheless, Buddhist hermeneutics of interdependence (dependent co-arising) is undertaken in expression of the Truth in a relative-linguistic sense. For a Buddhist hermeneutic, Buddhist doctrine would never have the description of reality as an aim. It serves only as a method or a guide for the practitioner in his experience of the ultimate reality,[73] because the finger pointing to the moon must not be mistaken for the moon as such. Here we see narrative, symbolic, and metaphorical thought in the Buddhist Path to Dhamma, enlightenment and nirvana.

As the Buddha said, "He who sees the Dhamma sees me; he who sees me sees the Dhamma."[74] Dhamma is presented in the new sense of compassion, ethics, and wisdom to overcome the fragility of life, which overturns the Brahman ideology and caste social system in early Indian society.

The Buddhist epistemology of impermanence, no-self, and radical relationality can become the entry point for dialogue with evolution and quantum physics.[75] Although there is no theory of evolution mentioned in Buddhist texts, humanity, society, and the world are depicted as changing and evolving in accordance with the principle of interdependence between cause and effect. In the Theravada school of Buddhism, a new interpretation of the Buddha as a biologist comes to the fore, appreciating evolutionary biology as a dialogue partner. The revolutionary science reveals how

73. Nhat Hanh, *Zen Keys*, 47.

74. Collins, *Nirvana and Other Buddhist Felicities*, 245.

75. Capra, *The Tao of Physics*; Ricard and Trinh, *The Quantum and the Lotus*.

deeply embedded and interwoven humans are within the network of life and nature.[76]

The Buddhist Middle Way in the Chinese tradition has especially developed more ecologically, more cosmically, and more compassionately with a view to all living beings in dukkha (suffering). All sentient beings without exception enter into a universal relationship with Buddhahood, so that they become Buddha (nirvana or emancipation). The reality of identity and interdependence in Hua-yen Buddhism, as expressed in the *Avatamsaka (Hua-yen) Sutra*, is reflected by the image of the jewel net of Indra, expounded by Fa-tsang (643–712). This image provides a pivotal foundation for a socially engaged Buddhism by illustrating the holistic dimension of Indra's net for complementarity between Sunyata and Fullness (wondrous being). In Indra's net each jewel exists only as a reflection of all the others, thus having no self-nature. In the infinite world of Indra a jewel is placed at each knot so that each jewel is generated and sustained through the web of interdependence.

A creative interpretation of Nagarjuna's Middle Way and a notion of Buddha-nature (*tathagatagarbha*; imago Buddha in Christian terms) had evolved and culminated in the Hua-yen interpretation of the relation between the unobstructed interpenetration of phenomena (*shi-shi wu-ai*) and the unobstructed interpenetration of the absolute and phenomenal (*li-shi wu-ai*). This hermeneutical debate was fully realized in Tsung-mi's (780–841) systematization of the importance of the one true dharmadhatu—that is, the priority of the unobstructed interpenetration of the absolute and phenomenal (*li-shih wu-ai*) over and against the expression of the unobstructed interpenetration of phenomena (*shi-shi wu ai*).[77]

Seen in terms of cosmic and universal ecology, the opening of the third eye through spiritual awakening through Ch'an should lead to opening the fourth eye in the social and cultural context, especially highlighting social ethical commitment. As Thich Nhat Hanh argues, "If you have compassion, you cannot be rich. . . . You can be rich only when you can bear the sight of suffering. If you cannot bear that, you have to give your possessions away."[78]

For the Buddhist economic vision from the web of relations, Sulak Sivaraksa proposes the Buddhist symbol of Indra's Net. In this web of interdependence, we can stay close to nature as our life companion. In the cosmic envisioning of a community, individuals and communities determine their own direction asking for structural support and symbiosis. It de-emphasizes

76. Nisker, *Buddha's Nature*, 3, 17.

77. Gregory, *Tsung-mi and the Sinification of Buddhism*, 68.

78. Berrigan and Nhat Hanh, *Raft Is Not the Shore*, 102.

the structural hierarchies of institutions, and de-centralizes power structure.[79] This perspective of the Middle Way characterizes Buddhist understanding of economic life and eco-justice. Buddhist economics is critical of
the subject of self-interest. Self-interest (needs) expands its meaning and
scope to the extent that it includes desire and greed in accounting for the
motivation for profit. This pursuit for self-interest and increasing profit is
regarded as meaningful and rational only in light of human purpose in accounting for the civilization of Western modernity and capitalist economy.
However, the Buddhist Second Noble Truth of non-attachment suggests that
attachment to greed cannot be considered rational, since it causes suffering
to humanity, society, and planetary life, driven toward a myth of rampant
growth and competition.

A Buddhist contribution to economic justice and an alternative way of
modernity in East Asia was undertaken in Robert Bellah's study of Buddhist
economic rationality in his *Tokugawa Religion*.[80] During the Tokugawa period (1600–1867) and the Meiji period (1868–1912), Japan did not have
the cultural or religious resources to initiate the process of modernization
itself. However, the Tokugawa society was more readily adaptable to modernization than any of the other non-Western countries.[81] Buddhism put
an emphasis on selfless detachment in the interest of collaboration with the
people, helping build bridges, undertake irrigation and drain swamps. The
core values in Buddhist ethics are compassion and collaboration rather than
this-worldly asceticism coupled with self-interest and competition.[82]

Faith, Understanding, and Recognition

In our study of faith seeking understanding in the science-religion dialogue,
we have advanced theological engagement with scientific theory of evolution and ecology and further examined the Buddhist contribution in this
direction. For Anselm, theological rationality, seen in light of God's mystery as insuperability, may be socially engaged in recognition of the secular
contributions to God's life. His analogical theology has been enhanced and
critically revised in our hermeneutical frame of reference concerning God,
science, religion, and the world for a current post-foundational rationality. The Darwinian model of evolution is not an established truth, but as a
scientific research program assuming critical realism, it is still in need of

79. Sivaraksa, *Wisdom of Sustainability*, 38.

80. Bellah, *Tokugawa Religion*.

81. Ibid., 40.

82. Puntasen, "Individual and Structural Greed," in Sinaga, *Common Word*, 88–89.

revision by other scientific approaches to evolutionary process and ecology. Emergent creativity and novelty at the states far from thermodynamic equilibrium transcend a principle of natural selection and randomness. An evolutionary-ecological framework facilitates theological understanding of God's creative interaction with evolutionary process, conceptualizing it in a persuasive manner through chance, contingence, and necessity. God, the grand compassion in the life of the vulnerable, the extinct, and the victims, encourages our faith (coupled with created co-workers) to establish participation in and solidarity with what God continues to do in natural history and humanity. Natural history and human history are not divided, but complement one another in light of God's universal reconciliation brought up by the Cosmic Christ.

In the mystery of the triune God in the threefold sense of creation, the original creation in the past does not simply imply God's once and for all work done at a distance, but it includes a reflection of God's emancipatory work during the period of the Babylonian captivity. It further points to God's eschatological act of the resurrection of Jesus Christ. This revised understanding helps to set us free from the captivity to timeless eternity, envisioning a hermeneutical circularity between God's eternity in temporality and God's temporality in eternity. Paul's eschatological expectation of emancipation of the creation from its bondage to decay and its obtaining of freedom in terms of the glory of the children of God (Rom 8:21) culminates in John's apocalyptic description of a new creation by destroying those who destroy the earth (Rev 11:18). The hope of the Revelation is the Lamb of God, the eschatological Immanuel of God's Future in which the new Jerusalem (Rev 21–22) becomes an earth-centered vision of our future, thereby divine ecology. We received God's promised future as a gift of God through Jesus Christ, awakening us to become the created collaborators serving in anticipation of the eschatological coming of God.

Faith seeks understanding of life of evolution in reference to God's future standing in God's relationality and embodiment, which is on the side of the unfit, fragile, and victimized. Faith in search of understanding is encouraged by and remains in anticipation of God's promise of a future. God is not of the gaps, a Greek idol of *deus ex machina*. At this juncture, Bonhoeffer's prophetic voice deserves attention: "We have for once learnt to see the great events of world history from below, from the perspective of the outcast, the suspects, the maltreated, the powerless, the oppressed, the reviled—in short, from the perspective of those who suffer."[83]

---

83. Bonhoeffer, *Letters and Papers from Prison*, 17.

Driven by a hermeneutics from below, faith recognizes the Buddhist contribution to compassion, economic justice, and sustainable ecology, which is consonant with God's ongoing creation and companionship to all sentient creatures. Faith in understanding remains integral when it recognizes the dignity of the other through whose face God speaks to our faith in an unexpected and surprising manner. Our Christian self is shaped in our social, narrative character of selfhood. Our selfhood arises only in dialogue with others which characterizes our self as the narrative and communicative self. Through stories we expand our horizon of faith and understanding in encounter with and recognition of the stories of the others. Story enriches a sense of identity of the self and the Other. Our belongingness to the story drives our history, facilitating a reconstruction of a new meaning for the present and future.[84]

Christian identity is shaped by a biblical story about creation, reconciliation, and redemption. Faith shaped by a story invites the other to contribute to God's Shalom and the integrity of life through mutual respect and renewal. A fusion of horizons in dialogue and mutual learning nurtures our faith in understanding as faith in recognition. We see in Abraham's faith journey that God advocates for Hagar and Ishmael. God is pleased to help Israel through Cyrus, a pagan king, or Balaam despite the sinister origin. Emmanuel Levinas acknowledges in Abraham's journey "a departure with no return,"[85] characterizing Abraham as the prototype of life for the Other. Abraham is differentiated from Odysseus, a prototype of the Western philosophy of Sameness and self-identity, whose "adventure in the world was only a return to his native island—a complacency in the Same, an unrecognition of the Other."[86]

More than that, prior to God's covenant with Abraham, there was God's universal covenant with Noah, including the generations to come and all living creatures. Likewise, all nations are invited to participate in the story of God's covenant through Jesus Christ. A hermeneutical structure in the direction toward the Other shapes our faith journey in emphatic listening to God's act of speech as it continues to be heard in the figure of the Other—Buddha, the poor, and nature as the new poor. As the multiple stories continue to meet, God as the communicator of stories embraces the textual world and the social world, such that God acts in, under, and through the evolutionary-planetary drama, widening its rhythm of life for a much larger horizon of the open system toward God's Future as the Source of the whole of time and place.

---

84. Bellah, *Religion in Human Evolution*, 45.

85. Levinas, *Basic Philosophical Writings*, 49.

86. Ibid., 48.

6

Ted Peters

Prolepsis, Divine Action, and Grace

Ted Peters, a prolific scholar, is a systematic theologian and public ethicist. His proleptic theology, which is elaborated in the context of evolutionary theory and other scientific insights, is a fulcrum for advancing theology of divine action, theology of nature, and graced life. Although he does not write in the area of postcolonial theology, his proleptic theology, held in a postmodern hermeneutical frame of holism, entails a strong component of public ethics in critically dealing with political rhetoric of self-justification and supporting the integration of distributive justice and restorative justice. Embedded within the life of beatitude, Peters envisions proleptic ethics from God's Future—a promise characterized by restorative justice imbued with divine love and symbolized by new creation in the kingdom of God.[1] This perspective enables us to incorporate his achievements into *postcolonial* public theology.

In the study of Ted Peters' theology, for the most part I shall deal with proleptic eschatology, hermeneutical epistemology and postmodern holism, a theological-scientific spectrum of divine action, genetic research in connection with human freedom, and proleptic ethics grounded in living of beatitude. After examining his important arguments and contributions, finally, my interest comes to a comparative study between proleptic theology and public theology in terms of appreciation, critical questions, and further development. I begin by analyzing Peters' concept of hypothetical consonance in dealing with the relation between theology and science.

1. Peters, *God—the World's Future*, 392; Peters, *Sin Boldly*.

Theology and Science in Hypothetical Consonance

For advancing science-theology dialogue, Peters is concerned with bringing science and theology into mutual interaction to purse creative development and revision, which goes beyond the warfare model. He also seeks to transcend limitations of the two-language theory. The warfare model is represented by ecclesiastical authoritarianism in the Roman Catholic tradition and scientific creationism of Protestant fundamentalists.[2] The two-language theory argues that science deals with natural facts while religion with ultimate meaning. There is the so-called NOMA, which stands for non-overlapping magisterial. For Stephen J Gould, science and religion occupy different domains, nonoverlapping rather than in conflict with each other.[3]

In driving the relation between science and religion in the direction of *hypothetical* consonance, Peters insists that scientists and theologians can find some areas of shared understanding and commonality to go beyond the two-language strategy. A notion of hypothetical consonance is in a weaker sense than the strong version of consonance as accord, or harmony. It identifies common domains of explorations for scientific understanding of the natural world and for theological understanding of God's creation.

The God question is not eradicated even within scientific reasoning, because scientists acknowledge the limitation of reductionist and materialist methods for the deeper question of the truth. The notion of the God of evolution (Denis Edwards)[4] indicates that the scientific theory of evolution facilitates actual knowledge for theologians to comprehend God's work in nature. Both the biblical teaching of Genesis and the theory of evolution help Christians rethink the triune God at work in creation.[5]

For his methodological procedure, Peters critically reviews scientism or naturalism, because scientific materialism is proven as an ideology in its atheistic orientation. Although acknowledging the existence of something divine, scientific imperialism claims knowledge of the divine exclusively for scientific research by conquering the territory of religious revelation. This perspective is seen in physicist Frank Tipler, a representative of scientific imperialism, who argues that quantum theory associated with the Big Bang

---

2. Peters, *Science, Theology, and Ethics*, 16–17.
3. Gould, "Nonoverlapping Magisteria."
4. Edwards, *The God of Evolution*.
5. Peters, *Science, Theology, and Ethics*, 20.

and thermodynamics is in a better position to explain the future resurrection of the dead than Christian theology.[6]

Against this, however, Peters pays attention to Paul Davies, who is willing to acknowledge the importance of faith within the context of scientific rationality, because ultimate questions always transcend the scope of empirical science.[7] Peters' hypothetical consonance fits Robert John Russell's dialectic between consonance and dissonance in which science and theology take different paths, while acknowledging the dissonance. Russell's model of creative mutual interaction challenges theologians to revise their view of sciences, requiring also that scientists take into account theological truth claims in promoting hypotheses for research programs. Such mutual interaction could eventually lead to consonance.[8]

Furthermore, Nancey Murphy's use of the philosophy of Imae Lakatos deserves attention, because she incorporates Russell's consonance-dissonance dialectic into a progressive research program. Murphy cuts through the limitation of critical realism for the sake of postmodern reasoning. Her critique is cast upon the critical realist commitment to epistemological foundationalism, representational thinking based on the correspondence theory of truth, and finally excessive individualism of critical realism linked to insufficient attention to the community. For her theological-scientific agenda, the progressive nature of a research program must be a sufficient criterion in challenging the referentiality of critical realism.[9]

Informed by the Lakatos-Murphy distinction between the core commitment and the outer auxiliary hypotheses in a research program, Russell's understanding of *creatio ex nihilo* is valued as the core, because it says that the world is ontologically dependent upon God. *Creatio ex nihilo* as ontological dependence is what Big Bang cosmology in the sense of a t=0 confirms in a partial confirmation, not as a proof.

In Peters' account, Russell's contribution lies in drawing the distinction between finitude and boundedness. Ontological dependence maintains that the world is finite but not necessarily bounded. The world has a beginning, because it is finite in time. Big bang cosmology may become a character witness in its quantum form to the creation of the world.[10] It seems that Russell could qualify Schleiermacher's endeavor to defend religion against its despisers, while scientifically engaging in *creatio ex nihilo* as ontological

6. Ibid., 17.

7. Davies, *Mind of God*, 15.

8. Peters and Hewlett, *Evolution from Creation*, 151.

9. Peters, *Science, Theology, and Ethics*, 25.

10. Ibid., 32.

dependence of the world and humanity in interaction with the Big Bang cosmology.

Theologically, Peters' hypothetical consonance becomes allied with Wolfhart Pannenberg's notion of theological assertions as hypotheses because it understands God as the all-determining reality. What makes theological assertions hypothetical, hence scientific, is the theological idea of the eschatological kingdom of God. This is because a wholeness of meaning is not yet fully present, subject to future confirmation. The direct confirmation of the hypothesis is dependent upon the actual coming of the eschatological wholeness, but our faith assumes the form of a hypothesis in terms of the indirect confirmation in our understanding of finite reality. Peters' interest in Pannenberg's proleptic theology can be seen in his edition of Pannenberg's theology of nature constructed in dialogue with scientists.[11]

Hermeneutical Epistemology and Postmodern Holism

For proleptic hermeneutics, it is important to briefly review Pannenberg's theology. In elaborating the notion of God as the all-determining reality, Pannenberg employs a theology of word-event (Gerhard Ebeling), in which discussion of the word of God (theology) is related to human linguisticality. Speaking about God implies speaking about the all-determining reality which is conceived of as present and active in every event. Every human word is finally indebted to an unthematic, hidden presence of God underlying the dimension of linguistic consciousness.[12]

More than that, Pannenberg employs Gadamer and Dilthey, while reframing Gadamer's notion of the fusion of horizons in terms of universal history. Gadamer describes the encounter between the horizon of the past text and the present horizon of the interpreter, presupposing the totality of history as its ultimate frame of reference.[13]

However, in Pannenberg's judgment, Gadamer tends to speak of the texts in terms of the linguisticality of human reality alone, in which tradition or history is linguistically mediated as the history of effect. Hence, Pannenberg argues that the fusion of horizons is also historically mediated, expanding such a linguistic dimension through Dilthey's concept of experienced meaning in historical life. The linguisticality of human reality via the historical life connection requires that meaning is accessible only in

11. Pannenberg, *Toward a Theology of Nature.*

12. Pannenberg, *Theology and the Philosophy of Science*, 281–82.

13. Ibid., 284.

the anticipation of divine future, which has proleptically occurred in the resurrection of Jesus of Nazareth. By grounding proleptic hermeneutics in the universal-historical framework of God as all-determining reality, Pannenberg rightly comprehends the intelligibility of the natural world through scientific discipline.

Let us move to Peters' hermeneutical concern. For him, hermeneutical questions and answers belong to the center of the modern theologcial enterprise. This is an issue of making the Christian faith, as articulated in ancient culture, meaningfully relevant to our life today in which we experience in a worldview, dominated by natural science, challenged by secular self-understanding, and demanded by autonomous freedom.[14]

The hermeneutical question characterized by the modern context entails critical consciousness or doubt, which is articulated primarily in the Cartesian principle *cogito ergo sum*. This position finds its apex in the masters of suspicion (Karl Marx, Friedrich Nietzsche, and Sigmund Freud), sharpening the principle of critical doubt in terms of economic basis, will to power, and the world unconsciousness.

As a theological response, hermeneutics is therefore located within the project of reinterpreting the original meaning of biblical narratives and symbols, seeking new formulation of their out-of-date symbols and articulating them in a meaningfully relevant way for the new situation. However, the translation model does not exhaust the language of Christian faith, although it is constituted in a linguistically translatable web of meaning from one language to another. For Peters, certain basic symbols tied to the original experience from God are irreplaceable and non-translatable, which circumvents a postcolonial notion of interpolation as translation.[15]

What allows the gospel to travel from one culture to another is the protean power of the biblical symbols to generate meaning in new contexts rather than its translatability.[16] Peters appreciates a hermeneutic of symbol (Paul Ricoeur) to prevent a modernist notion of translation from exhausting biblical symbol, metaphor, and narrative.

Nonetheless, our interpretation of the basic symbolic self-God-world relation finds its meaningfulness in the context-dependent manner. In

14. Peters, *God—the World's Future*, 7.

15. Peters' perspective finds parallel with my critique of a limitation of the postcolonial-deconstructive notion of translation, which reduces all of the biblical languages and symbols into indigenous language and particular locality. There are still zones of untranslatability, because it is hard to translate a kerygmatic thought in the Bible to a totemic system of thought or multireligiously fused cultural realty in Asia. Chung, *Hermeneutical Theology*, 365.

16. Peters, *God—the World's Future*, 16.

contextualization of biblical symbols, self-understanding can shift or change according to the context.

Peters also cites a provocative statement of Marit A. Trelstad:

> When one views the imperialistic tendencies of a whole nation or overall environmental abuse of the earth, one may hold the cross to be an antidote to pride. When one views the personal effects of domestic violence and sexual abuse, one may say the punitive image of the cross furthers the abuse. . . . Simply put, the vantage point from which one sees the cross influences one's interpretation significantly.[17]

Moreover, Peters distinguishes the deconstruction type of postmodernity from the reconstruction type of wholeness. The deconstructionst train of thought is characterized by abandoning the credibility of metanarratives (Jean-Francois Lyotard) inclusive of the whole of reality. Postmodernists denounce such universalism because it disguises the perspectivalism of the one dominant interest in its power over another. It rejects a confidence in the foundationalism upon which human knowledge is built on the foundation of the *cogito*. It refuses universalism of Cartesian modernity in generating confidence in progress through science and technology.

Peters' approach to postmodern holism is differentiated from postmodern deconstructionism in the fashion of Jacques Derrida.[18] Rather, holistic postmodernism aims at recovering meaning, not its deconstruction or dissolution. Peters' holistic train of thought can be summed up in Nancey Murphy's words: "a complex mutual conditioning between part and whole."[19] This means that the whole is greater than the sum of the parts.

Epistemologically, a holistic understanding of human reasoning or imagination includes both thinking and feeling, placing the human being in a context of intelligibility or meaning that includes both. Ontologically, it upholds the epigenetic view. Evolutionary theory rejects the notion of a completed beginning in the past. Evolution is not merely a process of change and its new forms are not merely fashioned out of the old materials. Rather the sum of reality is progressively increasing in the course of evolution, creating both new materials and new forms by synthesizing the new with the old materials.[20]

17. Trelstad, "Introduction: The Cross in Context," in Trelstad, *Cross Examinations*, 4. See Peters, *Sin Boldly*, 197.

18. Fair enough. However, Derrida is far more constructive in his later work, particularly in relation to religion, namely, the *via negativa* and the mystics.

19. Murphy, *Anglo-American Postmodernity*, 34.

20. Smuts, *Holism and Evolution*, 89.

This perspective presents evolutionary development as an epigenesis, creating new things, thus entailing freedom for the future. This view breaks the bondage of the past coupled with its fixed predeterminism. The evolutionary and epigenetic ontology maintains that the pull of the future is essential to the life of an organism, the push of the past. The new wholes are the center and creative source of reality.[21]

Proleptic consciousness refers to our awareness and anticipation of the future whole. God's promise and faith in God's faithfulness provides such awareness and anticipation, in which the gospel of Jesus Christ is essentially comprehended as a promise for the future. More than that, it actually embodies ahead of time the future that God has promised for the whole of creation, that is, new creation. What is real is future-oriented. In light of the God-determined whole which is not yet actual, we can apprehend that all the world processes and human enterprises will be integrated into God's whole, transforming separated and fragmented parts into an integrated unity. The God-determined whole has been revealed ahead of time in the life, death, and resurrection of Jesus, whose life is a proleptic life, the future life actualized ahead of time.[22]

Peters' postcritical hermeneutics based on postmodern holism unites what has been fragmented and divided through binary opposition. For systematic constructive theology, the principle of holistic thinking articulates the deeply experienced human need for healing and salvation. Vision of a divinely graced whole facilitates articulating the content of Christian faith in our context.

The other principle is hypothetical reconstruction. Theological hypothetical reconstruction is of postcritical character, to the degree that we live in a world of meaning.[23] By making the gospel meaningful to the new context, Peters is committed to postcritical thinking, which is personally participatory, integrative, holistic, and reconstructive. By questioning and understanding Christian symbols, which give us thought, we can move beyond the desert of criticism and meaninglessness.

Classic epistemology—faith seeking understanding—does not necessarily mean one-sided fideism, but expresses interaction between faith and reason. Classic epistemology helps us to pursue a post-Cartesian version of St. Anselm's definition of theology as faith seeking understanding. As Peters states, "Once we have entered the belief-understanding circle, the process of

---

21. Ibid., 115–16.

22. Peters, *God—the World's Future*, 21.

23. Ibid., 32.

interpreting Christian symbols begins to illuminate our own life and makes it understandable in relation to the divine reality."[24]

Peters' postcritical theology is world-reconstructive because of its participatory quality. In the act of belief in the transcendent God our life is reoriented in this world toward God's action in our midst. The ineffable God touches the mundane realm, revealing divine self-communication through the revelatory act of Jesus Christ, that is, the prolepsis of divine Future.

Spectrum of Divine Action in the Midst of Evolution

An analysis of the hermeneutical dimension in Peters' proleptic theology leads us to the next move, which is concerned with his concept of divine action in the interaction with evolutionary theory. His proleptic theism depicts God as constantly engaged in driving the world out of nonbeing and then leading it into existence with the eschatological aim of consummating in the future. God is dependent upon the world in an eschatological way, since God will not be fully God until God's kingdom is fulfilled. Peters' perspective is therefore best understood as eschatological panentheism.

For the proleptic model between creation and redemption, Peters first considers the theological order of redemption (Gerhard von Rad). A theology of creation in the Jahwist context was related to the eleventh century BCE, which was further developed by Second Isaiah and the Priestly writers in later periods. The Hebrews developed their own particular view of creation in terms of their experience of the Exodus redemption, interacting with the genesis myth, which was common to the ancient Near East.

However, according to the theological priority of creation (Terrence E. Fretheim), Israel interpreted the experience of redemption within a wider frame of creation. God has a cosmic purpose behind God's redemptive work for creation, making a new life within the larger creation.[25]

Given this conflict of interpretation, Peters, based on Isa 44:24, advocates an inextricable connection between creation and redemption for eschatology, because the prophets take the precedence of future over the past. God's creative work is comprehended in terms of God's work of redemption. *Creatio ex nihilo* is the key metaphor which affirms that God is the Creator, challenging the notion that the world was created out of preexisting matter by God's ordering a preexisting chaos.[26]

24. Ibid., 30.
25. Ibid., 134.
26. Ibid., 138. This is seen in the circle of process theology, which rejects the notion

Based on the integrative model between redemption and creation, the proleptic epistemology seeks to explain the integration between creation and redemption in view of scientific theories such as the Big Bang. Peters observes a classic notion of *creatio ex nihilo* in consonance with the Big Bang cosmogony with the concept of finite time (beginning at t=0), comprehending *creatio ex nihilo* in terms of God's first gracious gift of futurity. God's first act is bestowing an open future upon the world, opening up the possibility of its becoming something new, with the power of change. In the gift of the future new things can occur.[27]

Furthermore, nonequilibrium thermodynamics (Ilya Prigogine) indicates that time is monodirectional from past through the present and toward the future, thus irreversible. Thereby, it affirms that it had a beginning and will have an end.[28]

The theory of evolution (Darwin) maintains that producing the human race took considerable and deep time and creativity transpired in the gradual epigenetic appearance of new species according to mutations and natural selection. Creativity is epigenetic, not archonic, hence creation is ongoing. Peters is convinced of epigenesis which helps to comprehend *creatio continua* as anticipatory of eschatological transformation, implying the possibility of emergence of new wholes. In light of holistic epistemology, evolutionary history testifies to the emergence of living creatures as organisms which constitute wholes, giving new meaning to the parts.[29]

But we are also creators, using our personal freedom, cultural power, and scientific discovery in changing the course of evolutionary events. Peters values a notion of "created co-creator" (Philip Hefner), because it means that we, in collaboration with God, are participants in the ongoing creative advance.

Given this constructive mediation between theology and science, Peters states that "God creates from the future, not the past."[30] This important, yet provocative thesis maintains that the source of life and being is the continuing divine work of future-giving. God's creative activity from the future incorporates the postmodern notion of holism in which parts are defined by the whole as greater than the sum of the parts. It is applied to the proleptic notion according to which God's eschatological whole determines God's past and present reality. Proleptic theism contends that every divine action within the world is performed "in, with, and under" the things of

---

of *creatio ex nihilo* in the sense of creation out of absolute nothingness.

27. Ibid., 143.
28. Ibid., 140.
29. Peters and Hewlett, *Evolution from Creation*, 28.
30. Peters, *God—the World's Future*, 142.

the created world, thus aligning with a non-interventionist model without interfering in or violating the natural course or events.[31]

A principle of proleptic theism affirms God's purpose for the cosmos and life on earth, which will be revealed at the eschatological advent of the new creation. Proleptic theism therefore offers a constructive proposal within the larger context of theistic evolution by coupling together God's creation with the future promise of new creation.

Free Will Defense and Theology of the Cross

The natural world governed by natural selection and survival of the fittest has included untold suffering of countless sentient beings throughout time. History of nature is seen with the extinction of species whose waste is un-redeemable. It is difficult to reconcile natural selection and survival of the fittest with God's gracious, active work.

For the divine action spectrum, we pay attention to the school of theistic evolution in many verities and branches, which for the most part favors a noninterventionist model of divine action. A free-will defense within the larger group of theistic evolutionists contends that God acts to self-limit divine action to permit freedom and autonomy to nature. The classical notion of God's will and human freedom resurfaces in the schemes of theistic evolution, creating a space for natural selection as the mechanism for speciation.

Arthur Peacocke, the representative of free-will defense, argues that God is *semper Creator*, immanent to the creative activity of the natural world, while the world is a *creatio continua*. God is all powerful and any limitation on God's power is the result of God's free decision. The self-limitation of God allows pain, suffering, and death in natural history, because this is inevitable for the development of life, consciousness, and human freedom. However, self-limitation does not mean that God is absent, because God shares in the suffering of creaturely life. "God suffers in, with and under the creative process of the world with their costly, open-ended unfolding in time."[32]

At this juncture, there is an affinity of a free-will defense theology with theology of the cross, in which God is understood as a victim of suffering and evil. In the scientific framework of the theology of cross, the theory of

---

31. Peters and Hewlett, *Evolution from Creation*, 145. Nevertheless, Peters insists that the divine will is imparted to what happens, including miracles, through the holistic vision.

32. Peacocke, *Theology for a Scientific Age*, 126.

evolution is utilized to facilitate our understanding of the way God works in the natural world.

The God of evolution requires Denis Edwards to rethink a Trinitarian theology of divine work in creation.[33] A Trinitarian God is self-giving as well as relational. The internal life of God is affected by what happens in the created world. Evolution completed with deep time, natural selection, and common descents is fully incorporated into the relational Trinitarian theology. Natural selection is not so cruel, not necessary to impose personalized value upon an impersonal natural process. Divine self-limitation makes a space for creation, allowing for random chance in nature and free will in humanity. The Trinitarian God, in creating, freely accepts the limits of physical process of creation and of human freedom.[34]

According to Peters, however, the fallacy in the discourse of divine self-limitation presupposes a conflict between divine power and creature power. God's self-limitation opens up space within creation for contingency, chance, and self-organization, and makes human freedom possible. Evil and suffering in the natural world are understood as inevitable because of human freedom.

In Peters' account, free-will defense theology is characterized by the schizoid combination of divine self-withdrawal in allowance for natural self-organization and God's ongoing creation. In order to comprehend issues of theodicy, suffering, and evil in the physical world, the theology of the cross must be utilized. However, insofar as a doctrine of the self-limitation of God is proposed in favor of natural selection, a Christian faith would remain without hope for God's redemptive and liberative power.[35]

This said, John Haught's deliberation is more compelling than other theologians among free will defense, because he conceptualizes God's participation in the struggle and pain of the world, connecting God's power of future with evolutionary biology. God's grace for the world can be seen in withdrawing and allowing creative self-organizing through natural selection. The power of God's Future can best account for the three cosmic qualities: chance, lawfulness, and temporality—the law stuff of biological evolution.[36] Evolutionary creativity derives from God's promised future in the comprehensive renewal of creation

More than that, Peters endorses Robert John Russell who offers a more detailed description of God's active participation in the world in an appeal

---

33. Edwards, *God of Evolution*, 13.

34. Ibid., 44.

35. Peters and Hewlett, *Evolution from Creation*, 143.

36. Haught, *God after Darwin*, 94.

to redemption. Although suffering, evil, and death are natural today, eschatological new creation will make these not necessary. The triune God as Creator guides the evolutionary life toward the fulfilling of God's eschatological purpose.[37]

Examining the diverse spectrum of theistic evolution, Peters makes a constructive proposal, taking a shift from creation to new creation, since God's Future will appear as something new, a new creation. This move tries to overcome a tendency among theistic evolutionists to identify the theodicy problem such as suffering, violence, and death with natural process or as a value-neutral issue. Peters critically incorporates the Darwinian interpretation of nature into God's eschatological consummation, affirming that God has purpose for nature rather than locating purpose within nature.[38]

Nonetheless, Peters challenges a combination of evolutionary biology with technological progress, which provides scientific justification for a naturalist ethic in support of horrendous moral problems, laissez faire capitalism, racism, eugenics, colonialism, and militarism.[39] Transcending the limitation of Darwinian evolution, Peters' substantial thesis reads: "God creates from the future, not the past."[40]

Unlike the theologians of free-will defense, first, Peters sees the futurity-characterizing openness in terms of divine power in creation, rather than a divine self-limitation.[41] God's gift of futurity to the world is, first, openness, building its dynamism, contingency, self-organization, and freedom as the corollary of God's liberating gift of an open future into physical reality. Second, God gave the world promise, thus in the end everything would be "very good" in a qualified sense. God's Future means fulfillment, future-giving as God creates the world, redeems it, and finally will consummate it.

Human Freedom and Genetic Determinism

New knowledge gained from genetics research demonstrates a challenge to ethical questions. Are we playing God? How could theological insights guide and direct ethical deliberation in matters of genetic determinism? Moral controversy has brought genetics to espousal of ethics, namely, *genethics*.[42]

---

37. Peters and Hewlett, *Evolution from Creation*, 157.
38. Ibid., 159.
39. Ibid.
40. Ibid., 169.
41. Ibid., 160.
42. Peters, *Genetics*, 2.

Sociobiologists, together with the popularity of Richard Dawkin's book *The Selfish Gene*,[43] argue that our genes determine our behavior in biological terms, shaping a widespread cultural parlance: "It's all in the genes." Edward Wilson remarks, "The genes hold culture on a leash. The leash is very long, but inevitably values will be constrained in accordance with their effects on the human gene pool."[44] However, scientists for the most part agree that nurture remains an important factor.

Peters characterizes the contemporary notion, "It's all in the genes," as a gene myth. Two versions of the gene myth are puppet determinism and Promethean determinism. According to puppet determinism, we are presumed to be victims of our genes while Promethean determinism argues that we can take charge of our genes.

It is significant to mention the 1993 discovery of a possible genetic disposition to male homosexuality, because a gene influences sexual orientation. The possible gay gene is preferentially transmitted and inherited through the maternal side. This scientific knowledge poses a challenge to theological teaching of original sin. Peters affirms his position: "*The scientific fact does not itself determine the direction of the ethical interpretation of that fact.*"[45]

To advance his position, Peters critically engages in Augustine's teaching of original sin. For Augustine, sin is naturally unnecessary, because God created Adam and Eve good. However, it is historically inevitable, because they committed sin, thus fallen. This original sin affected their biological nature such that Adam's original sin becomes inherited sin for us. The propensity for sinning became an inherited trait. As Augustine writes, "We have derived from Adam, in whom all have sinned, not all our actual sins, but only original sin; whereas from Christ, in whom we are all justified, we obtain the remission not merely of that original sin, but of the rest of our sins also, which we have added."[46]

Augustine became the defender of a theory of biologically inherited original sin. The whole human race finds the redemption from inherited sin only in the forgiving and resurrecting power of Jesus Christ, because he is the eternal Logos, the true *imago Dei* under the conditions of humanity.

Given this Augustinian scheme, the issue of homosexual predisposition, together with homophobia, would constitute signs of a fallen human nature, because we have been born with an inherited predisposition toward

43. Dawkins, *The Selfish Gene*.
44. Wilson, *Sociobiology*, 4.
45. Peters, *Genetics*, 22. Italics in original.
46. Cited in ibid., 25.

sin. However, the question—whether homosexuality is sinful or not—is a matter of dispute. There are theological arguments whether the sexual dimorphism and a binary system of gender statuses correlate with God's order of creation. It is argued that sexually coded culture would be the system of cultural meanings about sexuality, which have been brought into being by a social power mechanism. This perspective presents sexuality as a historical construct, challenging a unified understanding of human sexual nature.[47]

At any rate, what is important for Peters is seen in the "Statement on the Gay Gene Discovery," in which we read, "There is a rich variety of theological reflection both in the religious traditions and in recent developments which leads us to affirm that the theological questions raised by this genetic research are profound and subtle. We recognize that genetic diversity requires a response of love, respect and justice."[48]

Peters is not content with Augustine, because evolutionary history has no room for an Eden story. Together with the Big Bang theory, it views nature itself as history rather than fixed or eternal, because it is subject to contingency and change. Nevertheless, theological teaching remains suspicious of arguments in seeking moral approval on the basis of genetic determinism.[49]

In evolutionary history we are free creatures capable of arising creatively in the evolutionary process. Philip Hefner's position becomes crucial: "The freedom that marks the created co-creator and its culture is an instrumentality of God for enabling the creation (consisting of the evolutionary past of genetic inheritance and culture, as well as the contemporary ecosystem) to participate in the intentional fulfillment of God's purpose."[50]

God creates new things and divine activity includes promises and fulfillments of promise. God is not restricted to the old, but God promises new realities and brings them to pass. The idea of new creation which is yet to come encourages us to trust God's creative and redemptive activity in the future. Genetic science may contribute in a positive way ecological sustainability, including contribution to the health and nutrition of all humanity.[51]

47. Postmodern deconstructionists regard sexual identity as shaped under the control of Western bourgeois norms and criteria. They argue that the exclusionary function of power plays an important role in determining knowledge of sexuality.

48. Peters, *Genetics*, 25.

49. Ibid., 24

50. Hefner, *Human Factor*, 45. Italics in original.

51. Ibid., 34.

Proleptic Advent and Ethical Vision

For Peters, the biblical promise of God's Future, which is grounded in the prophetic mode of thinking in the Hebrew context, implies that the power of being arrives to us from God's Future. Our time is yet open to God's eschatological future. The *telos* is God's promised new creation and our resurrection into it, which refers to the everlastingness of God's promised new creation rather than a timeless eternity.[52] This perspective seeks to overcome the limitations of Augustine, who separates God's eternity from temporality. For Augustine, times are not coeternal with God.[53]

According to Ilya Prigogine, the second law of thermodynamics requires us to think of natural processes as stochastic, future-oriented, and irreversible. Appreciating this scientific view, Peters, more importantly, insists that the Hebrew concept of time cannot be adequately understood from historical events. Event has an ontological priority, because time is event-dependent. Theologically speaking, events coming from divine action come ontologically prior to the time in which they transpire.

Robert John Russell deserves attention when he states, "Nature provides the necessary causes, but God's action together with nature constitutes the sufficient cause of the occurrence of the event. In short, and metaphorically, . . . what we normally take as 'nature' is in reality the activity of God + nature."[54]

Peters' preference of prophetic eschatology values the idea of *adventus* over the idea of *futurum*. The term *adventus* refers to the appearance of something radically new rather than the actualization of existing potential or the effect of past causes. Pannenberg's notion of eternity as the whole of time finds also inspiration for Peters' notion of God's eschatological future as the ground of all beings that exist.[55] Accordingly, Peters' incorporation of Moltmann's *adventus* eschatology entails a strong public ethical thrust.

The kingdom of God comes to us as an advent in which creation undergoes genuine and transforming renewal. This future renewal of all things, which will be brought about in the eschatological kingdom of glory, had taken place ahead of time in the person of Jesus from Nazareth, who is the proleptic advent of the eschatological rule of God. Thus the Easter resurrection is not merely a matter of remembering it as the past event, rather it is a matter of participating in or anticipating an as yet outstanding future of

52. Peters, *Science, Theology, and Ethics*, 63.

53. Augustine, *Confessions*, XI.14.

54. Russell, "Does the God Who Acts Really Act in Nature?," in Peters, *Science and Theology*, 89.

55. Peters, *Science, Theology, and Ethics*, 75.

God. The real presence of Christ in the Eucharist is the proleptic presence without being exhausted upon the arrival of the future. A proleptic configuration of Lutheran "est" is taken along with eschatological orientation.[56]

Correlating *creatio ex nihilo* with the scientific theory of the Big Bang, a proleptic eschatologist maintains that God bestowed a future on the universe, opening up the possibility of becoming something new through *creatio continua*.[57]

This perspective reframes ethical responsibility for a just and sustainable society in harmony and peace with the environment for a future way of thinking. Peters depicts the present state of environmental injustice as a humanly produced state of evil. The term "anthropogenic evil" refers to "evil that arises indirectly through the growth in human populations, industrialization and the economy, leading to the production of pollutant wastes which then have devastating impacts on other species and on human populations through processes such as climate change and habitat destruction."[58]

Our ethical task is to overcome anthropogenic evil, establishing a new level of justice, environmental justice. For a vision of the coming just and sustainable society, it is necessary to integrate creation with new creation. The theological resource of eschatology can make a genuine contribution to the public discussion and policy by projecting a vision of the coming new world order. This future project entails a public commitment to envisioning the world as a single, worldwide planetary society, which is united in devotion to the will of God. It should be sustainable within the biological capacity of the planet and harmonized within the system of the ecosphere. A political organization is required to preserve the just rights and voluntary contributions of all individuals, while being economically organized to guarantee the basic survival needs of each person. Social organization is required to respect and protect dignity and freedom in every quarter to develop the quality of life for the generation to come.[59]

Proleptic Ethic, Beatitude, and Justice

As we already saw, proleptic ethics begins with a vision of God's promised future symbolized in the new creation of the kingdom of God. According to this vision, God's Future will be characterized by restorative justice imbued with divine love. This divine promise provides the theological foundation

56. Ibid., 70.
57. Ibid., 76.
58. Deane-Drummond, *Eco-Theology*, 116. Peters, *Sin Boldly*, 51.
59. Peters, *Science, Theology, and Ethics*, 21.

for ethical reflection. In the transition from God's grace to human ethics, Luther's dictum remains undercurrent for Peters' fundamental ethical principle: *crede in Christum et fac quod debes,* that is, believe in Christ and do what you must. In other words, sin boldly.

Peters' notion of justice is distributive and restorative in his proleptic ethic. Distributive justice is the principle by which to determine the distribution should take place in a fair way. John Rawls grounds his entire theory of justice on the foundation of fairness. Justice *is* fairness. The aim of justice as fairness, for Rawls, is "the symmetry of everyone's relations to each other."[60] Where injustice is sponsored by institutions or social systems, it causes unfair distribution and structural violence. Liberation theology takes a stance for a preferential option for the poor. Uneven distribution of wealth is a sign of injustice.[61]

Karen Lebacqz interprets distributive justice in terms of social justice: "discrepancies of wealth indicate a situation in which some fail to remember that the goods of the earth are given for use by all; such a situation is unjust because it violates both the social nature of human beings and the purposes for which God gives the riches of the earth."[62]

Peters sees that Lebacqz's position starts from the present situation of injustice, invoking the ideal of distributive justice, and then working toward reformative or restorative justice. Distributive justice uncovers and exposes cultural lies in the act of self-justifying lies, maintaining unfair racial and gender privilege in Western society. Moe-Lobeda advocates truth-telling to expose misdistribution regarding structural violence, which takes the form of white racism and economic exploitation.[63]

On the other hand, restorative justice, sometimes called reparative justice, has reconciliation, harmony, and peace as its goals in replacement of retributive justice. Restorative justice requires distributive justice, while seeking to end the spiral of vengeance and violence, which is caused in every act of retribution. Nelson Mandela is one of the greatest examples, because he sought restorative justice in the midst of apartheid in South Africa.

Accordingly, Peters advocates for restorative justice and distributive justice, while bracketing retributive justice. Peters says that beyond

---

60. Rawls, *Theory of Justice,* 1, 3.

61. The U.S. Conference of Catholic Bishops' *Economic Justice for All: Pastoral Letter on Catholic Social Teaching and the U.S. Economy* (1985) affirms that fulfilling the basic needs of the poor is the highest priority, such that investment policies should be directed to benefitting those who are poor or economically insecure.

62. Lebacqz, *Six Theories of Justice,* 75.

63. Cynthia Moe-Lobeda, "Being Church as, in, and against White Privilege," in Streufert, *Transformative Lutheran Theologies,* 198–99.

justification-by-faith lies the *Life of Beatitude*. Symbolized by new creation and the kingdom of God, God's promised future becomes present in faith; and faith expresses itself in beatitudinal living. Peters fuels the Christian vision through a beatitudinal eschatology for the proleptic ethics. Beatitudinal eschatology treasures the purity of heart among the humble in their specific time and place. Beatitudinal eschatology acknowledges that transformation is cosmic in scope, yet embraces all creation at all times and all places. The eschatological event is imminent without being consummate, emitting power and grace and transformation breaking into the present moment.

Still more importantly, each moment God releases us from past bondages and opens up a freedom for unprecedented newness. Jesus communicated this in his Beatitudes in a proleptic structure. The future God has promised is present today, perhaps in a fragmented yet anticipatory way, when we find ourselves poor in spirit, mournful, meek, pure in heart, hungering and thirsting after justice, merciful, and striving to make peace. The future God is present in the lives of those who live, beatitudinally. The eschatological banquet which Jesus employed in so many of his parables reinforces what the Beatitudes say (Matt 22:1–14; Luke 14:16–24). Beatitudinally, one's life on the margins today may be exchanged for life in the center of God's domain tomorrow.

This ethical vision imbued with a beatitudinal epistemology supports a *theologia crucis*, emphasizing our thirst for justice and heartache at injustice. Qualifying the dimension of graced life in beatitude, Luther took a stand against the prosperity gospel, reminding us that a person who lives in financial poverty can very well enjoy a closer walk with God. In fact, Luther rightly worried that personal wealth could distract us from reliance upon God's grace and God's promise of everlasting life. In Luther's statement: "This is what it means: In our heart we should be able to leave house and home, wife and children. Even though we continue to live among them, eating with them and serving them out of love. . . . A rich man may properly be called spiritually poor without discarding his possessions."[64]

Luther is asking for a beatitudinal life that experiences freedom from the attachments that enslave, a freedom that enables the person of faith to give his or her possessions to help the poor and to do so with joy.[65] Bonhoeffer follows in the footsteps of Luther by describing those who actually do live beatitudinally. "They have an irresistible love for the down-trodden, the sick, the wretched, the wronged, the outcast and all who are tortured

64. Luther, "The Sermon on the Mount," LW 21:15.

65. This aspect can be seen in Bonhoeffer's reflection of a battle between the spirit and the world in the Christian life. Bonhoeffer, *Cost of Discipleship*, 121.

with anxiety."[66] Poverty of spirit grounded in Beatitude remains the driving force for our struggle for justice. This is an anticipation of the promise for us as a people of hope.

Conclusion: Proleptic Theology and Pubic Theology

The proleptic theology with advent-transformation penetrates all theological issues that Peters deals with in the science-religion dialogue concerning Big Bang cosmology, evolutionary theory, the genetic research program, and the like. As previously noticed, postcritical hermeneutics embedded within postmodern holism qualifies the very eschatological vision, to embrace the divine retrieval of the small and the humble and the local, in which a divine celebration of each particularity is undertaken within the scope of its universal meaning.

However, Vitor Westhelle is more concerned about the diversity and specificity of little stories, community biographies that have been side-stepped by historians of dominant cultures and their metanarratives. The universal vision risks imposing a hegemonic meta-narrative, marginalizing humble spaces and local uniqueness.[67]

For me, the prefix "post" implies the project of the future in light of the coming of the kingdom of God toward which Jesus demanded *metanoia* from the wrongdoing in the past. First, I ground public theology in a postcolonial fashion in the act of God's speech event through the face of the Other, incorporating the spatial dimension of the eschatology into the integrative model of time and place in the kingdom of God. Jesus Christ is *Dabar*-Logos for our faith and hope in anticipation of his final coming. The eschatological presence is of analectical character in our midst, awakening us to attend to God's act of speech through the world and in the otherness of the Other. This is helpful for a new hermeneutic to comprehend Jesus as the future person in reference to Jesus's anamnestic solidarity with those who are fragile, vulnerable, and broken.

Theologia crucis in eschatological form is presented as Jesus the slain Lamb related to the suffering of all victims in world history and the healing of creation, in which the creation itself will obtain the freedom of the glory of the children of God (Rom 8:20–21).

Philosophically, I appreciate a strategy of irregularity to develop postcolonial public theology. The irregularity can be compared to a notion of

66. Ibid., 124.

67. Westhelle, *Eschatology and Space.*

Lichtung (light and clearing), involved in deciphering and remembering the subjugated knowledge of the innocent victims in anticipatory recovery of the meaning for the future.[68]

Scientifically, I accept a notion of irregularity from the science of chaos and complexity in order to overcome the limitation of evolutionary theory and the modernist science of determinism.[69] Irregularity in regularity and disorder in order support a holistic science on the totality of the whole and the parts in mutual influence. If evolution depends on the initial conditions, its prediction of the future is impossible according to the butterfly effect.

Given this, the proleptic theology tied to postmodern holism and an epigenetic view of reality remains inspiration for *postcolonial* public theology, cutting through the setback and limitation of neo-Darwinian theory based on natural selection, random mutation of genes, and genetic determinism. Epigenesis and emergent holism display novelty and creativity, cutting through the archonic view linked to the bondage of the past and its fixed predeterminations imbued with an ideological form of competition, survival of the fittest, developmental progress, and colonialism. The proleptic thesis of God's creation from the Future argues that God creates by integrating into wholeness,[70] such that God's gift of futurity can be metaphorically seen in creativity and novelty of the emergent whole in the evolutionary process.

Actually, creativity and novelty in the evolutionary process emerge out of a state of chaos, far from thermodynamic equilibrium. Complexity implies self-organizing systems which produce emergent creativity and novelty along with the edge of chaos.[71] God works through chaos and complexity, in other words, through irregularity in nature and history, to bring up new order and new life, which characterize postcolonial shaping of rationality.

The irregular perspective sharpens our understanding of the freedom and emancipation of God's act of speech in, under, with, and through world and creation, especially through the face of the downtrodden and silenced in history and society. The epiphany of the face is of ethical character, such that the integration between expression and responsibility remains the essence of language in light of God's Saying.[72]

This said, I seek to emphasize the spatial dimension of public theology in terms of three life arrangements (*ecclesia, politia,* and *economia*) for the

68. Gandhi, *Postcolonial Theory,* 34.
69. Trinh, *Chaos and Harmony,* 107–10.
70. Peters, *Science, Theology, and Ethics,* 86.
71. Haught, *Science and Religion,* 154.
72. Levinas, *Totality and Infinity,* 200.

sake of God's lifeworld. God' Future is God's Place for the world in light of a new Heaven and a new Earth.

Faith, which seeks understanding, is also active in love seeking God's righteousness, solidarity, and shalom in the world. The kingdom of the gospel is in deep conversation with the kingdom of nature, which is reconciled in Christ, but analectically expecting the coming of kingdom of God (*regnum gloriae*) to be realized in our midst. God's Future is connected with a new Heaven and a new Earth, in which God will finally dwell among God's people, that is, God's final rest in God's place.

Accordingly, I comprehend God as the infinite horizon of speech-event in relation to God, the *topos* of the world, the place-provider. "Lord, Thou hast been our dwelling place" (Ps 90:1). The broad place (Job 36:16) refers to the living-space as the safe stronghold enclosed by God. Jesus goes to prepare a place for the disciples (John 14:2–3).

This perspective facilitates an interpretation of a model of God's two kingdoms or strategies, upholding its orientation to lifeworld against its colonization under the dominion of the Empire. The realm of creation (*regnum naturae*), which is the place of God's reconciliation, entails goodness of God who guides, fulfills, and completes it at the eschatological advent of the new creation. Hence public theology in the postcolonial relief emphasizes the bodily dimension of our life, incorporating a spatial dimension of eschatology in emphasizing the moral shift to the *Other*.

In the body of Christ, there is a penultimate-eschatological embodiment of God's *topos*, on behalf of the least, the fragile, and the voiceless, who are ascribed and granted a special place in God's grace and reign. This new perspective takes a classic notion of natural theology as the reconciled realm of creation to overcome its traditional, deistic form while contextualizing it to promote the collaboration with other religious people and secular humanists for the sake of God's shalom, justice, and the integrity of life.

This perspective poses a question about the tension between theology of nature and natural theology within the proleptic theology which is in commitment to theology of nature against natural theology. What is at the center of theology of nature is God's self-revelation in the cross of Jesus Christ and God's promise in the Easter resurrection of Jesus Christ as a lens through which to view the natural world as investigated and comprehended by empirical research and scientific reasoning. Theology of nature takes into account Scripture, tradition, experience, and reason. This approach challenges natural theology in the deistic fashion of William Paley, which continues to surface in models of intelligent and transcendent Designer with biological processes. However, for Peters, the Designer imagery is nothing more than the Designer of violence, suffering, death, and enormous waste.

Nature itself does not speak the voice of grace, providing the promise of renewal.[73]

On the other hand, the proleptic theology supports Thomas Aquinas' argument from an efficient cause for the existence of God. Science deals with the secondary cause methodologically and empirically, such that the law of the universe investigated by science is secondary to the divine action as the primary causation. However, the Thomist approach entails a traditional notion of *theologia naturalis* in its argument from the secondary cause for God as the primary cause.

Certainly, a proleptic ethic transcends an evolutionary ethic which lacks the ground for projecting transformative vision, because of its justification of the status quo. Nevertheless, the Thomist theory of primary and secondary causation is utilized to interpret divine action "in, with, and under" the natural process, while sharpening the distinction between the primary causation and the secondary causation in terms of the epigenetic-proleptic view of *creatio continua*. This perspective transcends a deistic tendency inherent within the framework of God as the unmoved mover, only working through secondary causation.

Given the affinity and difference between public theology and proleptic theology, Peters' theological achievement and insights remain the driving force for those who are faithful to the public mission of the church and its ethical responsibility in commitment to making society, culture, and the world a better place in light of God's Future, who has made the in-breaking embodiment prophetically in Jesus Christ.

---

73. Peters and Hewlett, *Evolution from Creation*, 173.

PART III

Public Theology, Prophetic Dialogue, and Justice

7

Ernst Troeltsch

Public Theology, Historical-Critical Inquiry, and
Hermeneutical Reorientation

Theological ethics in a broader sense is defined as the theory of the conduct of human life in light of the word of God, in which ethical questions become life questions and thereby construct meaning. Integration between public theology and ethics may reinforce Christian social ethics to critically analyze human life in social, political, economic, and cultural realms. This analytical endeavor undergirds a public discourse of the academy and church in ethical responsibility for God's reign in society and the world.[1] More than that, public theology qualifies theological ethics to get more involved in public issues such as interreligious dialogue and comparative religious ethics, cutting through the religious temptation toward individualism.

Given the integration between public theology and social ethics, this chapter deals with Ernst Troeltsch's contribution to Christian public ethics and comparative religious study. Critically reframing Troeltsch's sociological method and his public ethics, I shall turn to Gadamer's appreciation of Aristotle's ethics and Jürgen Habermas' communicative discourse ethics. In a hermeneutical reorientation, I shall move Troeltsch's study of comparative religious ethics toward public religious theology. In this long route, I shall attempt to critically appraise and revise Troeltsch's historical-critical

1. Dorrien, *Social Ethics in the Making*, 2–4.

method for postcolonial public theology, by grounding public religious theology and ethical humanism in global solidarity ethics.

Ernst Troeltsch and Social Ethics

Ernst Troeltsch (1865–1923) can be regarded as a public theologian, who was involved in his social and political context in seeking to make a religious ethical contribution to the future course of history. His task was to bring the sociological significance of Christianity to contemporary relevancy, while refusing to relegate its meaning only to the private, personal sphere.[2] Concerning the relation of the Christian ethos to the social environment, Troeltsch regards ethics as the apex of theology, which entails a comprehensive horizon to shape the future afresh.[3]

Troeltsch's project is undertaken in the context of the whole religious, cultural situation of the time as well as through the standpoint of historical consciousness. Religion should find concrete expression in the real world, because it is not separated from history. He is concerned with the further development of Christian thought and life in frank interaction with the forces of the modern world.[4]

Troeltsch analyzes the social ethics of churches, because Christian social teaching depends on the sociological conditions of the churches in a specific place and time. For Troeltsch, the Enlightenment breaks through European culture dominated by the church and theology, employing "a complete reorientation of culture in all spheres of life."[5] However, it is in part a religiously inspired process of liberation, which discovers the autonomous self-legislating individual as the most important feature of the modern world.[6]

There is a parallel between Ernst Troeltsch and Max Weber, who also maintains that a sociological method, based on the ideal-typical meaning, investigates the meaning of an individual's social action in regard to religious ethos. Weber's sociological method of the ideal becomes an undercurrent in Troeltsch's historical-critical inquiry.

---

2. Chapman, *Ernst Troeltsch and Liberal Theology*, 4–8. See further Gayhart, *Ethics of Ernst Troeltsch*, 232.

3. Gayhart, *Ethics of Ernst Troeltsch*, 182.

4. Troeltsch, *Social Teaching*, 1:19.

5. Chapman, *Ernst Troeltsch and Liberal Theology*, 152.

6. Ibid., 153, 155–56.

Ideal Types and the Church's Social Teachings

We observe that Weber's ideal type remains influential in Troeltsch's study of the social teachings of Christian churches coupled with the church-sect-mystic type distinction. The basic distinction of the three types of Christian churches implies that the church type and its principle is universal, open, and in accommodation to the world through the communication of grace and salvation. The church-sect-mysticism distinction shapes Troeltsch's social teaching in order to present the whole of Christian history. It comprehends the social teachings of the gospel, the early church, the Middle Ages, and the post-Reformation confessions in relation to the formation of the new situation in the modern world.[7]

Any ethical compromise has to take place in the conditions of the contemporary world for a new synthesis and construction, which are valid to the present life and situation. Nowhere does an absolute Christian ethic exist, which only waits to be discovered, or an absolute ethical transformation of material life or human nature. What matters is a constant wrestling and struggling with the problems. A Christian ethic of the present day and the future will only be an adjustment to the world-situation, desiring to achieve what is practically possible.[8] Christian theology can thus be understood as public ethical theology because of its involvement and continued evolution in light of pressing world dilemmas.

Historical Relativism and Ethical Involvement

In Troeltsch's study of social teachings of Christian churches, there is a mutually reciprocal relationship between the historical development of Christianity and its social context, exploring the influence of the social context upon Christianity. Social location becomes the arbiter in characterizing Christian public attitude and religious ethos. Here we perceive that a sociological-realistic-ethical outlook is critically juxtaposed with Christianity's historical self-understanding.

In an article on "Historical and Dogmatic Method in Theology" (1898) Troeltsch indicates that in the realm of history there are only judgments of probability, varying from the highest to the lowest degree in any religious tradition. Christianity is credited no privileged status by historical-critical

---

7. Troeltsch, *Social Teaching*, 1:25. Similar to Weber, Troeltsch insists that Calvinism in its form of ascetic Protestantism had attained comprehensive historical significance, and created a completely comprehensive social ethic. Troeltsch, *Social Teaching*, 2:603.

8. Ibid., 2:1013.

method. Criticism of history is possible on the basis of the principle of analogy, which provides us with the key to historical criticism. Assuming a basic
consistency of the human spirit in its historical manifestations, a principle
of the analogy finds its importance in comprehending cultural, historical,
and religious differences and similarities.

This analogical approach makes difference comprehensible, while also
rendering empathy possible. Furthermore, historians acknowledge and recognize the interaction and interplay of all events in a historical life setting
in terms of the principle of correlation. The method of correlation concerns
the interaction of all phenomena in the history of civilization, because there
is no point within the history of civilization that reaches beyond correlative involvement and mutual influence. Correlation, which stands in favor
of historical relativity, places limitations on all absolute claims of human
knowledge. Troeltsch applies the historical method to Christian theology
with a view to grounding theology on the historical-critical inquiry. His
concern with Christianity is both religious and ethical in this framework.[9]

For Troeltsch, the entire domain of the ethical standard is relative,
since it is embedded within historicism based on the triadic principle of
analogy, critique, and correlation. An analogical critique can be undertaken
by observing similarity in the historical activities of human beings, despite
their difference. In the principle of correlation, all is made relative as it is embedded within interconnection, knit together in embracing correlation.[10]
However, it does not necessarily mean a rampant and aimless relativism,
that is, denial of the values appearing in the individual configurations.
But it refers to cultural relativity, implying that all historical phenomena
are unique and individual configurations are acted on by influences from a
universal-particular context.

Since there is no absolute ethical transformation of human nature,
Christian ethics must interact with the situation, pursuing what is possible in the present context.[11] This historical influence comes to bear on all
historical phenomena and individual configurations in varying degrees of
immediacy.[12] Troeltsch's analogical critique has a hermeneutical character
in shaping Christian theology as public theology through its approach of
historical effectiveness, which I shall pursue later in dealing with H. G.
Gadamer.

9. Molleur, *Divergent Traditions*, 76–78.

10. Welch, *Protestant Thought*, 2:281–89.

11. Troeltsch, *Social Teaching*, 2:1013.

12. Troeltsch, *Absoluteness of Christianity*, 89.

A particular significance of historical relativity for Christian social ethics is expressed in terms of compromise, which describes the historically inevitable relationship and accommodation of Christianity to its historical and social context in different epochs. Compromise also refers to "the phenomenology of involvement."[13] Its task is to think through and formulate the Christian world of ideas and life, in terms of unreserved and practical involvement in the modern world.

For Troeltsch, Christian ethos is a constantly renewed search for the compromise, while providing a fresh opposition to the spirit of compromise and engagement.[14] This does not refer to the process of accommodation, but a critical endeavor to qualify the public and ethical relevance of Christian religion. The complexity and diversity of ethics in our world is essentially incapable of completion and is open-ended. But it is always searchable and practicable in each new case.[15] In interaction with history and society, ethicists are in search of its feasible form as context is constantly shifting. Christian public theology is in the making, remaining a creative act through faith, which is expressed in ethical decisions in a responsible and decisive act. It will be made anew as a creative act, because an ethical assertion of validity remains relative for us in the particular present.[16]

For Troeltsch, Christian public theology in its ethical orientation is undertaken by connecting religious ideas with social involvement in the present situation, because all Christian thought and dogma depends on fundamental sociological conditions. By grounding the Christian ethos on the future kingdom of God, all social life and aspiration focuses on a goal that reaches far beyond all the relativities of this earthly life. At issue here is to advance public theology in light of the kingdom of God, in which Christian eschatology promotes ethical involvement and social interaction with cultural and political life.

However, Troeltsch is excessively attached to religious individualism and historical relativism within the European ideal of Enlightenment and humanity. This ensnares Troeltsch to relegate an idea of the kingdom of God to Christian asceticism in opposition to all social utopias. The kingdom of God is within us. Thus, the Christian ethic can be a form of adjustment and accommodation to the world situation.[17] This remains a tension within

13. Reist, *Toward a Theology of Involvement*, 161.
14. Troeltsch, *Social Teaching*, 2:999–1000.
15. Welch, *Protestant Thought*, 2:299.
16. Ibid., 301.
17. Troeltsch, *Social Teaching*, 2:1013.

Troeltsch's public theology, because of his relegation of the kingdom of God to individual responses.

Hermeneutical Inquiry and Moral Reasoning

In the method of the history of religions, Troeltsch refines his triadic epistemology in terms of analogy, critique, and correlation, which is embedded with social context and historical effectiveness. I find his critical method to be the start of hermeneutical inquiry. On the other hand, Troeltsch does not qualify his critical theory of interpretation to overcome limitations of historical relativism. I find a hermeneutical inquiry of moral reasoning and praxis to be helpful in our quest for comprehending the integration between public theology and sociohistorical context for the sake of reconstructing Christian public identity, cutting through the limitations of historical relativism.

Gadamer's hermeneutical theory deserves attention, since he articulates a hermeneutical epistemology relevant to Aristotelian ethics. In the Kantian framework, the logical basis of judgment subsumes a particular under a universal and recognizes a situation as an example of a rule. Thus judgment requires a principle to guide its application of the rule to a particular context in a universal manner. However, the logical basis of judgment cannot be demonstrated and taught in the abstract, because it can only be practiced from case to case. What matters is not the application of the universal but internal coherence.[18]

Unlike Kant, Aristotle grounds the good on practice and ethos. Encountering the good in the form of the particular practical situation, the task of moral knowledge is to determine what the concrete situation asks of the acting person. When knowledge cannot be applied to the concrete situation, it remains meaningless and even obscures what is called for in the situation. Such an ethical perspective demonstrates a methodologically difficult problem because ethics is not capable of achieving the extreme exactitude of mathematics.[19]

Likewise, the hermeneutical problem is clearly distinct from pure knowledge, which is detached from any particular kind of being. Because the interpreter belongs to the tradition that he or she is interpreting and understanding, the interpretation itself is an historical event. Moral knowledge is not standing over a situation that a person merely observes; rather, the knower is confronted with what he or she sees in the particular context.

18. Gadamer, *Truth and Method*, 31.

19. Ibid., 312–13.

Hence, Aristotle makes a distinction between moral knowledge (*phronesis*) and theoretical knowledge (*episteme*). Knowledge of the particular situation is necessary to supplement moral knowledge. The moral task of application or correlation between understanding and context is also central to the problem of hermeneutics.[20]

For Aristotle, sympathetic understanding stands beside *phronesis*, the virtue of thoughtful reflection. Understanding is seen as a modification of the virtue of moral knowledge. Given this, Gadamer incorporates Aristotle's analysis of moral knowledge into the problem of hermeneutics. In reading a traditionary text, for Gadamer, the text is not given as something universal. In no way does the reader understand it universally, but rather interprets it for a particular application.

Against this mechanical application, Gadamer argues that the interpreter seeks to understand the text, what it says, and what constitutes the text's meaning and significance. In so doing, the interpreter's own thought plays a role in re-awakening the text's meaning in a fusion of horizons between the text and the reader.[21]

We understand the text in a different way, because in all understanding the efficacy of history is at work. For Gadamer, language is the universal medium in which understanding takes place. In other words, understanding transpires in interpreting. The linguistic dimension of understanding is the concretion of historically effected consciousness.[22] Projecting a historical horizon is overtaken by our own present horizon of understanding (incorporating our proleptic expectation of future). As the historical horizon is projected, it is also superseded. A concept of historically effected consciousness is to bring about this fusion in a regulated manner.[23]

This perspective circumscribes the historical-critical method, because the latter does not explore the dimension of correlation between inquirer and historical object of research in light of fusion of horizons, which would create a new meaning by avoiding the pitfall of historical relativism. A phenomenology of language in Gadamer's sense suggests that all morality is socially constructed and historically conditioned, and communicatively expressed. This perspective helps us to refurbish Troeltsch's notion of historical relativism through a historically effected consciousness for the sake of acquiring a new meaning in our communal public ethics and proleptic expectation of God's kingdom. A proleptic understanding of the kingdom

20. Ibid., 315.
21. Ibid., 324, 388.
22. Ibid., 388–89.
23. Ibid., 307.

of God interacts with the horizon of Christian public theology embedded within social historical context, creating a new meaning in each different place and time. Be that as it may, this perspective does not necessarily mean discarding the triadic procedure, namely analogy, critique, and correlation, when the public theology engages with history, society, culture, and the world.

A hermeneutical situation acquires the right horizon of inquiry for the questions that evoked by the encounter with tradition and in a conversation with the Other in the social context. A hermeneutical inquiry offers an insight to mediate and connect a historical-critical approach to social teachings of Christian religion in different contexts (according to Troeltsch), explicitly undergirding intercultural moral theorizing and praxis in dialogue with the Other.[24]

This perspective also helps equip and reinvigorate hermeneutical inquiry with a critical reasoning. A public theology, comprehended in social-hermeneutical frame of reference, is socially situated and historically affected in recognition of the social cultural life-setting of the self. The morality of the religious individual finds its validity in relational terms, realized and fulfilled in community with others. A notion of historical relativism and religious individualism is critically revised in terms of the common good and Christian ethics of responsibility in light of the kingdom of God, which transcends the inward and private sphere of the religious individual.

Discourse Ethics and Communicative Rationality

Advancing hermeneutical inquiry to moral reasoning, I find it significant to sharpen such inquiry in the project of discourse ethics grounded in communicative rationality and the reason of anamnesis in remembrance of the reality of the innocent victim and mass suffering. Social discourse should function, as inherited types of discourse, in incorporating an explanation of the role of discourse, which creates public ethics in attending to the otherness of the Other. It is therefore necessary to develop a social biographical approach to ethics by critically analyzing the ideological aspect of distorted communication and language in the public realm. This is where Gadamer leaves off in his discussion of history as effect, sidestepping power relations within the dialogue.

Circumscribing Gadamer's hermeneutics, Jürgen Habermas conceptualizes discourse ethics based on communicative rationality, which has contributed to a sociological understanding of morality in terms of a

---

24. Twiss and Grelle, *Explorations in Global Ethics*, 1.

double framework of lifeworld and system. His discourse-communicative ethics provides a critique of ideology (communicatively distorted language and discourse) regarding history as effect. It also refines self-reflection on emancipation and undergirds a social critical deliberation of public ethics in taking a stance for lifeworld against a mechanism of the system, that is steered by money, politics, and mass media. In the framework of systems, language becomes a medium for domination and social power, hence it is ideological. The process of emancipation aims at revealing and overcoming systematically distorted communication by critiquing dominion and power in a given society.[25]

Habermas refers to morality as the foundational question of right and wrong in the Kantian sense, while the term 'ethical' refers to the question of living a good life in a particular time and place. He differentiates the issue of the moral from the evaluative, ethical issue for a good life.[26] He justifies the principle of universalization as a rule of argumentation and confines plurality of lifeworlds and moral difference to the universal of communicative rationality.

Habermas also provides an important insight for public theology, because civil society entails the plurality of institutions, associations, and movements emerging out of the lifeworld. Religion, speech, and association are important realms that support civil society. Religious community and ethical norms can be seen in the social space of communication, in which religious community and ethical practice are advanced through the public process of interpretation and through a network for communication, information, and consensus. Religious discourse is asked to be free of all forms of coercion, dominion, and authority in search of communicative reason and action. Public theology takes issue with the religious language, decision, statement, and ecclesial policy, which would be undertaken by hierarchical authority and institutionalized power structures.

Habermas' perspective helps the religious community concerning whether it is on the side of lifeworld for civil society or the mechanism of system steered by the hyperreality of global capitalism and military intervention. The unfortunate alliance between the altar and the crown in the Christian tradition needs to be critically analyzed for the sake of the prophetic, ethical factor in proleptic-advent expectation of the in-breaking reality of the kingdom of God in our midst.

Nonetheless, Habermas' communicative ethics tends to show a lack of theoretical sophistication concerning the discourse of those who are

---

25. Habermas, *Theory of Communicative Action*, 2:119.

26. Habermas, *Justification and Application*, 8, 117.

unfit, deviant, and underprivileged in the public sphere.[27] Articulating the priority of anamnestic-archeological reasoning over the communicative rationality, we uncover power relations embedded within social discourse of marginalized and subjugated people.

Hermeneutics of Involvement and Religious Validity

In the previous arguments, we have endeavored to review Troeltsch's public theology and his sociological method. Improving on limitations of Troeltsch, we have incorporated Gadamer's hermeneutics and Habermas' ethical distinction into public theology in order to improve historical effectiveness, critique of ideology, and power relations.

Theology and ethics are integrally related, with distinct disciplines, methods, and themes. Underlying ethics as "an intensified form of theology,"[28] public theology is concerned with human relationships, predicaments, and obligations involved in human action and accountability concerning God, humanity, and the world. Public and contemporary questions force theologians and ethicists to meet their challenges in a theologically intensified manner. Public theology therefore becomes ethical theology.

More than that, ethics implies a tradition. A way of life includes a specific worldview and ethos that are influenced by history, tradition, and culture. It is also mediated socially and culturally through the universal-particular medium of language. A fusion of horizons can be performed in many more ways than Gadamer expects. First, it transpires in correlation or interplay between tradition and one's historical consciousness in reading and understanding classic texts. In the process of understanding, one's historically effected consciousness is co-shaped by one's place in social location in which language as social discourse (power, knowledge, and dominion) influences and also distorts one's identity. It is also conditioned by socioeconomic formation through labor, capital, and market. Religion is not merely subsumed under an institution or material life formation. Diversity, difference, and plurality in religious cultural worldviews are important factors in shaping and characterizing our understanding of morality and religious ethics in a comparative manner for public theology.

As previously noted, Troeltsch presented diverse forms of Christian teaching in social contexts. He comprehends Christianity among the great religions as "the strongest and most concentrated revelation of personalistic

27. Chung, *Hermeneutical Self*, 169.
28. Rendtorff, *Ethics*, 1:7.

religious apprehension."[29] His notion of Christianity is established as the culmination or focal point. Although Christianity is "the focal synthesis of all religious tendencies and the disclosure of what is in principle a new way of life,"[30] we cannot prove that it will always remain the final culmination. Absolute truth belongs to the future appearing in the judgment of God.[31] I find a future-oriented dimension in Troeltsch's study of religions indispensable to reframe public theology in a comparative religious manner.

Troeltsch's construction of the supreme validity of Christianity seeks to provide an adequate synthesis between relativism and absolutism. But later, his endeavor shifted toward a more relativistic notion of cultural validity in an article on "The Place of Christianity Among the World Religions."[32] His notion of relativity as historical individuality and individual configuration[33] can be sharpened and reinforced in the notion of the cultural circle in which religious people grew up. A concept of historical individuality is not so neatly reconcilable with the notion of supreme validity. This perspective is already manifest in Troetlsch's *Social Teaching*.[34]

However, Troeltsch lacks understanding of the traditional Christian concepts and symbols in the ontological analysis of religious history and the present situation. He does not comprehend *kairos* and *kairoi* in light of the symbol of the kingdom of God. A religious study of ultimate concern can be undertaken in sacramental-mystical-prophetic framework. For such a challenge we pay attention to Paul Tillich, who is interested in refining the method of the history of religions. Insofar as religious symbols are not stones which fall from Heaven, Tillich argues that a historical-critical method needs to integrate the reinterpreted concepts into our present religious and cultural situation.[35] Tillich offers a clue to renew Troeltsch's historical-critical method in terms of hermeneutical theory of symbol, relating the symbol of Christ as the *kairos* to *kairoi* in the history of religions.

29 Troeltsch, *Absoluteness of Christianity*, 112.

30. Ibid.,114.

31. Ibid., 115.

32. Troeltsch, *Christian Thought*, 35–63.

33. Troeltsch, *Absoluteness of Christianity*, 89.

34. Troeltsch, *Christian Thought*, 51.

35. Tillich, *Christianity and the Encounter of World Religions*, 77.

Religion and Ethics in a Sociological Frame of Reference

In approaching the value and diversity of cultural validity and richness of pluralist abundance of religious individualities, we are not in a position to ontologically transcend hermeneutical necessity under the influence of historical effect. A hermeneutical notion of history as effect circumvents the privileged locus of critical reason in historical critical method, which stands in favor of relativism and the mystery of God.

Within the diversity of religions, a new and unique meaning of religions may emerge between interpreter and his/her own religious and cultural tradition by encountering other religious traditions. No historical situation could be understood except in its own terms grounded on the social situation.

Beyond the confinement of historical relativism and religious individualism, religion is an eminently social and cultural entity, implementing its spiritual and cognitive meaning. Spiritual experience of religion or its social ethical teaching is embedded within a sociohistorical and cultural framework. Religions exist because human beings exist only as social beings and in a humanly shaped world,[36] though it is expressed in diverse ways concerning social and ethical teaching.

In the cultural dimension of religious study, sacred symbols work in a way of synthesizing a people's ethos and moral configuration.[37] Religion as a system of symbols does not necessarily de-emphasize its political, economic, and material dimensions, because such aspects relate to evaluating ideology as a cultural system in favor of the politics of meaning.[38]

In Robert Bellah's study of religion in the Axial Age, we perceive that a world of absolute nonviolence and social justice plays an important role in the prophetic vision (Isa 65:17–19, 21–22, 26) in connection with other religions in the Axial Age. Bellah argues that the hallmark of Confucian utopianism is based on the rule of virtue by ritual and moral example, which replaces the rule of war and punishment by establishing and promoting the peaceful unification of the world.[39]

Religions have resources for ethics in a time of many worlds, underlying a practical construal of the world in different sociohistorical settings

36. Durkheim, *Elementary Forms of Religious Life*, xix.

37. Geertz, *Interpretation of Cultures*, 89.

38. Ibid., chs. 8 and 11.

39. Bellah, *Religion in Human Evolution*, 587, 476, 576. Here we see that Bellah's argument transcends a limitation of Weber's assumption against a utopian element in Judeo-Christianity and Confucianism. Weber, *Religion of China*, 145.

for moral aspirations. Thus, a public theology in a comparative religious context has the task of respecting the integrity of life, enhancing the imperative of ethical responsibility, recognizing the moral value and dignity of the Other in order to contribute to peace, justice, and integrity of creation.

Prophetic Dialogue and Ethical Humanism

In a new path to public theology in a comparative religious context, it is necessary to adopt hermeneutical reorientation. A dialogue with people of other religions and cultures is inevitable in our global context, which seeks to transcend the conflict, violence, and scapegoating ensuing in the aftermath of colonialism.

Postcolonial public theology is suspicious of any attempt to deploy a singular master metaphor capable of articulating and including the entire moral space of life. A religious tradition is more complex than one root metaphor. Hence, many metaphors are necessary, existing in a moral lexicon, without exhausting the meaning of life and its dignity.[40]

By correlating interreligious dialogue (practical engagement) with comparative religious scholarship (theoretical foundation and elaboration), public theology provides further theoretical and practical sophistication. In mutual interaction and collaboration, interreligious involvement provides a more practical and persuasive rationale, agenda, and orientation with the scholarly field of public religious ethics. The latter, in turn, offers critical inquiry, conceptual clarity, and framework, helping the interreligious dialogue to deepen and enhance its practical effectiveness and public relevance.[41]

Seen in this light, public theology seeks to shape its point of departure in terms of enriching identity of the self in recognition of the Other. Public theology in a comparative religious context, or public religious theology, can be recognized as a distinct field of theological and ethical inquiry, which entails a possibility to be profoundly challenged and renewed as a result of comparative process and prophetic moral dialogue.

This said, it is substantial to begin comparison by the critical study of another religion and classic texts, reinterpreting the classic texts, art, rituals, and ascetic practices of the home tradition in view of the other traditions. The critical mutual correlations are taken in recognition of similarity, without undermining difference. Both similarity and difference in the sense of analogical critique are of significance for the sake of correlation in attending to its alterity and appreciating its transformative power. Ethical awareness

---

40. Schweiker, *Theological Ethics and Global Dynamics,* 214.
41. Twiss and Grelle, *Explorations in Global Ethics,* 3.

and public responsibility becomes crucial as it considers those who are buried and sacrificed in religious fanaticism and its demonic history of effects.[42] This perspective prophetically advocates an attempt to shape Christian faith in accordance with anamnesis, subversive memory upon God's humanity in Jesus Christ.

Given this, theological-philosophical sophistication of God's humanity in light of God's Saying (or God's act of speech) through the face of the Other upholds an analectical critique through the remembered story of the Other and sharpens religious experience as moral reasoning by underscoring ethical responsibility and solidarity for a new form of humanism. "Saying," therefore, leads to a vital activity in the life of responsibility and solidarity as *parrhesia*—witnessing to God's humanity in Jesus on behalf of the dispossessed, displaced, and marginalized.

For Levinas, in the phenomenological account of self, responsibility, and religiosity, a notion of God as infinite Saying lies underneath a cry of ethical revolt, prophetic responsibility.[43] This helps to gain nuanced insight of the Other as an ethical, cultural, and political question. It entails a site of the subaltern-Other's speech or discourse under illeity of God, emphasizing God as infinite Saying through the others in the entanglement of world religions and indigenous spiritual cultural traditions. A perspective for solidarity ethics finds its validity by reconfiguring a hermeneutical theory of speech-event grounded in God's Saying and the Other. This provides an imperative for public religious theology to be involved in interreligious dialogue in order to shape its ethical horizon in accordance with biblical prophetic tradition and the gospel of Jesus Christ about the kingdom of God.

Seen in light of the coming kingdom of God, a hermeneutical correlation between creation and reconciliation remains a fulcrum for a concept of moral goodness and common good more amenable to an age of ethical plurality, religious plurality, and the co-existence among religious communities. Moral diversity implies the ethical challenge of pluralism, offering an opportunity to reflect and deepen the multidimensional meaning of diversity in terms of moral theory and public religious ethics. This aspect acknowledges that the life story and social biography of an individual or communities can be comprehended as the history of relations with the Other. The world is already constituted as a social entity, which shapes a background for any specific actions, intentions, or moral obligations.[44]

---

42. Tracy, *Plurality and Ambiguity*, 93, 102.

43. Levinas, "God and Philosophy," in Levinas, *Basic Philosophical Writings*, 147.

44. Berger and Luckmann, *Social Construction of Reality*, 28.

Conclusion: Public Theology and Solidarity Ethics

A notion of social ethics in an American context became a public discourse in the circle of the "Social Gospel movement" in the early 1880s. The social ethical mission of the public theology was to transform the structures of society in the direction of social justice and solidarity. Theologians and ethicists have construed the social meaning of Christian religion as the public religion in this direction. Reinhold Niebuhr's influential blend of realist politics and neo-Augustinian theology, together with H. Richard Niebuhr's ethics of the responsible self, remains a catalyst and watershed in propelling the further development of public theology as social ethical theology.

Max Stackhouse, together with Martin Marty, presents public theology in appreciation of Niebuhr's biblical realism while connected with the tradition of the Social Gospel movement of Walter Rauschenbusch, who greatly influenced the American public. Theological language and discourse were utilized to interpret and guide the basic ordering and fabric of the common life, examining the basic aspects of the human condition under God's reign.[45]

Eurocentric notions of modernity, upon which Troeltsch's public theology is grounded, have brought the tremendous new knowledge of humankind and heightened the material standard of living in the progression of science, technology, and capitalism. On the other hand, it has increased destructive forms of cultural and structural dominion and violence in social cultural life, as well as in ecological-planetary life (for instance, climate disaster and acceleration of species extinction).

In the study of Troeltsch I have made an effort to employ critical-emancipatory reasoning in a hermeneutical-communicative frame of reference, critically revising his historical-critical method by way of postcolonial notion of God's Saying through the face of the Other, such that emphasis is given on anamnesis and solidarity with those fragile, vulnerable, and victims. This postcolonial shift to the *Other* also qualifies American public theology and its social ethics to be more relevant to the public-global reality under the spell of the Empire. This said, a critical, emancipatory notion of public theology takes interest in advancing a shift from a Eurocentric modernity to a transmodernity,[46] which seeks to articulate a global project of solidarity and recognition of religious others for ethical humanism.

A discourse of God's solidarity, which is framed within the reconciliation of Jesus Christ embracing the Other, critically revises Troeltsch's public

---

45. Stackhouse, *Globalization and Grace*, 88.
46. Duchrow and Hinkelammert, *Transcending Greedy Money*, 175.

theology and his historical-critical study via a discourse ethics (in the fashion of Levinas) and *parrhesia* (in the fashion of Bonhoeffer, Habermas, and Foucault).[47] This perspective helps public theology to articulate an ethically infused understanding of hospitality, recognition, and engagement. Public theology in a global context is concerned with issues of historical and cultural experience across geographies with a transnational and transcultural sensitivity.[48]

The postcolonial solidarity ethics takes issue with a global responsible ethic in a Weberian (coupled with Troeltsch) sense which always asks realistically about the foreseeable consequences of our actions in taking responsibility for them.[49] According to Weber, disenchantment with religious-metaphysical worldviews is coupled with the emergence of modern structures of consciousness. It has also brought progress and liberation while causing the inevitable bondage of the iron cage.

Weber's endorsement is an acknowledgement of the powerful reality of impersonal forces and polytheism in the biblical sense of the dominion of lordless powers rather than de-mythologizing and challenging the reality of the iron cage.[50] Weber's pessimism finds its ethical contour only in an individual hero, namely a parliamentary charismatic leader.[51] However, a notion of an individual charismatic leader becomes questionable in our experience of evil charismatic leaders throughout history. Such a global ethic tends to belittle the more silenced voices of oppressed minorities in the cultural and religious tradition.[52]

Against this, postcolonial public theology and its solidarity ethics gain a form of critical and emancipatory theory concerned with considering not only human relations but of the human relationship to nature as a whole. A theological discourse of God's humanity in Jesus Christ upholds a critical and emancipatory notion of public theology, implying that *Gloria Dei, vivens homo* (the glory of God is a human being fully alive—Irenaeus of Lyon). However, this perspective does not necessitate a modernist notion of *over*humanism, but includes the dignity of the web of life in our planetary context.

Public ethics must be imbued with awareness of co-existence with other creatures for the sake of ecological sustainability, because nature is

47. For a study of *parrhesia* in the thought of Bonhoeffer, see chapter 2 above.
48. Drabinski, *Levinas and the Postcolonial*, 13.
49. Küng, *Global Responsibility*, 30.
50. Chung, *Church and Ethical Responsibility*, 53.
51. Weber, "Politics as a Vocation," in Weber, *From Max Weber*, 128.
52. Twiss and Grelle, *Explorations in Global Ethics*, 2.

a living organism, calling for a new dialogue with humans as created collaborators. The biblical notion of creation, in correlation with reconciliation, entails openness toward a pluralistic reality, related to abundance and fecundity and the integrity of life.[53] Creation is ongoing in anticipation of the coming of the kingdom of God, which will bring the creation to final consummation, thereby in the vision of a new Heaven and a new Earth.

More than its assumption of reality, public ethics for Christian eschatology critically unfolds the social structure of reality in respecting the lifeworld of the Other. This seeks to articulate that ethical subjectivity can be framed in interaction with the Other. This postcolonial reconstruction of public theology, undertaken in critical appraisal and revision of Troeltsch's insight, takes a step further in conceptualizing hermeneutics of intertextuality in terms of God's speech-event through the face of the vulnerable, fragile, and victimized in the reconciled world through Jesus Christ.

53. Schweiker, *Theological Ethics and Global Dynamics*, 31.

8

Public Religious Theology
Christians and Buddhists

Anselm's epistemology *fides quaerens intellectum* (faith-seeking-understanding) can enhance epistemology in interreligious dialogue for public religious theology. A concept of God as mystery remains central in Anselm's approach to God as insuperable (such that nothing greater can be conceived). I find Anselm's argument significant to advance public religious theology in analectical approach to the discourse of religious Other, for commonality in difference.

This perspective undergirds an approach to public religious theology in interreligious dialogue, especially regarding Buddhist contributions to economic justice and an evolutionary-ecological view of reality. Actually, analogical language is an alternative vocabulary to a univocal language (where all is the same) or an equivocal language (where all is different). This analogical imagination, embedded with the reality of social discourse, when it is sharpened in attention to social and religious discourse of other religions, facilitates our preparation for risking all present self-understanding, acknowledging the claims of the Other.[1]

Accordingly, I focus public religious theology on respecting the integrity of life, ethical maturity and responsibility, as well as recognizing the moral source and dignity of the Other in different religious traditions. Without intentional learning and appropriate understanding of the culture, religion, and spiritual experiences of those in other contexts, Christian public theology cannot be developed as a viable project. I advocate a

---

1. Tracy, *Blessed Rage for Order*, 32.

hermeneutics of plurality and recognition, arguing that interpreting the religious classics includes our exposure to the difference of the Other. In the project of public religious theology, it is necessary to get involved in the study of religious classics, which attend to their plurality, difference, and ambiguity in characterizing religious discourse in terms of commonality in dissimilarity between different religions and affecting it in the nexus of religious knowledge and its social power.

A theological epistemology (faith-seeking-understanding) endeavors to bring one religious tradition (home tradition) critically and constructively in conversation with another religion.[2] In the critical study of another religion, comparative procedure is taken in reading and understanding classic texts, and in dialogue with the practitioners of other religious traditions. In such a process and engagement, we do not discard difference for the sake of generalization but uphold the otherness of the Other. This procedure belies an underlying project of public religious theology for collaboration and mutual encouragement.

Given this, this chapter presents public religious theology by utilizing the sociological study of economic ethics in interreligious engagement. Focus is given to the analysis of Max Weber's and Robert Bellah's distinct investigations of Buddhism, including Buddhist responses to economic justice and an ecological view of the world. Second, we shall attempt a critical analysis of Weber's evaluation of the Reformation and his economic traditionalism. Then we will move on to developing a trans-scriptural reading to compare Buddhist texts of compassion and wisdom to *theologia crucis* as articulated in Dietrich Bonhoeffer's poem. Buddhists and Christians together contribute to global ethics through compassion and solidarity. Thus, faith-seeking-understanding is in ongoing renewal through the creative activity of interpretation and participation in interreligious engagement, which is involved in the mystery and freedom of God as Ultimate Reality.

Comparative Study of Religion in a Sociological Framework

According to Max Weber, religious ideas and economic interests are explored in terms of selective affinity between them in order to comprehend human rational conduct. Religious ideas, such as the Calvinist doctrine of predestination, entail a selective affinity with the capitalist spirit. The capitalist ethos has been developed among Puritans and Calvinists, since profits are rationally organized and continually reinvested in profitable and rational

2. Clooney, *New Comparative Theology*, x, xiii.

enterprises. Weber defines capitalism as "the pursuit of profit, and forever renewed profit, by means of continuous, rational, capitalistic enterprise."[3] The production of profit becomes an economic ethos and attitude underlying a way of life, which drives this-worldly asceticism. The Puritan Calvinists are the example of this model of selective affinity, since they have propagated constant self-control in every aspect of daily life, engendering an ascetic way of life.[4] Although there is an ethos of capitalism among all the religions, Weber argues that there is no evolution among them toward the capitalist spirit in the sense of distinctively ascetic Protestantism.[5]

Buddhist Path toward Economic Rationality

It is certain that Buddhists made a concerted effort to comprehend the meaning of life in the sense of otherworldly mystical experience by flight from the wheel of karmic causality.[6] In Weber's evaluation, however, Buddhism was not concerned with social issues in any direct and immediate way. Because of the monk's indifference to the world and idealization of a life of devotion to contemplation and nirvana, he sought enlightenment through "absorption into the eternal dreamless sleep of Nirvana."[7] Although the Buddhist emperor Ashoka (ca. 264–226 BCE) made a religious commitment to the centuries-old oral tradition of Buddhism,[8] Weber argues that there is no path in the world-rejection of Buddhism toward any rational social economic ethic.[9] However, scholars find Weber's thesis inadequate, arguing that Buddhism entails a genuine social ethic. Because of his insufficient knowledge of Buddhism, Weber had neglected the positive potential for changing society in Buddhism, in terms of its different notion of rationality.[10] The Buddhist doctrines of karma and no-self do not necessarily become an obstacle to social reform and nation-building. Buddhist teaching is consonant with a form of this-worldly nonattachment, which disagrees with a natural expression of acquisitiveness and greed in a capitalist economy.[11]

---

3. Weber, *Protestant Ethic*, 17.

4. Ibid., 175.

5. Weber, *Sociology of Religion*, 269.

6. Ibid., 266.

7. Ibid.

8. Bendix, *Max Weber*, 169.

9. Weber, *Sociology of Religion*, 269–70.

10. Harvey, *Introduction to Buddhist Ethics*, 207.

11. Ibid., 208.

All life is suffering through change (*dukkha*), the first Noble Truth, implies that all things are subject to impermanence, change, and vulnerability in the world of the endlessly cycled wheel of unsatisfactory lives. According to the second principle of the Four Noble Truth, the root cause of social evil lies in the greed of human persons craving for material things, in attachment to external and material things. The suffering caused by greed entails an economic reality in the teaching of Buddha: "Thus, from the not giving of property to the needy, poverty became rife, from the growth of poverty, the taking of what was not given increased, from the increase of theft, the use of weapons increased, from the increased use of weapons, the taking of life increased—and from the taking of life, people's life-span decreased, their beauty decreased."[12]

In the Buddhist tradition, the accumulation of wealth is endorsed for the purpose of merit-making and generous donation and deed. Generous donation is the most effective way to advance social concerns and contribute to social and economic influence. The Buddhist precept of right livelihood in the Eightfold Path also teaches that one's means of livelihood must not be dishonest, imprudent, and deceiving. It seeks to overcome wrong livelihood that is beset by trickery, stealing, or greed. In dialogue with Dighajanu, the historical Buddha advised persistent effort, good friendship, and balanced living, expressing one's skillfulness and diligence. For balanced living, one's income and expenditures should be balanced without being extravagant or miserly.[13] This perspective encourages people to use wealth properly for the self, the family, and community in a moral, compassionate, and generous manner.

A Historical Example of Modernization in a Buddhist Context

The Buddhist economic ethic helps us to examine the Buddhist Path toward modernization in a Japanese Context. In his study of *Tokugawa Religion*,[14] Robert Bellah argues that a this-worldly asceticism played an important role during the Tokugawa period (1600–1867) and the Meiji period (1868–1912). In Tokugawa society, commerce had developed in the new, unified national market. Success in this life was appreciated in the form of an abstemious

---

12. Ibid., 197.
13. Bodhi, *In the Buddha's Words*, 124–25.
14. Bellah, *Tokugawa Religion*.

attitude, because it supported advancement of the good opinion of others and material rewards.[15]

In Bellah's evaluation, the Tokugawa society was readily open and adaptable to modernization.[16] Although Japan did not have the cultural, religious resources to initiate the process of modernization itself, the Tokugawa society was more readily adaptable to the acceptance of modernization than any other non-Western country.[17] During the Tokugawa period, Buddhism put an emphasis on selfless detachment in collaboration with the people, especially in the case of Soto Zen monks. Work itself is accepted as Buddha-action, that is, the work of a Bodhisattva. One's work as a Bodhisattva leads to enlightenment for the benefit of all in the Japanese context: "Perform your work as a public service to the Righteous Way of Heaven . . . producing the five cereal grains, worship of the Buddha and the kami [Shinto gods]. Make the great vow to sustain the life of all men and to give alms even to insects and other such creatures, recite 'Nama-Amida-Butsu, Nama-Amida-Butsu' with every stroke of the hoe."[18]

Seen in light of the Bodhisattva spirit, Bodhisattva deeds are identified as the deeds of merchants and artisans. The business lives of merchants and artisans were appreciated for the sake of the community.[19] The merchants of Omi province, who were under the influence of the Jodo Shin sect, were known for their diligence, hard work, simplicity of life style and dislike of waste.[20]

Buddhist Critique of Economic Injustice and Ecological View of Reality

Buddhist scholars articulate a Buddhist way of life based on the Middle Way between materialist heedlessness and traditional immobility, providing a corrective to the onslaught of modernization and economic globalization.[21]

15. Harvey, *Introduction to Buddhist Ethics*, 211.

16. Bellah, *Beyond Belief*, 125.

17. Bellah, *Tokugawa Religion*, 40.

18. Harvey, *Introduction to Buddhist Ethics*, 212.

19. Bellah, *Tokugawa Religion*, 120.

20. Ibid., 120–21. Nonetheless, I do not undermine the political problem of Japanese Zen sect in accommodation to the Japanese military system tied to Samurai tradition, which served as an imperial ideology during the Japanese politic of colonialism. D. T. Suzuki, the cardinal representative of Zen Buddhism in the United States in the 1960s, justified Zen militaristic expansion and its ruthless colonial rule and plundering of China and Korea in the 1930s. Žižek, *Puppet and the Dwarf*, 27–29.

21. Payutto, *Buddhist Economics*.

Modernization and the disenchantment of the world have brought pollution, urban ugliness and slums, and rampant unemployment in the peripheral countries. A Buddhist notion of economic integrity sees the meaning of civilization in the purification of human character and compassion.

Buddhist economic theory is critical of the subject of self-interest central in the civilization of Western modernity and capitalism. The attachment to greed cannot be considered rational. The pursuit for self-interest and increasing profit causes suffering to humanity, society, and planetary life. The core values in Buddhist ethics are compassion and collaboration, which counter self-interest and competition.[22] Thus, Sulak Sivaraksa denounces economic globalization as free-market fundamentalism, that is, a new form of colonization. The myth of global capitalism is perpetuated by structural violence and Western dominion, which originates in the Western notion of modernity and individualism.[23]

Likewise, Thich Nhat Hanh presents a social vision grounded in the Buddhist principle of dependent origination as expounded in the *Heart Sutra*—all things inter-are, in other words, inter-being. The meaning of civilization is seen as enhancing the wellbeing of all creatures based on the wisdom of inter-being. For the sense of identity grounded in inter-being or interrelationship, Nhat Hanh introduces a story of a young Vietnamese girl, the daughter of woodcutters, whose father is killed in battle when she is seven. To alleviate her sadness, she takes her bamboo flute into the forest and plays. One day, while she is playing, a plane drops chemical defoliants, which leaves her blinded. Now totally blind, she plays her flute for the birds to come. She meets a golden bird that sings to her for nine days. As time goes by, she becomes more and more part of the world of the forest. Little by little, she forgets that she is a young girl. Rather, she becomes a tiny creature living in the forest. The flute sounds, resonating with the cries of the other creatures. Tree, moss, grass, and roots dance as she becomes one with the forest. Her pain is finally resolved. The sense of inter-being or interconnection with all beings helps her gain a new sense and horizon of identity and empathy.[24]

Given this, Paul F. Knitter in Buddhist-Christian engagement maintains that awakened beings grounded in universal compassion toward others are interconnected and part of all beings, growing in awareness of one's real interconnectedness with others. This Buddhist perspective would turn

---

22. Puntasen, "Individual and Structural Greed," in Sinaga, *Common Word*, 88–89.

23. Sivaraksa, *Wisdom of Sustainability*, 28–29.

24. Nhat Hanh, *Moon Bamboo*, 7–8.

Jesus's commandment ("Love others as you love yourself") to "love yourself as you love others!"[25]

Furthermore, we have observed that the Buddhist Middle Way in the Chinese context has especially developed more ecologically, more cosmically, and more compassionately in the face of the reality of all living beings. All sentient beings without exception enter into a universal relationship with Buddhahood, so that they become Buddha (nirvana or emancipation). The reality of identity and interdependence in Hua-yen Buddhism, as expressed in the *Avatamsaka (Hua-yen) Sutra*, is reflected by the image of the jewel net of Indra, expounded by Fa-tsang (643–712). This image provides a pivotal foundation for a socially engaged Buddhism by illustrating the holistic dimension of Indra's net for complementarity between Sunyata and Fullness (wondrous being). In Indra's net each jewel exists only as a reflection of all the others, thus having no self-nature. In the infinite world of Indra a jewel is placed at each knot so that each jewel is generated and sustained through the web of interdependence.

A creative interpretation of the Middle Way and a notion of Buddha-nature (*tathagatagarbha*; imago Buddha in Christian terms) evolved and culminated in the Hua-yen interpretation of the relation between the unobstructed interpenetration of phenomena (*shi-shi wu-ai*) and the unobstructed interpenetration of the absolute and phenomenal (*li-shi wu-ai*). This hermeneutical debate was fully realized in Tsung-mi's (780–841) systematization of the importance of the one true dharmadhatu—that is, the priority of the unobstructed interpenetration of the absolute and phenomenal (*li-shih wu-ai*) over and against the expression of the unobstructed interpenetration of phenomena (*shi-shi wu ai*).[26]

Seen in terms of cosmic and universal ecology, Thich Nhat Hanh argues, "If you have compassion, you cannot be rich. . . . You can be rich only when you can bear the sight of suffering. If you cannot bear that, you have to give your possession away."[27] For the Buddhist economic vision from the web of relations, Sulak Sivaraksa proposes the Buddhist symbol of Indra's Net. In this web of interdependence, we can stay close to nature as our life companion. In the cosmic envisioning of a community, individuals and communities determine their own direction asking for structural support and symbiosis. It de-emphasizes the structural hierarchies of institutions, and decentralizes power structures.[28]

25. Knitter, *Without Buddha*, 34.

26. Gregory, *Tsung-mi and the Sinification of Buddhism*, 68.

27. Berrigan and Hanh, *Raft Is Not the Shore*, 102.

28. Sivaraksa, *Wisdom of Sustainability*, 38.

This perspective of the Middle Way characterizes a Buddhist under-standing of economic life and eco-justice. Buddhist economics is critical of the subject of self-interest. Self-interest (needs) expands its meaning and scope to the extent that it includes desire and greed in accounting for the motivation for profit. This pursuit for self-interest and increasing profit is regarded as meaningful and rational only in light of human purpose in ac-counting for the civilization of Western modernity and capitalist economy. However, the Buddhist Second Noble Truth of non-attachment suggests that attachment to greed cannot be considered rational, since it causes suffering to humanity, society, and planetary life, driven toward a myth of rampant growth and competition.

Given this, Ulrich Duchrow, theologian and economist, appreciates Buddhist insight into economic life and justice, because the capitalist main-stream economics has made the core mistake in branding up self-interest with desire and greed. Buddhist approach corresponds to Aristotle's argu-ment in which the means of life for the household (*oikos*) runs counter to a chrematistic economy. The latter utilizes money only as a means of exchange and unit of account. Furthermore, the Buddhist consideration concurs completely with the biblical approach to an economy of enough for all, in other words, a prophetic economy in the service of life and empower-ment of the people.[29]

Christian Contribution: God's Oikonomia and Economic Justice

Buddhist contributions to economic justice, local economic integrity, and a sustainable web of ecology entail ethical compassion for those who are economically weaker and all sentient beings. This marks an important field for dialogue and collaboration with Christian theology of God's *oikonomia*. Economy (*oikonomia*) as the law or the management of the household con-sists of *oikos* (household) and *nomos* (law or management). *Oikos* retains the relationship with the living household and includes family, institution, market, state, and nature. God's *oikos* articulates a connection between God's shalom and the political and economic realm.[30]

In the Hebrew Bible, God's grace of righteousness summons us to up-hold a corresponding action, because faith in the God of Torah is active and effective in love and service of our fellow humans as well as care for other creatures. If our relationship to God is influenced by economic realities,

29. Duchrow and Hinkelammert, *Transcending Greedy Money*, 81–82.
30. Meeks, *God the Economist*, 33.

unjust economic conditions can ruin the true worship of God. Worshipping God in distorted ways leads to the dehumanization of economic life.[31] The biblical notion of God versus mammon helps the church contribute to the renewal of the economic system and structure in its current dehumanizing form, while promoting the integrity of a life-enhancing direction in ecological sustainability.[32] The biblical perspective of God's economy challenges the notion of possessive individualism, as seen in the tradition of Thomas Hobbes, John Locke, Adam Smith, and, to some extent, Max Weber.

For Weber, Western civilization has generated a consequence of what he calls the disenchantment of the world. He argues that Luther's theology of vocation was indifferent to the spirit of capitalism, because Luther regards society as independently fixed and sanctioned by the divine order of creation. This remains an obstacle for Luther to develop ethical rationalism, because he was not capable of establishing a reliable religious attitude toward worldly economic activity.[33]

In contrast to Weber, we have already observed in our study of Martin Luther (see chapter 1) that Luther was keenly aware of the importance of economic life and justice in his theological deliberation of God, as articulated in the connection between the first commandment and the seventh commandment in his Large Catechism. Luther prophetically criticized the Christian character of capital accumulation at this time, as seen in the practice of usury, speculation, and hoarding in early capitalism, as clearly seen in the political-economic alliance between the Catholic Church, Charles V, and the Fuggers.

Luther defined the social reality of early capitalism in terms of the system of "devouring capital." Those who think they have God and everything they need (money and property) but demonstrate no concern for anyone else have a mammon-god. They set their "whole heart" on money and property, and this, Luther says, "is the most common idol on earth."[34] He takes issue with mammon as a system of totality in which people want to be god of the whole world through mammon and to make themselves worshipped as such.[35] Luther's sharp critique of the devouring system of capital accumulation entails a prophetic voice against the Christian character of early capitalism in reference to colonialism in America.

31. Chung, *Hermeneutical Theology*, 159.

32. Ibid., 159–60.

33. Weber, *Protestant Ethic*, 85.

34. Luther, Large Catechism, *BC* 387.

35. Duchrow, *Alternatives to Global Capitalism*, 176.

This perspective makes Max Weber's evaluation of Luther's theology questionable in matters of economic justice. For Weber, Luther regarded society as already produced and sanctioned by the divine order of creation. Although Luther made an attack upon the great merchants of his time, it ironically represents economic traditionalism. Thus Luther has a lack of ethical rationalism because of his incapability of maintaining a fundamental relationship of worldly activity with religious principle.[36]

In contrast, Luther's prophetic stance against structures of mammon linked to the system of devouring capital is grounded in God's justice and economic righteousness in the biblical-prophetic tradition. This helps us to advance a substantial impulse for the church's responsibility for economic justice, promoting an endeavor of creating fair and just life arrangements.[37]

Compassion and Solidarity: A Trans-scriptural Reading

Christian self is shaped in the social, narrative character of selfhood, emerging out of dialogue with others. Through stories we expand our horizon of faith and understanding and enrich the identity of the self in encounter with and recognition of the stories of others.

The familiarity with the story, which characterizes history and shapes social biographies of communities, provides us with a platform for reconstructing a new meaning for the present and future in the presence of the Other.

Buddhist contribution to economic rationality and eco-justice marks one of the important fields with Christian understanding of God's economy versus mammon. More than that, interreligious dialogue, seen in the context of sociological, comparative study, aims at pursuing interreligious learning and enrichment for the sake of fresh theological insights into the newly encountered traditions as well as the home tradition. Thus, public religious theology is a theological, practical response to religious diversity by interpreting the world in light of engaged faith traditions. Many religious traditions are built upon rich and complex commentarial traditions.

Religions have resources for ethics in the time of many worlds, leaving a construal of the world for moral aspirations. Religious pluralist sources can be appreciated and analyzed in religious moral diversity, underpinning ethics of responsibility, compassionate social engagement in a comparative religious framework. A hermeneutical correlation between creation and

36. Weber, *Protestant Ethic*, 85.
37. Chung, *Church and Ethical Responsibility*, 38–40.

reconciliation, which relates to abundance and fecundity and the integrity of life, support a concept of moral goodness more amenable for an age of religious pluralism and its co-existence. If faith seeks understanding, faith and understanding come together in a hermeneutical, ecological view of the web of life, rather than expressing one-sided fideism.

Driven by hermeneutics from below and the Other, faith recognizes the Buddhist contribution to compassion, economic justice, and sustainable ecology, which find a consonance with God's ongoing creation and companionship to all sentient creatures. Faith in understanding remains integral when it recognizes the dignity of the other through whose face God speaks to our faith in an unexpected and surprising manner.

As an act of comprehending the language of faith in the comparative framework, I introduce a Buddhist poem that characterizes the compassion of the Bodhisattva:

> May I become the protector of those without protection, the guide for those on the path, the boat, the bridge and the causeway for those wishing to go to the other shore.
> May I become a lamp for those desiring a lamp, a bed for those desiring a bed, a slave for all beings desiring a slave.
> May I become the wish-fulfilling gem, the miracle urn, a successful mantra, a universal remedy, the wish-fulfilling tree and the wish-fulfilling cow for all beings.[38]

Buddhist compassion is universally applied to all sick beings in the world. This compassion is socially engaged to alleviate the pain of thirst and hunger and in support of those who are poor and destitute.[39] According to the Buddhist monk and philosopher Santideva (eighth century CE), the Bodhisattva is characterized by the spirit of self-sacrifice in an attitude of readiness to offer his body to those who beg for it.[40] Behind compassion is seen the Bodhisattva's refusal of entering into Enlightenment, underlying the path of renunciation. Instead of benefiting from Enlightenment for him/herself, the Bodhisattva goes to the *samsaric* ocean full of suffering by identifying him/herself with those who are sick, hungry, thirsty, poor, and destitute. Compassion as praxis of empathy undergirds non-dual identification in the path of renunciation and readiness to self-sacrifice.

A Christian perspective on the practices of tolerance and patience, as advocated in Matt 5:38–42, shows relevance with Mahayana Buddhism in the context of bodhisattva ideals. "Love your enemies and pray for your

38. Brassard, *Concept of Bodhicitta*, 46–47.

39. Williams, *Mahayana Buddhism*, 203.

40. Brassard, *Concept of Bodhicitta*, 49.

persecutors" is also known as the *Compendium of Practices* in a Mahayana Buddhist text. Santideva asks, "If you do not practice compassion toward your enemy then toward whom can you practice it?" The presence of an enemy is crucial in our spiritual path, providing us with the opportunity to enhance and advance tolerance, patience, and love. As the gospel says, "the sun makes no discrimination where it shines." This gives a wonderful sense of compassion, impartiality, and all-embracing nature.[41]

Buddhist qualified non-dual, analogical language may express God's wisdom in God's foolishness, which "no eye has seen, nor ear heard, nor the human heart conceived" (1 Cor 2:9). "Surely he has borne our infirmities and carried our diseases. . . . But he was wounded for our transgressions, crushed for our iniquities . . . by his bruises we are healed. . . . He was oppressed, and he was afflicted, yet he did not open his mouth; like a lamb that is led to the slaughter" (Isa 53:4–7).

The distinctive feature of faith in the crucified and risen Christ is driven toward life, emancipation, and reconciliation. For the message about the cross (1 Cor 1:18) we observe that God chose the foolish, the low, and the despised, in the world to shame the strong and the powerful. Jesus as Lamb of God demands conversion from mammon-worship (Matt 6:19–24), identifying himself as the Liberator living in solidarity with the lowest of the low. God against mammon or the reality of the powers and principalities, which is the foundation for Christian theology and praxis, can be promoted in interreligious engagement and solidarity on behalf of God's preferential option for the poor, the marginalized, and the victimized.

A *theologia crucis*, which is grounded in a slaughtered lamb, expresses God's compassion and forgiveness in the act of embracing all, while denouncing the crucifix of crusade, a symbol of racial discrimination or exclusivism, and genocide.

As Bonhoeffer poetically writes during the period of National Socialism:

> God goes to every man when sore bestead,
> Feeds body and spirit with his bread;
> For Christians, pagans alike he hangs dead,
> And both alike forgiving.[42]

A theology of the cross cannot be adequately comprehended without God's reconciliation in forgiving both Christians and non-Christians. As a prophetic relief Christ's reconciliation summons the church to be faithful to

41. Dalai Lama XIV, *Good Heart*, 49.

42. Bonhoeffer, *Letters and Papers from Prison*, 349.

and responsible for God's compassion for and solidarity with those who suffer. The confession of the church is seriously taken concerning the silence about "the spoliation and exploitation of the poor," while justifying "the enrichment and corruption of the strong."[43] Bonhoeffer insists: "In the body of Jesus Christ God is united with humanity, the whole of humanity is accepted by God and the world is reconciled with God. . . . There is no part of the world, be it never so forlorn and never so godless, which is not accepted by God and reconciled with God in Jesus Christ."[44] A theological doctrine does not overwrite the embracing grace of God in Christ, but the grace of God as the ultimate reality guides and shapes the meaning of the Christian confession in service of the world.

Bonhoeffer's *theologia crucis* grounded in God's reconciliation in Christ sharpens the meaning of grace in terms of hermeneutics from the Other. Only the suffering God "encompasses even the most abysmal godlessness of the world."[45] This irregular hermeneutics from below and the Other is embodied in anamnestic-archeological inquiry, because our memory of the subversive action of Jesus, the representative of subaltern-*minjung*, becomes socially engaged in light of the learning from those irregularized in the world. This perspective reinforces interreligious engagement to attentively listen to those on the margins and innocent victims, because the world is driven by "the perspective of the outcast, the suspects, the maltreated, the powerless, the oppressed, the reviled."[46] That is the standpoint of those who suffer (in dukkha).

A theological insight into God's reconciling embrace of the world can be seen in the fashion of a Buddhist hermeneutic of experience. As Thich Nhat Hanh states, "as reality can only be lived and experienced, Buddhist doctrine would never have as an aim the description of reality; the doctrine serves only as a method, as a guide, to the practitioner in his experience of this reality."[47] Buddhism and Christianity are "not one," but "not two" in articulation of the deep compassion and reconciling agape for the sake of the praxis of justice and emancipation regarding those who are weak, poor, and despised—thereby God's Lazarus in today's context.

---

43. Bonhoeffer, *Ethics*, 115.
44. Ibid., 202–3.
45. Ibid., 72.
46. Bonhoeffer, *Letters and Papers from Prison*, 17.
47. Nhat Hanh, *Zen Keys*, 47.

9

Public Theology
and World Economy

Prophetic *Diakonia* and Economic Justice

Max Stackhouse, who is influenced by Reinhold Niebuhr's biblical real-ism, pursues a rationale for public theology in the field of political economics, in which a vision of economic stewardship is elaborated for public life. Driven by Scripture, Christian tradition, reason, and experience, his public theology attempts to include other ethical resources to the contemporary context. Stackhouse argues that possessive individualism in the tradition of Adam Smith does not fit biblical teaching. The notion of possessive individualism drives selfish interest in calculating costs and benefits, contradicting a biblical notion of *imago Dei*.

The biblical root metaphor of the kingdom of God plays a central role in shaping Stackhouse's public theology, which critically integrates the prophetic tradition of the Social Gospel for public discussion of economic activity and political democracy. Persons in communion live under God's justice toward God's kingdom. This personal-communal principle is connected with a transcendent point of reference, externally to God's truth, justice, and love known in Jesus Christ. This transcendent point of reference in light of the kingdom of God functions as a yardstick to measure the life of people and institutions of the community.[1]

In Stackouse's notion of public theology, the biblical image of the kingdom of God is the overriding symbol for the future, providing a necessary

1. Stackhouse, *Public Theology and Political Economy*, 64.

conceptual norm and criterion in anticipatory connection with eschatological motifs. Here, humanity and community are fulfilled and transformed within a social, political sphere, while embracing the cosmos and creation. The vision of the kingdom of God breaks through proleptically in Jesus Christ, only in a provisional way, expecting the breaking of the possibilities of the future into the reality of the now.[2]

Given this, he maintains that the church has continually fixed the vision of the kingdom of God on the spiritual realm, neglecting its social, political and cultural realms. Undertaking prophetic articulation of the kingdom of God needs to be done in the midst of the social political realm in which God may be also present, emphasizing the specific responsibility of religious leadership and institutions in the face of public issues.[3] Public theology attempts to provide reliable warranted guidance about human life in the public sphere in the face of social, economic, political realities.

Stackhouse understands a theory of globalization in terms of an inevitable consequence of the technical advancement and economic transformation in 19th century Europe. Driven by expansion and penetration of capital movement transcending national boundaries to the global economy, globalization inevitably pursues capital accumulation and world market. The reality of globalization includes "a worldwide set of social, political, cultural, technological, ethical and ideological motifs."[4]

In his study of globalization he further advances a rationale for public theology as an alternative to political theology, in a conviction that the public should be more determinative of politics rather than prioritizing politics for society and religion. Thus, he maintains that religious faith, faith-based ethics, and religious institutions are a decisive component in the fabric of civil society. The public is the driving force to the republic and the moral and spiritual fabric of civil society.[5]

More than that, Stackhouse remains a strong defender of economic globalization as an alternative to postmodernism, because the image of a complex and holy civilization tied to economic globalization has come to us by God's grace.[6]

Given the economic globalization and the postmodern theory of Empire, however, I take a step further in shaping public theology in terms of

2. Stackhouse, *Ethics and the Urban Ethos*, 103–4.

3. Ibid., 106. See Stackhouse, *Public Theology and Political Economy*, 92.

4. Stackhouse, *Globalization and Grace*, 80.

5. Ibid., 103.

6. Ibid., 249. See further a critical-constructive study of Stackhouse and public theology in Chung, *Hermeneutical Theology*, 258–69.

a global-critical and postcolonial perspective on world economy and economic justice. In order to shape the public theology and political economy in terms of prophetic *diakonia*, I shall explore the relationship between *diakonia* and economic justice in light of ecumenical endeavors to promote the church's responsibility for economic justice. A postcolonial reorientation of *diakonia* toward issues of economic justice for public theology shall be featured in the midst of world economy. First, an analysis is given to the global-critical perspective on world-economy and colonialism.

Word Economy and Global-Critical Perspective

According to a periphery epistemology on Western colonialism and world economy, it is inadequate to attribute the genesis and development of capitalism only to the Great Transformation of the industrial revolution. Certainly, the industrial revolution is heavily indebted to Western colonialism in Latin America in the wake of Columbus's conquest. The year 1492 entails a historical tragedy of colonial dominion and power structure in terms of the inauguration of centuries of European expansion, conquest, and massacre in colonization of non-Western countries. Thus, it is hard to relate the origins of capitalist modernity only to the Renaissance, Protestant Reformation, and the Enlightenment.

In the colonial context in Latin America, the conquistadores served the interests of the empire while driving their own desires often in tension with the crown. In Vitor Westhelle's account, a conflictual logic of colonialism cannot be seen only in light of the interest of the Spanish Empire and desire of the conquistadores. A complex colonial logic and discourse reveal a binary juxtaposition of oppressor and oppressed.

Europe began to organize the initial world-system, placing itself as the center of world history over and against Latin America, Africa, and Asia. Theologically, the colonial project, woven into a complex web of interests and desires, was upheld in religious sanction under ecclesiastical authority as the primary strategy for mission.[7] Colonialism had divided the world into metropolis and satellites, whose relationship was marked by the unequal development of capitalism. This establishment reveals binary opposition brought by the metropolis, such that the economic-material conditions of colonial rule are inseparably connected with colonial hegemony and division.

Each regime of capital accumulation is coupled with political, military, territorial forces. In the first phase of the capital power of Genoa, the

7. Dussel, *Invention of the Americas*, 9–10, 132.

Spanish conquered and confiscated minerals, particularly gold and silver, and nearly extinguished the indigenous people. The feature of the second phase, mercantilism under Dutch hegemony, was reinforced by triangular trade. In Africa slaves were captured and shipped to the Americas for labor on the plantations to produce raw materials like cotton. These goods were shipped to Europe to be manufactured and sold all over the world, killing more than 70 million slaves. The transatlantic commerce and trade system increased and produced investment capital for the industrialization of Western Europe.[8] Consequently, in Latin America, capitalism has generated "the development of underdevelopment" in terms of the structure and function of the world system.[9]

Globalization, Modernization, and Empire

A global-critical perspective on world economy takes issue with global capitalism embedded with economic globalization and its wide-ranging effect. The endless accumulation of capital has generated constant technological change and a constant expansion of frontiers (geographical, psychological, intellectual, and scientific) on a global scale, expanding over time to cover the whole globe.

In the previous period, nation-states were the primary actors in the imperialist organization of global production and exchange. The creation of a world market is already a given in the concept of capital itself. Any kind of barrier or obstacle is to be overcome. The capital looks outside itself to discover non-capitalist markets. The search for additional constant capital and world market maintains imperialism through pillage, theft, and the ransacking of the whole world. The capital creates the world "after its own image," such that civilization and modernization mean capitalization.

Capital has entered a new phase of international development defined by monopoly, in which capitalism could achieve a real political and economic unification of the world market. The dynamic of imperialism has progressively undermined the distinction between the inside and outside of capitalist development, in either the dominant or the subordinate countries. Capital must eventually overcome imperialism, destroying the barriers between inside and outside.[10]

This perspective is perpetuated in the context of economic globalization. That is a shift from the dynamic of imperialism to a state of Empire

8. Chung, *Church and Ethical Responsibility*, 27–28.

9. Frank, *ReOrient*, xvii.

10. Ibid., 234.

and from the nation-state to the political regulation and sovereignty of the global market. In the era of globalized economy national boundaries are overcome in the world market. Life relations are commodified and bound to colonization of the lifeworld by the political, economic, and administrative system which has been spurred by an imbalanced modernization through capital accumulation. The international economic system (codified by the IMF and the World Bank associated with institutions such as the Trilateral Commission and the G 7/8 or G 20 countries, among others) appears to be in control and have dominion as an imperialist hegemony.

Sociologically speaking, a theory of modernization assumes a multidimensional and interdisciplinary character, because a one-dimensional economic approach to modernization has proven inadequate. The sociological dimension in the model of modernization has drawn upon a general theory of action (Talcott Parsons), which has incorporated the insight of Durkheim into the functional need met by differentiated social structures. This structural-functional approach demonstrates an integrated framework for research and policy concerned with modernization processes in particular. When this theory is applied to the study of modernization in the aftermath of colonialism, the development process under colonial regimes has continued itself, adopting Western attitudes, values, and institutions, as well as democratization, industrialization, mass education, and secularization.

Modernization theory entails a notion of "blaming the victim" based on the paternalistic assumption, which emphasizes the internal causes of underdevelopment and ignores the external depredation by Western imperialism. The United States served as the ideal model of modernization as Americanization. U.S. interventions in developing nations, which are driven by self-interest, are regarded as benign and effective.

A number of neoliberal economists have critiqued the basic presuppositions of Keynesianism and argued against state intervention in the economy. Grounded on economic doctrines and policies of Friedrich von Hayek and the monetarist approach of Milton Friedman, they attributed failures of development theory to its Keynesian underpinning, swinging a powerful blow to a former modernization theory. In the evolution of market capitalism we observe that the economic and political power is aggregated in the large transnational corporations that dominate the global economy generating environmental degradation. Neoliberals urged the World Bank, IMF, and other international development agencies to adopt market-oriented policies in Britain and America. The new "Washington consensus" promoted deregulation, privatization, reduction of state expenditures, tax reform, trade liberalization, and removal of barriers to foreign investment. This marks a shift from liberal modernization to neoliberal globalization.[11]

Postcolonial reality may be another term for identifying the globalization of cultures and histories with the structural violence of Western modernity tied to economic globalization, such that the colonial aftermath does not put an end to colonialism. The postcolonial perspective seeks to debunk a logic of possessive individualism as adhesion to politics of neo-colonization and neoracism. This entails a comprehensive critique of the Western notion of modernity and developmental projects for the sake of an alternative transmodernity.

In a postmodern model of Empire, capitalism focuses on informational accumulation, which plays in the processes of postmodern primitive accumulation and the ever-greater socialization of production. The revolution of informational accumulation points beyond the era of capital toward a new social mode of production.[12] Empire is emerging today as the central support of the globalization of productive networks, deploying a powerful police function. It understands the U.N. organizations together with the multinational and transnational finance and trade agencies as the supranational juridical constitution. This globalized biopolitical machine makes nation-states merely instruments to serve the flow of commodities, finance capital, and the population in motion.[13]

Empire, the new global form of sovereignty, is a decentered and de-territorializing apparatus of imperial rule, progressively incorporating the entire global realm within itself and transforming the modern imperialist geography of the globe into the anonymous Empire. It is formed "on the basis of the capacity to present force as being in the service of right and peace."[14] The definitive decline of sovereign nation-states, the deregulation of international markets, and the end of antagonistic conflict among state subjects characterizes the new paradigm of Empire as imperial authority.[15]

As Rieger asserts, "Empire seeks to extend its control as far as possible, beyond the commonly recognized geographical, political, and economic sphere, to include the intellectual, emotional, psychological, spiritual, cultural, and religious arenas."[16]

11. McCarthy, *Race, Empire, and the Idea*, 209.

12. Hardt and Negri, *Empire*, 259.

13. Amin, *Capitalism in the Age of Globalization*, 31.

14. Hardt and Negri, *Empire*, 15.

15. Ibid., 13.

16. Cited in Pui-lan et al., *Empire and the Christian Tradition*, 3.

A model of Empire envisions a gradual weakening of imperialist contradictions which leads to ultra-imperialism. This perspective envisages a dismantling of all the contradictions inherent in imperialism, for instance, the antagonism between capital and labor in the metropolitan countries and the semi-colonies, and the intensification of inter-imperialist rivalry among superpowers. Free-market capitalism proved historically to be exploitative and generated unequal distribution of social wealth. The rules of the free-market game in global capitalism are under the most powerful players who dominate international associations, agencies, and agreements (the IMF, World Bank, the G-7/8 and World Trade Organization). Neoliberals, who gained political power in Britain, America, and elsewhere, mobilized value-free advice for free trade in the shift from Keynesian to neoliberal policies. A neoliberal policy for free trade is actually based on unfair competition, driven by monopolistic capital agencies under the control of powerful nations. The once-powerful nations are actually under control of the capital agencies (transnational corporations) through lobbying—the new corruption.

Postcolonial Struggle for the Kingdom of God against Empire

As a rule, postcolonial theology attempts to transcend the aftermath of colonialism by moving beyond the colonial or neocolonial forms of global domination. Postcolonial theologians take issue with the empire in present day globalization that produces postcolonial hybridity. In Foucauldian terms, the panopticon of globalization enforces a homogenization of narratives, forgetting and trampling over the countless indigenous and subalternized stories. In hybridity, however, postcolonial theologians in their deconstructive orientation recognize great potential for resistance against the economic reality and hegemony of Empire.

Empire entails massive concentrations of power permeating all aspects of life over which the Empire seeks to extend its control. This control and domination are based on top-down systems established on the back of those who are burdened by the political-economic reality of the Empire. This political-economic reality is tied to the growth of global capitalism that exerts power through cultural, ideological, and intellectual webs.[17]

A reality of the power of Empire in this regard is manifested as "biopower," that is, a power of regulation of social life from its interior side, putting together economic, political, and cultural forces.[18]

17. Rieger, *Christ and Empire*, 2–3.

18. Hardt and Negri, *Empire*, 23. For the concept of "biopower," see Foucault,

For Hardt and Negri, the national colors of the imperialist world map have merged and blended into the imperial global rainbow of Empire.[19] Postcolonial theology frames its epistemology in terms of Empire and bio-power. To the degree that the capitalist economy on a world scale is driven by growth and the maximization of surplus value and profit, the relations of production include all the fundamental relations between men, women, and the environment. Social formation confronts people in the form of capital, and human labor is subsumed under the dominion of capital as a whole. This refers to the dominion of the capitalist mode of production in the phase of late capitalism.[20]

In support of this principle of capital fetishism on a global scale,[21] neoliberal tenets and experiments have brought privatization in force. The whole point of privatization is simply to transfer wealth from the public purse to private hands. Under the dominion of monopoly, competition is the true motor of economic globalization, and victory in competition is the criterion of efficiency and capital accumulation. The owners of capital create a bubble in the financial markets, and various kinds of speculation drive up the desire for profit through so-called casino capitalism.[22]

Embedded within the global economy is a worldwide financial structure that has transcended the geographical barriers of the nation state, in which the encounter of multiple civilizations becomes inevitable. This reality of reification generates and multiplies the quantity of sign and image, establishing the regime of sign-value that penetrates, vitiates, and dominates our everyday life and consciousness. Sign-value laden with meaning characterizes the nihilism of the power accrued through identification between self and product. A sports-car, when driven, represents one's life and status in a hyperreality of simulation. Our lifeworld is produced, consumed, determined, and colonized in the society of simulation, which multiplies images and spectacles. Hyperreality upholds the powerful role of sign-value in interaction with human consciousness and knowledge. Technology, the proliferation of images, information, and signs implode into each other.

Jonathan Ingleby unfolds a notion of the kingdom of God going beyond Empire, emphasizing a nonviolent yet confrontational approach. He argues that the kingdom of God is fundamentally expressed in a way that is rooted in a particular locality, its unique stories and social biographies of

Discipline and Punish, 195–228.
19. Hardt and Negri, *Empire*, xii.
20. Mandel, *Late Capitalism*, 571.
21. Hinkelammert, *Ideological Weapons of Death*, 1–3.
22. Duchrow and Hinkelammert, *Property for People*, 92.

local communities. A slogan "leaving the local" is rescinded. Rather, he suggests that we seek appropriate economic, political and ecological strategies for the mission of God's kingdom.[23]

Here, context, as seen in light of the kingdom of God, is not merely the cultural shaping of theological contents, but the articulation of their embeddedness in power relations and self-interest. Postcolonial theology undertakes a thicker description of realities concerning the lived experience of those in very different social locations, especially the innocent victims and the subaltern, which finds their place in the kingdom of God.

God's kingdom, which has proleptically broken in through the life of Jesus, finds its analectical reality in our midst through God's act of speech transpiring through the life of the subaltern. Their social discourse marginalized under the dominion of the Empire should be taken into account in terms of Jesus's solidarity with *massa perditionis*, inviting them to the table fellowship.

Insofar as all knowledge is infused with the fallibility of experience and power relations, there is no blind acknowledgement of privileged knowledge and dominant narrative. Privilege/inequality needs to be taken seriously as a social and cultural reality that conditions a neocolonial reality. The biblical image of the kingdom of God becomes the arching principle for postcolonial theology in emphasizing political economic solidarity with those victimized in society and healing the ecological wound under the global dominion and hegemony of Empire.

Diakonia and Economic Justice: Biblical-Prophetic Perspective

For the political economy of public theology, I retrieve the biblical notion of *diakonia* to articulate the mandate of service and God's solidarity with the poor in the discussion of the relevance between *diakonia* and economic justice to our task of globalization. In experience of exodus, God is the One who listens to the outcry of the enslaved people, allowing non-Jewish people to join God's grace of liberation (Exod 12:38). God stipulates the Torah and the commands in the socio-cultural realm, demonstrating special concern for the poor, the old, the widows, the orphans, the strangers, and the slaves. God's liberative option for the poor and the needy, which is expressed in Exod 20:2, penetrates and emphasizes the whole dimension of *diakonia* in the Hebrew Bible. We read of God's diaconal interest in Lev 19:9–18. The

23. Ingleby, *Beyond Empire*, 70.

Jubilee year also belongs to the category of social *diakonia* and rights for granting freedom and protection for the stranger (Deut 10:17–18).

God's liberating will in Torah is articulated in Jesus's ministry as movement for the kingdom of God. Jesus is a primal example of a mutual helping-serving life (Luke 22:24). *Diakonia*, which belongs to the essence of Christ, shapes and characterizes the life of the church in a publicly responsible manner. Jesus and his disciples turn upside down the relationship of domination and the criterion of value for the sake of God's coming reign. In Mark 10:41–45 Jesus introduces *diakonia* as a counter-concept against political and economic oppression, promoting an anti-patriarchal twist against the male competition of the disciples. In Matt 25:31–46 we read the Magna Carta of *diakonia*.

Furthermore, *diakonia* can be seen in Paul's mission to the Gentiles, as the Gentile mission is related to supporting the poor and hungry in Jerusalem, Judea, and Macedonia (Acts 11:29; 2 Cor 8–9; Gal 2:10). *Christos diakonos* is a point of departure and its aim for the theological discourse of *diakonia*, because Jesus is a circumcised *diakonos* (Rom 15:8), and also a slave (Phil 2:6). God chose the weak, the plebeians, and the despised to shame the strong (1 Cor 1:26–28).

In the Synoptic Gospels, we observe the social emphasis on *diakonia* and economic solidarity in Luke, because the problem of poverty and wealth is sharply recognized (Luke 16:19–31). The rich are awakened to social responsibility for the poor, because the conversion to Jesus is connected with *metanoia* from the previous wrongdoing, undertaking social engagement with the poor (Luke 19:8–10). In the final analysis, the greatness of *diakonia* is expressed in our participation as servants of the Lord's Table in eschatological fulfillment (Luke 22:28–30).

The biblical story of the rich man and the poor Lazarus found its prophetic voice in the Uppsala Conference of the World Council of Churches, emphasizing the church's responsibility in policies of economic development.[24] The task of the church in terms of proclamation of the gospel and *diakonia* comes together with the perception of economic justice. Engagement for the victims is the first demand of freedom and emancipation is bestowed by God's grace of justification. The Gospel of the forgiveness of sin entails the ramification of the church's solidarity with those who are fragile, vulnerable, and victimized on the underside of the world.[25]

---

24. Gollwitzer, *The Rich Christians and Poor Lazarus*.

25. Chung, *Church and Ethical Responsibility*, 233.

This perspective of justification and justice remains an inspiration for us to advance the relationship between *diakonia* and economic justice in the midst of economic globalization in the aftermath of colonialism.

Given this, I seek to redefine public theology in God's salvific economic activity, *oikos* through the discourse-event that challenges a global reality of lordless powers, which is steered through world-market, international politics, information systems of mass media and Empire ideology, and the hyperreality of global capitalism. The God-*oikos* relationship implies a God-economy correlation in the socioeconomic situation as seen in God's self-introduction in relation to the seventh commandment: "You shall not steal." This aspect takes issue with a market logic of self-regulation, which has made a biblical God superfluous in the socioeconomic field.

A neoliberal theory allied with global capitalism and its possessive market individualism needs to be critically analyzed and challenged by God's *oikos* for choosing and enhancing life, which entails a special partisanship with those who are economically weaker and innocent victims. God's economic concern, which is revealed in Torah (Exod 20:22—23:33; Lev 17–26; Deut 12–26) and in the life of Jesus Christ, should be a form of solidarity with those who suffer in the culture of Moloch generating "ideological weapons of death."[26] God's solidarity can be practiced in our emphatic listening to the voice of those on the margins, while creating a space for them to speak of and for themselves. A prophetic-ethical form of *diakonia* which is shaped in accordance with God's *oikonomia* implies an alternative faith community opposed to the tyranny and dictatorship of global capital monopoly and its accumulation. It is important to review the ecumenical church's endeavor about God's justice and economic life, in which the reality of economic globalization is critically analyzed and challenged.

Ecumenical Church and World Economy

Within the framework of the conciliar process for Justice, Peace and the Integrity of Creation (launched in Basel in 1989 by the 6th Assembly of the WCC), Ulrich Duchrow undertook a study of Europe in the World System from 1492–1992. He advocates for a new approach to the church's responsibility for economic justice, maintaining that meeting the basic needs of concrete human beings and ecological sustainability must become the point of departure.[27] It is significant for us to sharply dismantle the reality of neoliberal economic globalization as an ideological weapon of death against the

26. Hinkelammert, *The Ideological Weapons of Death*.
27. Duchrow, *Europe in the World System, 1492–1992*.

life of God. Defining Empire as the visible hand of the absolute possessive market, Duchrow provides a reliable source for transcending the limitation of postmodern theory of Empire (Negri and Hardt) by revealing the imperialism of nation states. An alternative for rebuilding the system of ownership from below is envisioned against the Empire for the sake of communal life and the common good. A theological, prophetic epistemology grounded in the God of justice and life fights against the irrationality inherent in the civilization of imperial globalization, leading to the instrumental logic of greed, dominion, and self-destruction.[28] This perspective helps us to advance a prophetic *diakonia*, strengthening the church's mission to God's life in terms of economic balance, people's rights of dignity, and ecological sustainability.

The church's responsibility for economic justice characterizes *diakonia* as an essential element of the church's life—grounded in Christ's way to incarnation and reconciliation. It upholds the church's engagement with public and global issues, which are imbued with the signs of the times on behalf of God's Shalom, justice, and the integrity of life. The God who forgives is the One who demands justice. Economic justice is an indispensable part of the church's responsibility and prophetic *diakonia* for society. Given globalization and the prophetic call for economic justice, it is significant to note documents of WCC expressing suspicion of the neoliberal reality of world economy. How do they combat the dark side of globalization? How do they call people to respond the needs of the least of these?

In a 1995 document of the World Alliance of Reformed Churches, we read that the global market economy has been sacralized and elevated to an imperial throne. The African reality of poverty caused by an unjust economic world order calls for a *status confessionis*. In 2004 at its 24th General Council in Accra, Ghana, WARC made a confession in the tradition of the Barmen Theological Declaration against Nazism (1934): "We reject any claim of economic, political, and military empire which subverts God's sovereignty over life and acts contrary to God's just rule."[29] Likewise, the Lutheran World Federation denounces neoliberal economic globalization as the false ideology in its 10th Assembly in 2003. This false ideology is critiqued as idolatry, leading to the systematic exclusion of those with no property and destruction of cultural diversity and the earth.

The WCC document of the 9th Assembly of the World Council of Churches (held in Porto Alegre, Brazil, 2006) discerned the signs of the times tied to the civilization of globalization. Human dignity, human rights, and social justice must be basic values and the yardstick by which to judge

---

28. Duchrow and Hinkelammert, *Property for People*, 158.

29. Cited in Rieger, *No Rising Tide*, 126.

economic activity on a local or global scale. WCC documents critique global inequality and express a worry about the ecological devastation tied to the process of globalization. An ideology of neo-liberalism is chided as a myth of Procrustes who waylaid travelers and chopped short their legs to fit into "one size fits all." This characterizes the principle of neo-liberal economy which chops the legs of the poor nations for the sake of the economic program of rich countries.[30] The WCC in its AGAPE Document ("Alternative Globalization Addressing People and Earth") demonstrates the results of a seven-year global study of the church's response to economic globalization, emphasizing the church's responsibility for the victims of economic globalization, in accordance with the gospel.[31]

Furthermore, in the WCC study, *Justice Not Greed,* we observe the church's effort to analyze and seek solutions to the current financial and economic system of global capitalism, addressing inequality, poverty, and ecological devastation, including the greed line.[32] Ecumenical study of world economy and economic justice facilitates our endeavor to conceptualize a postcolonial reorientation regarding the relationship between *diakonia* and economic justice.

Public Theology in Postcolonial Reorientation

Public theology in postcolonial reorientation takes into account the political economy in the context of world economy and articulates a vision of God's *oikonomia* and democratic economic system in terms of the biblical outlook on God's kingdom and economic order. The notion of prophetic *diakonia* is articulated in a political economic realm to sharpen the meaning of the gospel about the kingdom of God. *Diakonia* must tackle the cause of political and economic evil at the social and cultural roots. It takes into account economic classes, their conflicting interests and ideologies, and social divisions.

Church action of *diakonia* is driven by prophetic action and advocacy for emancipation and solidarity in awareness of the signs of the times. A prophetic and emancipatory *diakonia* struggles to remove social problems of neoracism and neocolonialism by engaging the liberating Word of God. The interpretation of our time and all its historical and social documentations needs to be undertaken in a socio-historical manner and under the

30. Rivera-Pagan, *God, in Your Grace . . .*, 214.

31. Ibid., 221–23.

32. Brubaker and Mshana, *Justice Not Greed*, 21. See further Mshana and Peralta, *The Greed Line.*

social and economic category of understanding, promoting *diakonia* as the church's witness to God's in-breaking reality and Jesus as the partisan of the subaltern-*minjung*. The table fellowship of Jesus with *ochlos* (publicans and sinners) is the cardinal example for the church's *diakonia* of solidarity with *massa perditionis* (the mass of the damned or the lost multitude), which qualifies a theology of the cross to be embodied in the flesh of the poor.

An alternative movement for global civil society against the Empire finds its voice in some areas of Asian countries in a semi-peripheral or economically developing context. Along with this, World Christianity epistemology critiques an elitist notion of mission as the white man's burden. In a biography of Rudyard Kipling, we read about the imperial mission to the world to "take up the white man's burden" for the colonization of the Philippines. This phrase effectively frames the missionary approach of the colonizer to civilize the savages.

Postcolonial theory challenges the cultural and economic legacy and aftermath of colonialism which continues in previously colonized countries. It helps us to identify a hidden regime of power and dominion and guide a new strategy of resistance in counter hegemony against the neocolonial reality of the Empire ensuing in the aftermath of colonialism. In a postcolonial reorientation to *diakonia* and economic justice, it is essential to conceptualize God's *oikos* in dealing with how God and economy are correlated in the political economic context. Economy (*oikonomia*) is the law or management of the household, which is a compound of *oikos* (household) and *nomos* (law or management). *Oikos*, which is in access to livelihood and its relationship to the living household, includes family, institution, market, state, and nature.[33]

If economic realities influence our relationship to God, unjust economic conditions would threaten the true worship of the triune God. If our concept of God influences our economic life, worshiping God in a distorted manner would generate the dehumanization of economic life. The biblical notion of God versus mammon helps the church contribute to the renewal of the economic system and structure in its current dehumanizing form, while promoting a life-enhancing direction through ecological sustainability.[34] The issue of *diakonia* and economic justice, as seen in the horizon of God's economy, challenges the notion of possessive individualism in the tradition of Thomas Hobbes, John Locke, and Adam Smith, who were attached to the modern market society.

33. Meeks, *God the Economist*, 33.
34. Chung, *Hermeneutical Theology*, 159–60.

God's household which is constituted by *diakonia* helps articulate how to uphold Christian praxis and discipleship following the economic work of God in the public realm. This perspective becomes the driving force for us to undertake postcolonial reorientation to *diakonia* and economic justice in light of God's *oikonomia* concerning God's act of speech through the church, the world, and in the otherness of the Other. This epistemology emphasizes double listening to the Word in the church as well as to God's irregular voice marginalized in the world. It further develops archeological rewriting of those who are economically fragile and victimized through the analysis of the material formation of labor, capital, and marketing in relation to the word-economy and the Empire.

Given this, public theology in postcolonial reorientation, accentuates an anamnestic reasoning of not-forgetting the mass suffering of the innocent victims in the context of political economy. Their own affairs and struggles have been violently cancelled and erased from the collective memory. Their history and society must be seen in light of God's economy and God's act of speech, which addresses and awakens our discipleship to be responsible for them in our midst.

Given this, I seek to critically revise postcolonial hermeneutics in terms of interpolation, palimpsest, archeology, and a new form of re-presentation. A palimpsest was originally a piece of manuscript on which the previous entry had been rubbed out and replaced by another. No inscription is indelible. A place may be re-appropriated and given new meaning by the people who continue to live.[35] Archeology performed with a palimpsest, is undertaken to unearth indigenous forms of culture buried by the colonial experience and dominion of the powerful in our society. A strategy of archeology aims to uncover what has been foreclosed, forgotten, and subjugated under the dictate of Western dominant scholarship, ecclesial authoritative structure, and a dominant form of world economy. Postcolonial hermeneutics entails a substantial moment of de-centering the centered narrative and knowledge-power system, underlying socio-historical, critical analysis of politics, hyperreality of global economy, and social discourse propagated through mass media.

This archeological strategy is driven by anamnestic reason grounded in a subversive memory of Jesus on the cross in connection with his resurrection tied to God's Future. Jesus as a deacon of the circumcised (Rom 15:8) continues to embody God's economy in deep solidarity with public sinners and tax collectors and in his identification with the hungry, the thirsty, the stranger, the naked, the sick, and the prisoner—thereby "one of the least of

35. Ingleby, *Beyond Empire*, 54.

these who are members of my family" (Matt 25:40). Our preferential option for the gospel about the kingdom of God, which is tied to metanoia from the wrongdoing in the past and present, can be embodied in our trustworthy commitment to Jesus in deep solidarity with those who are fragile, vulnerable, and broken.

Thus, it is significant to undertake a postcolonial reorientation of God's *diakonia* and economic justice in ways of qualifying and sharpening interpolation, archeology, and a new form of re-presentation,[36] especially in light of God's *oikonomia* in anticipation of the coming of God's Future.

God's grace of justification and righteousness become the driving force for public theology to clarify the relationship between faith in the God of love in Christ and Torah in order to make God's *oikonomia* and care relevant and effective to our society and the creaturely life. Torah, which includes God's economy and grace, is a catalyst for guiding the life of righteousness and equality in God's household, favoring the weaker members of society based on the ethos of the Exodus.

The good news (Luke 4:18–19) is announced in a preferential option for God's reign in solidarity with the poor, the captives, healing the blind, and for liberating the oppressed. This view cannot be adequately understood without connection to the prophetic legacy of Isaiah (Isa 61:1). Torah-Gospel correlation helps us to develop a theology of God's *oikonomia* based on God's Shalom and justice for underpinning the church's responsibility and prophetic *diakonia* for the sake of the integrity of life and emancipation.

Conclusion

If God's activity is conceptualized in a Trinitarian-economic sense, it takes the form of God's salvific economy for the world. Insofar as the gospel is expressed in relation to ethical commandment and the church's *diakonia*, in a critical and liberating manner, the postcolonial public theology seeks and encounters human life in the socioeconomic context by connecting God and economic justice. The economic Trinity integrates the life of the household and economic realms into God's salvific drama, making us into God's collaborators for the sake of God's Shalom, justice, and the integrity of life. This perspective helps us to comprehend a metaphor for God as the householder of political economy in relation to economic justice and global capitalism.

God is the One who provides the place of life arrangements, enhancing the integrity of life in contrast to the rule of Empire. God's *oikos* becomes

---

36. Ibid., 48–59.

a conceptual tool in the church's practice of *diakonia* in dealing with how God's economy and life arrangement take root in our planetary context, sustaining and enhancing people and earth. In *diakonia* constituted by God's household, God's reign is biblically and topologically grounded on Jesus's narration of remembrance, which is connected with the place of the fragile, vulnerable, and victimized. *Diakonia*—in orientation toward God's *Topos* of life—critiques an espousal between the Empire and the barbarism of neocolonialism in acceleration of neoracism and hyper-casino capitalism, threatening the poor and our planetary life. This offers a post-developmental notion for public theology to promote the church's commitment to prophetic *diakonia* and economic justice in anticipation of God's *oikonomia* and in-breaking Future in our midst.

Afterword

Public Theology, Ecology, and Confucianism

Introduction

Religion is not a private matter, because religious language is socially and culturally construed, considering and, at its best, enhancing human life. Public theology challenges the opinion of religion as a private affair and undertakes a critical, hermeneutical endeavor, bringing the vitality of Christian discipleship and responsibility toward the public affairs of society in light of actualizing the gospel about the coming of the kingdom of God. Public theology seeks to articulate and communicate the language of Christian faith to diverse and multiple realities of public life by critically and prophetically engaging the universal horizon of Christ's reconciliation with the pressing issues of public life.

Public theology establishes worldwide relevance by seeking emancipation from violence, poverty, and injustice, while acknowledging the otherness of God in God's solidarity with innocent victims and nature. It critically analyzes the extent to which our public life and environment is affected and vitiated in predominant social mechanisms of injustice and violence. It takes issue with the institutionalized policy of scientific technology in order to ensure quality of life on Earth.

Because of the pressing challenge of global climate change, the ecological issue is one of the main agendas in the public sphere. Religious systems include a public ecology, together with a public society, institution, academy, and church. Christian public theology can also be explored in engagement with cultural, religious pluralism and science of ecology.

Public theology necessarily engages in the science-religion dialogue about ecological awareness and the scientific understanding of the Earth and creaturely life. Public theology in a postcolonial frame of reference can be undertaken by a critical analysis of the economic, political, and cultural development linked to ecological degradation, which has grown through-out the tradition of Western modernity. Public theology provides essential reframing in dealing with environmental issues and challenges, introducing and exploring basic characteristics of eco-theology as public theology.

In addition, a comparative study of Confucianism marks an important field in enhancing public theology in the context of prophetic dialogue. A discussion of the Confucian teaching of the human-cosmic relationship, namely, Confucian ecology, deepens our ecological moral and responsibil-ity. Reinvigorating the relationship between theology and ecological sus-tainability in our globe as well as in public life, a comparative study in the Christian-Confucian context deserves significant focus.

As Christians, we may say that earthly life comes from God and re-turns to God, as God accompanies and sustains all living things through the Holy Spirit. All life is declared good by God. In our century there is a universal understanding of the importance of the earth as a whole, the welfare of nature and human kind, the interdependence of all. Christian theology provides a resource for a culture of peace, forgiveness, eco-justice, and reconciliation.

On the other hand, Confucianism as a living reality is not a dead past, but gives rise to a moral reconsolidation as well as our ecological awareness. It may offer an alternative to the Enlightenment's faith in progress, reason, individualism, market economy, and democratic polity, which is yet embed-ded within inequality, violence, self-interest, greed, and dominion. The new development of Confucian theory can be made more effective in an age of pluralism, social ecology, alternative modernity, and global civil society. A retrieval of Confucian ecology necessitates a new hermeneutical task for making the Confucian living tradition and bringing relevance of its moral ecology for our responsibility.[1]

Having said this, the afterword investigates and advances public theol-ogy in a social, ecological frame of reference through a comparative study of Confucian morality and ecology. It is significant to carefully consider the instrumentalization of our rationality, which leads us to hold abusive dominion. A dialogue between Confucianism and Christianity remains un-dercurrent in postcolonial public theology on the matter of ecology. Finally, this chapter provides a subversive critique of major polluting powers such as China and the U.S.

---

1. Tu, "Beyond the Enlightenment Mentality," in Tucker and Berthrong, *Confucian-ism and Ecology*, 3–21.

Public Theology and Ecology

Theology is fundamentally in the public realm, and it bears responsibility to participate in the global public sphere as it deals with the economic, social, political, and environmental reality under the dominion of globalization. Interwoven with public life in society and community, the church shapes and influences an integral part of human life in the world.

The global-ecological culture is socially relevant, becoming a major issue in the context of public theology and interreligious dialogue. Basically human though is socially and publicly embedded within the cultural life setting, such that we communicate and advance our knowledge of and attitudes toward life in a system of culture. The global-ecological culture as the fabric of meaning challenges us to interpret our experience and guide our meaningful action in the current network of social reactions and relations.[2]

Along with economic and social advances, the public sphere has become the realm of secularity. Public space generates a public opinion through discussion via various media. It is metatopical because it is nonlocal, transcending any one topic of discussion. Driven by the increasing influence of mass media, print capitalism,[3] and hyperreality, public space has agency, exerting power over public life and decision-making.

Ecology, defined as "the science of relations between the organism and the surrounding outer world" (Ernst Haeckel), studies the interdependence and interaction of living organisms and their environment.[4] Ecology becomes a new platform for global public theology, as theology begins to address the concept of sustainability through critical analysis of the tradition of modernity.

Public theology in a postcolonial frame of reference challenges the limitations of human self-invention grounded in competition, expansion, greed, and domination tied to the modernist values of overhumanism and androcentric culture. Thus it requires a new perspective of Earth-honoring values, respecting a network of interdependence while subverting the life-destroying systems at work in our global, public sphere. Thus, social, eco-ethical standards and norms can play an important role in the re-orientation of public theology toward reinforcing a public moral self as an ecological self.

In a short period of time the human species has emerged as the dominant species and their scientific reason has been utilized to increase human

2. Geertz, *Interpretation of Culture*, 45, 89, 145.

3. Taylor, *Modern Social Imaginaries*, 99. See Dalton and Simmons, *Ecotheology and the Practice of Hope*, 7.

4. Boff, *Ecology and Liberation*, 9.

power over nature on a massive scale. To the extent that humans have been successful in the pursuit of their material interests to control and manage nature, human ingenuity has been marked by a field of problems. Driven by modern economic progress, advanced science, and technology, nature itself is increasingly exploited and colonized by the system of capital and politics.

The wave of globalization has always been transformative, frequently destroying life-forms, institutionalizing the conquest of nature, and reducing habitat for animals and plants. As a result, it has induced and perpetuated climate change, generated polluted air and water, and finally created a burden of toxic wastes for future generations. Conquest and colonization is affected chiefly through commerce and financial capital expansion, threatening the poor and undermining the ecological web of life. Issues of environmental crisis continue to make front-page news and acquire broader attention in the global village.

A new scientific understanding of nature as a living organism has begun in the science of ecology, in which we learn that evolution has occurred and continues to advance within an ecological theatre. Accordingly, the theatre itself changes, varies, and advances through the autonomous dynamics of self-organizing and living systems.

In fact, the earth as a whole can be considered approximately closed, for it receives only energy from the sun. However, in the complex interactions among animals, plants, minerals, and the physical environment, we observe that the complex interweaving of living and nonliving systems operate throughout the ecosystem in an infinite web of all-inclusive relations. The dissipation of an open system becomes a source of order, because dissipative structures maintain themselves in a stable state far from equilibrium and may even evolve.[5]

This perspective challenges the great dualism of the Western tradition which affirms a way of dividing reality into polar opposites, that is, one pole superior and the other inferior. Against this dualistic frame, nature becomes a living nature, debunking a mechanical dualism. In learning about the life and beauty of nature, it is indispensable to adopt a new attitude toward nature in terms of respect, collaboration, and dialogue rather than dominion and control. This attitude is a radical change and transformation and may transpire in human approach to nature only through anew dialogue.[6]

Ecology reaffirms the interdependence of beings, and interprets all hierarchies as a matter of function and network, which becomes the crucial

5. A concept of a dissipative structure further than an open system includes the points of instability where new structures and forms of order can emerge. Capra, *Web of Life*, 180.

6. Prigogine and Stengers, *Order Out of Chaos*.

metaphor of ecology.[7] All creatures manifest and possess their own relative autonomy in which all beings constitute a link in the vast cosmic chain. This scientific epistemology requires public theology to be more socially engaged and ecologically responsible, concerned with the relationship between public life, technology, and ecological fitting.

Social Ecology and Ecological Holism

Ecology is becoming an architectonic discipline within which a new ethics of care for the earth and a green politics is nurtured and implemented in the public realm. Ecology at a broader level encompasses not only nature (natural ecology) but also culture and society (social ecology). In dealing with ecological awareness, a project of a vision of the whole does not derive from the sum of the parts but from the organic interdependence of everything. This ecological holism respects the web of all life, emphasizing the dependence of human life and its future heavily upon the wellbeing of the whole planet.

The situation of social injustice involves an element of ecological injustice, and an ecological critique is exercised in view of economics, politics, society, and gender. Our global public life would be alerted by the apocalyptic warning, which threatens and violates the planetary life of creation. Public life cannot be adequately comprehended without considering ecological injustice.

From the sixteenth century, with the advent of mercantile capitalism and then industrial society, we observe that the project of systemic exploitation of nature holds sway. Both free-market capitalism and authoritarian state socialism have been found guilty disseminating and encouraging abusive and exploitative views of nature.

Global capitalism today often hides its serious shortcomings, because its system is incapable of placing restrictions on rampant self-interest and unlimited profit. The aggressive pursuit of growth and profit may generate destructive resource extraction, exploiting workers through low wages, and accordingly, it violates and pollutes ecosystems.[8]

Violence against nature vitiates contamination of the biosphere and destabilizing ecosystems. Ecological sin is thus understood as a social sin because it affects life as a whole tremendously. The challenge of modernity and systemic destruction of the environment has become a global, public phenomenon, calling for our endeavor of a paradigm shift toward alternative

7. Capra, *Web of Life*, 10.
8. Martin-Schramm and Stivers, *Christian Environmental Ethics*, 15.

understandings of modernity or trans-modernity, in order to transcend the limitation of Western modernity and civilization.

This said, an ecological holism and social ecology needs to be critically introduced, challenging "sustainable development," which promotes economic development even at the expense of ecological disorder. As humankind is embedded within interaction with nature, social ecology is articulated with natural ecology. The task of social ecology refers to the study of social systems in interaction with ecosystems, while examining the way in which society and public policy are ecologically organized. Every member of the larger community, humans and nonhumans, has intrinsic value and value for others. Technology should become socially and ecologically responsible, considering ecological holism and paying attention to the life of those who are marginalized and victimized.

Nevertheless, powerful technologies are utilized frequently to damage nature's ecosystem, supported by economic and political systems to serve the powerful. This perspective has considerably shaped anthropocentric and privileged attitudes toward nature and the poor. The destruction of biodiversity causes environmental and social injustice. To the degree that industrialized people consume the most energy and resources, toxic pollution is distributed unevenly to people in poor countries who cope with unfair and disproportionate burdens. Ecological degradation has to do with public issues such as power, wealth, and privilege in the dominant globalized culture.[9]

Against this, it is important to understand the new scientific understanding of nature and earthly life. James E. Lovelock, in his book *Gaia: A New Look at Life on Earth*, presents the planet Earth as a living whole and a self-organizing system. A universal bio-cybernetic system possesses a trend toward homeostasis. This theory became known as the Gaia hypothesis. It does not imply a remystification of the earth or presuppose a petty deity, stern and tough with revenge to the transgressor. Rather it is a helpful scientific narrative of the Earth's environment as living organism, comprehending the total system of our planet as a system of interactions and feedbacks.[10]

The earth's atmosphere as an open system, far from equilibrium, strives to create the best possible environmental conditions for life through a constant flow of energy and matter. The earth lives and implements its own rhythm and dynamic interaction with its biosphere, together with the

9. O'Brien, *Ethics of Biodiversity*, 5–6.

10. Lovelock, *Age of Gaia*, 212. Lovelock's metaphorical argument goes too far when he states that Gaia is "stern and tough" and that she destroys "those who transgress." He writes, "Her unconscious goal is a planet fit for life."

atmosphere, the oceans and the expanses of land. Comprising all life and its environment, the earth forms a self-regulating entity.[11]

Theological Rethinking and Divine Ecology

In his classic 1967 article titled "The Historical Roots of Our Ecological Crisis," Lynn White argued that Jewish and Christian traditions have helped to contribute to the modern ecological crisis since they have entailed "an implicit faith in perpetual progress." Christianity in the Western context is "the most anthropocentric religion" and God's will is that the humans exploit nature for their proper ends, because they are made in God's image.[12] The doctrine of creation in both traditions places humans at the apex of the creation process over and against the rest of creation.

"Anthropocentric" Christianity has played a crucial role in shaping Western attitudes and practices by disenchanting and instrumentalizing the natural world. Signalizing "a wreck of Eden," the ecological challenge confronts and radically revises theology, because Christianity is co-responsible for the present ecological crisis[13] for the public project of "ecological" Christianity.

Furthermore, critically analyzing the relation between sexism and ecological exploitation, it is maintained that the ecological myopia deforms and generates socially constructed categories such as gender, race, and class. Eco-justice, on the socioeconomic level, analyzes the socially constructed nature of patriarchal society and culture on the cultural-symbolic level. The system of domination of women and destruction of nature was rooted in a larger patriarchal, hierarchical system, because of its transcendental dualism. The transcendental dualism is denounced as that imbued with binary opposition in terms of separation, polarization between sexes, classes, and human and nonhuman beings. Such a metaphysic supports infinite exploitation of the earth's resources for science, technology and production, perpetuating ecological destruction.[14] In this light, the Genesis story is critiqued to posit a patriarchal God who creates Adam as a generic human assumed to be embodied by the male patriarchal class.

Nonetheless, Gen 1:26–28 states that the terms "dominion" and "subdue" need to be understood in reference to image and likeness, rather than in any despotic sense. It is unfortunate to see that the words "dominion"

11. Lovelock, *Healing Gaia*, 12.

12. White, "The Historical Roots of our Ecological Crisis," reprinted in Gottlieb, *This Sacred Earth*, 189.

13. Dalton and Simmons, *Ecotheology and the Practice of Hope*, 2, 14.

14. Ruether, *New Woman, New Earth*, 194.

and "subdue" are taken literally in the modern world. The human being is intended to dominate and harness the forces of nature such that the biblical notion is exploited to uphold the scientific-technological project of rampant domination of nature.[15]

Against this charge of transcendental dualism, we must recover the social ecological meaning of the biblical message. In Gen 2:15, the human being is placed in the garden of Eden to till it and keep it. The human being is a friend of nature, working with the earth to till and safeguard, in terms of care and service, and with accountability to God. We are from the earth and go back to it. In fact, a biblical notion of creation is structured in an emancipatory, eschatological, and planetary-ecological character. The Genesis story reflects God's act of emancipation that the Israelites experienced during the period of the Babylonian captivity. This story also refers to God's historical-eschatological act of resurrection occurring in the life and death of Jesus in reference to God's final consummation of the new Heaven and new Earth.[16]

In the story of Genesis God is seen as a gardener, who is to be seen, in parallel, as the gardener in the story of the resurrection of Jesus in the gospel of John (John 20:15). In the parable of the mustard seed (Luke 13:18–19) the kingdom of God is compared to a "mustard seed that someone took and sowed in the garden; it grew and became a tree, and the birds of the air made nests in its branches." Garden, tree, branches, and birds are integral parts of defining God's paradise such that God's kingdom is connected with God's Eden.

Furthermore, God's Sabbath is a way of giving freedom and rest to humanity and all living creatures including the land. God calls us to serve as created coworkers for God's mission of emancipation and reconciliation in accordance with God's *oikos* and Sabbath. In Gen 9:9–10, God enters into relationship with Noah and his descendants including every living creature. Nothing created is a matter of indifference and negligence to God's eye. Every creature has its own dignity and its own rights, for they are all included in God's covenant. God's covenant with Noah provides the basis for fundamental human rights, the right of future generations, and the rights of nature. This goes beyond the androcentric viewpoint of the modern world. If the earth, together with all living things, is God's creation, then its dignity must be respected for God's sake, upholding God's creation in a social, ecological manner.

Public theology framed with social ecological orientation may be undertaken in terms of the Sabbath of the earth. The seventh day is rightly

15. Bauckham, *Living with Other Creatures*, 3.
16. Marquardt, *Eia, wärn Wir da*, 60.

called the feast of creation. The divine Sabbath is the pinnacle of creation, not the human being. Everything that exists was created for this feast as God's fellow celebrants, each in its own way. The Sabbath is important environmental policy for healing the wounded side of our life, other creatures, and the land.

In fact, Earth does not submerge into the eternal life of goddess Gaia. But as a contingent creation, it, together with all earthly living things, is under the compulsion of frustration and transience. It waits in hope for liberation from its bondage to decay and the revelation of glory (Rom 8:19, 21).

According to Exod 23:11, every seventh year Israel is not to plant or till the ground, but is to let it rest. The land shall keep its great Sabbath to the Lord (Lev 25:4). The social system is complemented and fulfilled by the ecological justice. God will scatter Israel among the nations and the land shall be desolation (Lev 26:33). The land shall rest, enjoying its Sabbath, as long as it becomes desolate, while Israel is in the hands of the enemy (Lev 26:42–43). Israel's Babylonian exile, seen in the context of divine ecology for the land,[17] entails a social ecological, emancipatory interpretation of Israel's captivity (Jer 9:12–13).

Public Theology as Eco-theology

Joseph Sittler is one of a group of pioneering thinkers in the field of environmental ethics and eco-theology. His 1962 speech at the Word Council of Churches at New Delhi put greater emphasis on the cosmic dimension, grounding the care of creation in Christology. The unity of church and the unity of all things are undertaken in the cosmic Christ (Col 1:15–20). In "Called to Unity" (1962), Sittler argues that a doctrine of redemption becomes meaningful only within the larger orbit of a doctrine of creation. God's creation of earth cannot be redeemed without connection to a doctrine of cosmos, God's home, and God's definite place. Physical nature cannot be treated "as the mere stage and setting of the drama of personal redemption."[18]

For the sake of Christian eco-theology and ethics, Larry L. Rasmussen argues that Christian theology must rediscover that all of the earth community and creation's well-being are at the center of Christian responsibility, including liturgical and contemplative practices. "God-Cosmos-Earth-Church" takes priority over against "God-Church-World."[19]

17. Moltmann, *God for a Secular Society*, 115.

18. Sittler, "Called to Unity," 411–12.

19. Rasmussen, "Is Eco-Justice Central to Christian Faith?," 415.

Eco-justice is central to Christian faith. The long term task is the conversion of Christianity to the Earth, building toward sustainable communities. Christian faith must be a form of Earth-honoring Christian communities.[20] Upholding the integrity of diverse Christian traditions, eco-theology valorizes Christian pluralism in its contribution to Earth's well-being and "[thinks] ecologically about ecumenism and ecumenically about ecological well-being."[21]

The basic motive of shaping public theology in terms of eco-theology articulates an attitude in conversion to Earth, that is in contrast to anthropocentric attitudes, enhancing greater appreciation for the welfare of nature. Issues of human justice deserve equal consideration with environmental preservation. Hierarchical attitudes toward nature are challenged because they are clothed in the garb of scientific management. Darwinian ideas of evolution, as grounded in survival of the fittest, competition, and nature red in tooth and claw, are replaced by a new notion of collaboration and symbiosis in nature.

A new perspective of critical eco-justice and its theological project becomes biocentric, egalitarian, cooperating, connected, and holistic.[22] This perspective characterizes the basic forms of public theology in a social ecological frame, meaning to be in solidarity with other people and creatures—companions, victims, and allies—in the earth community.

A project of eco-theology as public theology accentuates ecological sustainability—environmentally fitting habits of living and working—which enables life to flourish, utilizing ecologically and socially appropriate technology. Giving sustainability high visibility to ecological integrity and wise behavior, distributive and participatory justice is required in a world that is exceeding resource, pollution, and population limits. Socially just participation becomes a significant factor in decisions of how to obtain sustenance and to guide community life for the common good. In care for the variety of life on Earth, we are participants in that variety while acknowledging our dependence upon it. Thus an ethic of biodiversity assumes a holistic character[23] in a participatory and interdependent direction.

The ecological challenge brings new dimensions to theological revisioning that received little attention in the social context of ecology; it explores the complex relation between eco-justice and public morality, first in terms of a new biblical hermeneutics. The Bible as the source for theological

20. Hessel and Rasmussen, *Earth Habitat*, xi, 21.

21. Rasmussen, "Is Eco-Justice Central to Christian Faith?," 416.

22. Martin-Schramm and Stivers, *Christian Environmental Ethics,* 23.

23. O'Brien, *Ethics of Biodiversity,* 7.

reflection and ethical guidance, whose subject matter is a God of emancipation, forgiveness, reconciliation, and healing, becomes foundational for guiding the public ethical practice for ecological justice.

A theological orientation toward eco-justice rereads scripture as a basis for improving on limitation of theological tradition and retrieving the relatedness of faith to the realm of creation. In a reinterpretation of scripture and critique of tradition, an ecumenical consensus develops, decisively transcending the view that reduces nature as an object for domination and critiques justification of careless and destructive subduing of the earth. This reading strategy seeks to replace the current paradigm of mastery over the earth by way of a new model of human-Earth interrelationship that finds biblical resonance.[24]

Mediating sacramental sensibility and covenantal commitment in connection with sustainable community and public justice, public theology explores the link between ecological integrity and social justice in terms of ethics of eco-justice and solidarity with the innocent victims in our midst. In public theology imbued with eco-justice, the plight of the earth and people, particularly the most abused, are seen together. The diverse tradition of Christianity about the kingdom of God, Christian pluralism on solidarity, justice, and nature are considerable contributions to ecologically shaped public theology by way of a practical endeavor for the clean city in accordance with God's city, on behalf of the poor and nature.

God's *oikonimia* provides a dynamic framework for thought and action that fosters ecological integrity with social-economic and cultural justice. All beings on Earth make up one household (*oikos*), which benefits from an economy (*oikonomia*) taking ecological and social relationship seriously.

A reading strategy of Revelation reinvigorates Christian eschatology of hope to assume theology of *topos* for God's clean garden city. Revelation's critique of Babylon's prostitution, which is based on the portrayal of the harlot (17:1–6), is directed against Rome's exploitive trade and economic domination. This is because Rome's deforestation of conquered lands was notorious for stripping the landscape of its vegetation and forests. A reading of Babylon as a denuded wasteland (Rev 17:16) entails an ecological critique of Rome.[25] Furthermore, unlike American rapturism, people are not snatched from the earth for God's new Jerusalem, for it descends and is "rapurted" down to Earth from Heaven, to the point where it takes up residence and dwells in our midst (Rev 21:2–3). God's presence in all implies an Earth-centered vision of our future, with God dwelling among mortals.[26]

24. Hessel and Ruether, *Christianity and Ecology*, xxxviii.
25. Rossing, "River of Life in God's New Jerusalem," 210–11.
26. Ibid., 214–15.

In the eschatological-ecological hope, imagery such as the garden, the city, and the kingdom are sociologically interconnected. God as co-dweller in the future city is the core of social hope, because the city-utopia is essential part of radical social utopia, which has no death, no mourning, crying, and pain (Rev 21:4).[27] It is the new Jerusalem whose temple is the triune God, the Lord God the Almighty and the Lamb (Rev 20:22). As the temple city, it is filled with presence of God and the Lamb, since the glory of God is its light, and its lamp is the lamb. The river of the water of life flows from the throne of God and of the Lamb through the middle of the street of the city. The new city as the temple city entails a critique of the established religion, because human beings do not need a religion in the future city. God as the *topos* is in their midst, because the Lamb is the temple of the body (John 2:21).

Actually, an eschatological hope for the garden city is imbued with a social ecological vision in which the right is granted to the tree of life (Rev 22:14). The leaves of the tree are for the healing of the nations. God as the Alpha and the Omega is the God as the hope of the coming of God's kingdom, which is defined as the eschatological reality, for God comes in the creation of new Heaven and new Earth and will create the new humanity. The divine "making" (Hebrew *asah*; Rev 21:5) implies that the kingdom of God as *topos* is ecologically and sociologically structured in shaping anew that which has been created.[28] The eschatological secularity of the city is no longer negatively condemned, because it is grounded in the humanity and worldliness of God which transcends and ends the distinction between the holy and the profane. Eschatology is Earth-centered and aims to heal, for it entails the clean city in which God will wipe every tear from the eyes of the innocent victims (Rev 21:4).

Confucian Ecology and Human Life

Christian public theology in an ecological frame of reference may enhance its horizon in making a comparative study of a Confucian theory of life concerning moral and cosmic ecology. The resource for public ecotheology is also acquired in moral prophetic dialogue in an interreligious context for dignity and sustainability of nature.[29] Mutual learning in interreligious dialogue provides a platform for guiding our public ethical practice in collaboration with people of other faiths and cultures.

27. Marquardt, *Eia, wärn Wir da*, 238.
28. Moltmann, *Coming of God*, 271.
29. Martin-Schramm and Stivers, *Christian Environmental Ethics*, 36.

Many Christians in East Asia acknowledge the Confucian moral teaching and its ecological value for theological construction. They perceive and fear whether air pollution and ecological destruction would bring living in East Asia to the apocalyptic situation. For instance, China has serious pollution and public health issues because heavy industries emit nitrogen oxide. The nitrogen emissions worsen the condition of lungs and diminish human capacity to resist influenza and other respiratory infections. Heavier coal dependency in the north pollutes the air much more than the air in the south. As a result, the average life span in the north is much shorter (a full 5.5 years shorter) than in the south. Environmental anxiety is spreading, and pollution is the major reason for social unrest and protest in China. The year 2013 was the year of the horrific "airpocalypse" that saw deadly air pollution envelop Beijing. Air pollution is likewise a problem in Shanghai, Tianjin, Hangzhou, and other cities. In March 2014, top officials in Beijing waged a "war on pollution."[30]

East Asian cultural resources need to be explored to contribute an alternative to the ecological problem. As a living tradition Confucianism may find expression in its moral-cosmic interconnection, which is embedded within the unity of Heaven, Humanity, and Earth. The moral self is seen in the naturalistic-cosmic process and order, while it is guided in an ethic of responsibility and rectification in terms of honoring the mandate of Heaven, the right of people, and respect of the tree and mountains. It is well known that Menzi deplored the mindless deforestation of Ox Mountain in North China. Human nature can be effaced just as Ox Mountain was damaged and ruined badly. Moral self has put forth new growth, together with the mountain's vegetation.[31]

According to Zhu Xi (1130–1200), the most important representative of Neo-Confucianism, individual human beings were produced through spontaneous generation without having any progenitors, that is, evolutions of the Ether. Other creatures originated in a similar manner. The creation of human beings depends on the union of Principle with the Ether. The two Ethers (the *yin* and *yang*) must interact upon each other while condensing and creating.[32]

The human in the Confucian worldview is interdependent on other creatures and an active participant in the cosmic process, having the responsibility of care for life in the environment. Human participation in cosmic processes constitutes unity with Heaven and Earth, standing in

30. See Gardner, "China's Environmental Awakening."

31. Ivanhoe, "Early Confucianism and Environmental Ethics," in Tucker and Berthrong, *Confucianism and Ecology*, 68.

32. Fung, *History of Chinese Philosophy*, 2:551.

solidarity and empathy with all living creatures. Confucian ethics promotes respect for the Earth and life in all its diversity, in care for the community of life with compassion and empathy and in commitment to securing present and future generations. Human beings emerge as an integral part of nature, coming out of the primordial forces of production and reproduction (*yin* and *yang* in interplay of material elements), which generates mountains, rivers, and the whole of the planet. They occupy a distinctive place as moral beings in the evolutionary-cosmic drama.

Accordingly, Zhang Zai (1020–77) strengthens the cosmic-pneumatic vision of all lives through the unity of all creation. Material force is identified with the Great ultimate. *Qi* is the source of the universe and the driving force of endless change. The idea of both *yin* and *yang* and the five elements refer to generative forces, which express material force (*qi*) consisting of both matter and energy.[33] *Qi* as the vital material force runs throughout the creation, self-generating in a constant process of change, transformation, and nourishment.

The primordial *qi* without form (which is called the Great Void or Great Vacuity), by being contracted and consolidated, generates Heaven (*yang*) and Earth (*yin*). The Great Vacuity as the substance of *qi* is the primal undifferentiated material force and its function appears as the Great Harmony in the continual process of integration and disintegration.[34]

Given this, Zhang Zai calls the Great Harmony the Way (Dao, Moral Law), for it is the origin of the process of fusion and intermingling in overcoming and being overcome and in the process of expanding and contracting. Unless the whole universe is in the process of fusion and intermingling like fleeting forces moving in all directions, it may not be called Great Harmony.[35]

In the interaction between the *qi* of Heaven and the *qi* of Earth, *yin* and *yang* unite and give rise to the concrete, for *qi* moves and flows in all directions and in all manners. This dynamic cosmic function produced the multiplicity of things and human beings, constituting the great principles of the universe.[36]

Through the interaction of the *yin* and *yang*, the Ether becomes activated and condenses to form concrete objects (semblance). Though mutually opposed, such objects serve to compliment each other. With the dispersion of the Ether, the opposed objects revert to the Great Vacuity in terms of

---

33. Chan, *Source Book in Chinese Philosophy*, 784.
34. Tucker, "Philosophy of Ch'i," 192–93.
35. Chan, *Source Book in Chinese Philosophy*, 501.
36. Ibid., 505.

harmonization and dissipation. All products must eventually return to the Great Vacuity which implies the universal phenomenon of the world.[37]

For Zhang Zai, there is emphasis on the need for obliterating all distinction between the self and others so as to bring the individual into unity with the universe. "The nature is the one source of all things, and is not the private possession of one's own ego. It is only the great man who is able to exhaust its principle."[38] Human life as part of continuous flow of the cosmic process is connected with rocks, trees, mountains, rivers, and animals.

The cosmic and ecological perspective remains undercurrent in conceptualizing the unity of Heaven and Earth, humanity and the myriad things included. Every daily activity that is done under Heaven and Earth is comprehended in unity with the principle of the universe. This refers to the principle which means one but with its many manifestations.[39] In *Western Inscription*, he argues human relationship with Heaven as father and Earth as mother. He finds an intimate place in the midst of such a small creature, regarding all people as his brothers and sisters. All things are accepted as his companions.[40]

The *Western Inscription* entails a call to act in recognition of the interrelatedness of all things. The nature of the universe is described in terms of the identification of the commonality of material force and the nature of all things. More than that, a call is given for treating people as brothers and sisters, regarding all things as companions of life. Confucian ecology is of moral cosmological character.[41]

The principle of one with its many manifestations continues to take effect later in Zhu Xi's notion of the Principle by metaphor "the moon reflecting itself in ten thousand streams."[42] With emphasis on the Principle over against the Ether that Zang Zhai did not clarify enough, Zhu Xi states that the Supreme Ultimate is present and immanent, yet "it is not cut up into pieces. It is merely like the moon reflecting itself in ten thousand streams."[43] This perspective implies that the stream throws back the image of the moon,

---

37. Fung, *History of Chinese Philosophy*, 2:483.

38. Ibid., 492.

39. Chan, *Source Book of Chinese Philosophy*, 495.

40. Ibid., 497.

41. Wang Yangming (1472–1529) also moves in this direction, emphasizing moral action in connection with a single body of uniting all things throughout the universe. Wang, *Instructions for Practical Living*, 272. "When he observes the pitiful cries and frightened appearance of birds and animals about to be slaughtered, he cannot help feeling an 'inability to bear' their suffering. This shows that his humanity forms one body with birds and animals."

42. Fung, *History of Chinese Philosophy*, 2:542.

43. Ibid., 541.

such that the Principle is mirrored in its diverse, particular manifestations in earthly life connections. The Principle as Dao is manifested in the plurality of the world in its interdependence.

In a different route from Zhu Xi's analogical-meditative thinking, the philosophy of *qi* has made potential contributions to ecological cosmology which asserts a common ground for all living things through *qi*'s running through everything. It refers to reciprocity and relationship with all life-forms, which accounts for the role of the human to assist in changing, transforming, and nourishing Heaven and Earth in the cosmos.[44]

In the final statement in the *Western Inscription*, we read, "In life I shall serve [Heaven and Earth] unresistingly, and when death comes, I shall be at peace."[45] This characterizes the Neo-Confucian attitude toward life and death.

An eco-friendly ethics can be reformulated in a Confucian moral-cosmic worldview to support a more comprehensive global ethic for sustainable community, social justice, and peace. Humanity as an emergent part of a vast evolving universe is alive with a community of planetary life. We live in connection within an ever-emerging web of the fecundity and creativity of nature. Given the idea of the unity of Heaven and humanity embedded within inseparable dimensions of self, community, nature, and Heaven, a harmoniously sustainable relationship between the human species and nature provides a practical guide for nature, the role of humanity, and environmental ethics in companion with the rest of creatures.

Conclusion

As creatures we have come from God, and we are travelling, together with other creatures, toward God. In the story of creation, the human being is not found at the top but at the end of creation. Being antecedent to humankind, the world does not belong to humanity, but to God. Redemption implies not a replacement but a recovery of creation as a good creation.

Other cultural traditions are important factors contributing to an ecological ethics. The supreme good is to be found in earthly and cosmic integrity. The Confucian ethic based on duty-consciousness emphasizes social solidarity, eliciting a spirit of collaboration, emphasizing its connection with a whole body of social conventions and practices, and cosmos. Neo-Confucian self-cultivation is embodied in the perfection of the universe as a whole and embraces a proper sense to create a sustainable and balanced

44. Chan, *Source Book in Chinese Philosophy*, 108.
45. Fung, *History of Chinese Philosophy*, 2:495.

ecosystem. Confucian ecology includes both moral conduct in society and the universal duty, serving Heaven. The sphere of *ren* (humanity) forms one body with all things.[46] In companion with all things in the world, this community helps people live in peace and mutual support in moral exhortation through cultivating their own personal characters.[47]

God in companion with all is the font of life that sustains a variety of particular beings in co-existence in each generation, and sustains their life-giving in interdependence with each other. It is important to develop a public theology in a social, ecological framework in learning from the scientific understanding of biodiversity and the earth as a unique self-regulating organism. Through the constant absorption of solar energy, life is developed and sustained in the self-regulation of the planetary system, in which the planet's living parts are interlocked with its nonliving parts (rocks, oceans, and the atmosphere).

Scientific knowledge must no longer serve the interests of domination but be guided by the concern for shared life and survival, by way of collaboration, symbiosis, and respect. The human race could survive in terms of symbiosis, coordination, and concurrence with the total organism of the earth. By honoring Earth's life, the earth itself is alive, for God creates human beings together with the earth (Gen 1:26).

In eschatological hope, public theology exercises a creative influence on society and promotes a culture of public and ecological participation. Revelation's vision of God's future home on Earth can empower us to work to renew and transform our cities and our world in accordance with God's clean city. God's new Jerusalem is contrasted as the opposition to the polluted Babylon with its anti-ecological Empire, violence, unfettered commerce, idolatry, and injustice. As the new Jerusalem will have no sea, so no shipping economy and maritime trade in luxury goods will prevail, but they will collapse. The vision of God's radiant new Jerusalem is profoundly eschatological, entailing a social, utopian character. The image of city (*polis*) as the garden city, which is central to the book of Revelation, has no temple (Rev 21:22), because God's presence is not confined to a temple, but now extends to the entire creation. God as *topos* of the world in eschatological-ecological vision reinforces our commitment to eco-justice and healing for all creation, especially in deep solidarity with those who are marginalized and victimized in our midst.

46. Chan, *Source Book in Chinese Philosophy*, 761–62.
47. Tu, *Centrality and Commonality*, 49, 50, 56.

Bibliography

Althaus, Paul. *The Theology of Martin Luther*. Translated by Robert C. Schultz. Philadelphia: Fortress, 1966.

Amin, Samir. *Capitalism in the Age of Globalization: The Management of Contemporary Society*. London: Zed, 1998.

Augustine. *The Confessions of St. Augustine*. Translated by John K. Ryan. Garden City, NY: Image, 1960.

Barber, Michael D. *Ethical Hermeneutics: Rationalism in Enrique Düssel's Philosophy of Liberation*. New York: Fordham University Press, 1998.

Barbour, Ian G. *Myths, Models, and Paradigms: A Comparative Study in Science and Religion*. New York: Harper & Row, 1974.

———. *Religion and Science: Historical and Contemporary Issues*. Rev. and exp. ed. of *Religion in an Age of Science*. San Francisco: HarperSanFrancisco, 1997.

———. *When Science Meets Religion*. San Francisco: HarperSanFrancisco, 2000.

Barth, Karl. *Church Dogmatics I: The Doctrine of the Word of God*. Edited by G. W. Bromiley and T. F. Torrance. London: T. & T. Clark, 2004.

———. *Church Dogmatics II: The Doctrine of God*. Edited by G. W. Bromiley and T. F. Torrance. London: T. & T. Clark, 2004.

———. *Church Dogmatics III: The Doctrine of Creation*. Edited by G. W. Bromiley and T. F. Torrance. London: T. & T. Clark, 2004.

———. *Church Dogmatics IV: The Doctrine of Reconciliation*. Edited by G. W. Bromiley and T. F. Torrance. London: T. & T. Clark, 2004.

———. *Christian Life: Church Dogmatics, IV*. Pt. 4. *Lecture Fragments*. Translated by Geoffrey W. Bromiley. Grand Rapids: Eerdmans, 1981.

———. *Theology and Church*. Translated by Louise Pettibone Smith. London: SCM, 1962.

Bauckham, Richard. *Living with Other Creatures: Green Exegesis and Theology*. Waco: Baylor University Press, 2011.

Bell, Daniel A., ed. *Confucian Political Ethics*. Princeton: Princeton University Press, 2008.

Bellah, Robert N. *Beyond Belief: Essays on Religion in a Post-Tradionalist World*. Berkeley: University of California Press, 1970.

———. *Religion in Human Evolution: From the Paleolithic to the Axial Age*. Cambridge: Belknap Press of Harvard University Press, 2011.

———. *Tokugawa Religion: The Values of Pre-industrial Japan*. Glencoe, IL: Free Press, 1957.

Bellah, Robert N., and Hans Jonas, eds. *The Axial Age and Its Consequences*. Cambridge: Belknap Press of Harvard University Press, 2012.

Bendix, Reinhard. *Max Weber: An Intellectual Portrait*. Berkeley: University of California Press, 1977.

Benjamin, Walter. *Illuminations: Essays and Reflections*. Edited by Hannah Arendt. Translated by Harry Zohn. New York: Schocken, 1968.

Berger, Peter L., and Thomas Luckmann. *The Social Construction of Reality: A Treatise in the Sociology of Knowledge*. Garden City, NY: Doubleday, 1966.

Berrigan, Daniel, and Thich Nhat Hanh. *The Raft Is Not the Shore*. Boston: Beacon, 1975.

Berthrong, John H., and Evelyn Nagai Berthrong. *Confucianism: A Short Introduction*. Oxford: Oneworld, 2000.

Bethge, Eberhard. *Dietrich Bonhoeffer: Theologe, Christ, Zeitgenosse*. Munich: Kaiser, 1967.

Bevans, Stephen B., and Roger P. Schroeder. *Constants in Context: A Theology of Mission for Today*. Maryknoll, NY: Orbis. 2004.

Bodhi, Bhikkhu, ed. *In the Buddha's Words: An Anthology of Discourses from the Pali Canon*. Boston: Wisdom Publications, 2005.

Boff, Leonardo. *Ecology and Liberation: A New Paradigm*. Translated by John Cumming. Maryknoll, NY: Orbis, 1998.

Bonhoeffer, Dietrich. *Act and Being*. Edited by Wayne Whitson Floyd Jr. Translated by H. Martin Rumscheidt. Minneapolis: Fortress, 1996.

———. *Berlin, 1932–1933*. Edited by Larry L. Rasmussen. Translated by Isabel Best and David Higgins. Dietrich Bonhoeffer Works 12. Minneapolis: Fortress, 2009.

———. *Christ the Center*. Translated by Edwin Robertson. New York: Harper & Row, 1978.

———. *Conspiracy and Imprisonment, 1940–1945*. Edited by Mark S. Brocker. Translated by Lisa E. Dahill. Dietrich Bonhoeffer Works 16. Minneapolis: Fortress, 2006.

———. *The Cost of Discipleship*. Translated by R. H. Fuller, with some revision by Irmgard Booth. New York: Macmillan, 1959.

———. *Creation and Fall: A Theological Exposition of Genesis 1–3*. Edited by John W. de Gruchy. Translated by Douglas Stephen Bax. Dietrich Bonhoeffer Works 3. Minneapolis: Fortress, 1997.

———. *Ethics*. Edited by Eberhard Bethge. Translated by Neville Horton Smith. New York: Macmillan, 1955.

———. *Letters and Papers from Prison*. Edited by Eberhard Bethge. New York: Macmillan, 1971.

———. *London, 1933–1935*. Edited by Keith Clements. Translated by Isabel Best. Dietrich Bonhoeffer Works 13. Minneapolis: Fortress, 2007.

Bosch, David. *Transforming Mission: Paradigm Shifts in Theology of Mission*. Maryknoll, NY: Orbis, 1991.

Brassard, Francis. *The Concept of Bodhicitta in Santideva's Bodhicaryavatara*. Albany: State University of New York Press, 2000.

Brock, Rita Nakashima et al., eds. *Off the Menu: Asian and Asian North American Women's Religion and Theology*. 1st ed. Louisville: Westminster John Knox, 2007.

Brubaker, Pamela, and Rogate Mshana, eds. *Justice Not Greed*. Geneva: WCC, 2010.

Capra, Fritjof. *The Hidden Connections*. New York: Doubleday, 2002.

———. *The Tao of Physics*. Boston: Shambhala, 1999.

———. *The Web of Life: A New Scientific Understanding of Living Systems*. New York: Anchor, 1996.

Carson, Rachel. *Silent Spring*. Boston: Houghton Mifflin, 1962.

Chan, Wing-tsit. *A Source Book in Chinese Philosophy*. Princeton: Princeton University Press, 1963.

Chapman, Mark D. *Ernst Troeltsch and Liberal Theology: Religion and Cultural Synthesis in Wilhelmine Germany*. Oxford: Oxford University Press, 2001.

Chung, Paul S. *Church and Ethical Responsibility in the Midst of World Economy: Greed, Dominion, and Justice*. Eugene, OR: Cascade, 2013.

———. *Constructing Irregular Theology: Bamboo and Minjung in East Asian Perspective*. Leiden: Brill, 2009.

———. "Dietrich Bonhoeffer Seen from Asian Minjung Theology and the Fourth Eye of Socially Engaged Buddhism." In *Asian Contextual Theology for the Third Millennium: Theology of Minjung in Fourth-Eye Formation*, edited by Paul S. Chung et al., 127–45. Eugene, OR: Pickwick, 2007.

———. *The Hermeneutical Self and an Ethical Difference: Intercivilizational Engagement*. Cambridge: J. Clarke, 2012.

———. *Hermeneutical Theology and the Imperative of Pubic Ethics: Confessing Christ in Post-Colonial Christianity*. Eugene, OR: Pickwick, 2014.

———. *Karl Barth: God's Word in Action*. Eugene, OR: Cascade, 2008.

———. *Martin Luther and Buddhism: Aesthetics of Suffering*. 2nd ed. Eugene, OR: Pickwick, 2008.

Chung, Paul S., et al., eds. *Asian Contextual Theology for the Third Millennium: Theology of Minjung in Fourth-Eye Formation*. Eugene, OR: Pickwick, 2007.

Clooney, Francis X., ed. *The New Comparative Theology: Interreligious Insights from the Next Generation*. New York: T. & T. Clark, 2010.

Cobb, John B., Jr., and David R. Griffin. *Process Theology: An Introductory Exposition*. Philadelphia: Westminster, 1976.

Collins, Steven. *Nirvana and Other Buddhist Felicities*. New York: Cambridge University Press, 1998.

Cone, James H. *The Cross and the Lynching Tree*. Maryknoll, NY: Orbis, 2011.

Confucius. *The Analects*. Translated by Arthur Waley. Hunan: Hunan People's Publishing House, 1999.

———. *Confucian Analects; The Great Learning; and The Doctrine of the Mean*. Translated by James Legge. New York: Dover, 1971.

Dalai Lama XIV. *The Good Heart: A Buddhist Perspective on the Teaching of Jesus*. Translated by Geshe Thupten Jinpa. Edited by Robert Kiely. Boston: Wisdom Publications, 1996.

Dalton, Anne Marie, and Henry C. Simmons. *Ecotheology and the Practice of Hope*. Albany: State University of New York Press, 2010.

Davies, Paul. *The Mind of God*. New York: Simon & Schuster, 1992.

Dawkins, Richard. *The Blind Watchmaker*. New York: Norton, 1986.

———. *The Selfish Gene*. Rev. ed. New York: Oxford University Press, 1989.

Deane-Drummond, Celia. *Eco-Theology*. London: Darton, Longman and Todd, 2008.

De Bary, Wm. Theodore, and Irene Bloom, eds. *Sources of Chinese Tradition*. 2nd ed. New York: Columbia University Press, 1999.

D'Entrèves, Maurizio Passerin, and Seyla Benhabib, eds. *Habermas and the Unfinished Project of Modernity: Critical Essays on* The Philosophical Discourse of Modernity. Cambridge: MIT Press, 1996.

Depew, David J., and Bruce H. Weber. *Darwinism Evolving.* Cambridge: MIT Press, 1995.

Dillenberger, John, ed. *Martin Luther: Selections from His Writings.* Garden City, NY: Anchor, 1961.

Dirlik, Arif. "The Postcolonial Aura: Third World Criticism in the Age of Global Capitalism." In *Contemporary Postcolonial Theory: A Reader,* edited by Padmini Mongia, 294–320. New York: Oxford University Press, 1996.

Dorrien, Gary. *Social Ethics in the Making: Interpreting an American Tradition.* Chichester, UK: Wiley-Blackwell, 2011.

Drabinski, John. E. *Levinas and the Postcolonial: Race, Nation, Other.* Edinburgh: Edinburgh University Press, 2011.

Duchrow, Ulrich. *Alternatives to Global Capitalism: Drawn from Biblical History, Designed for Political Action.* Reprint, Utrecht: International Books, 1998.

———. *Europe in the World System, 1492–1992: Is Justice Possible?* Translated by Keith Archer. Geneva: WCC, 1992.

Duchrow, Ulrich, and Franz J. Hinkelammert. *Property for People, Not for Profit: Alternatives to the Global Tyranny of Capital.* Translated by Elaine Griffiths et al. London: Zed, 2004.

———. *Transcending Greedy Money: Interreligious Solidarity for Just Relations.* New York: Palgrave Macmillan, 2012.

Durkheim, Emile. *The Elementary Forms of Religious Life.* Translated by Karen E. Fields. New York: Free Press, 1995.

Dussel, Enrique. *The Invention of the Americas: Eclipse of "the Other" and the Myth of Modernity.* Translated by Michael D. Barber. New York: Continuum, 1995.

Ebeling, Gerhard. *Luther: An Introduction to His Thought.* Translated by R. A. Wilson. Minneapolis: Fortress, 2007.

———. *Word and Faith.* Translated by James W. Leitch. Philadelphia: Fortress, 1963.

Edwards, Denis. *The God of Evolution: A Trinitarian Theology.* New York: Paulist, 1999.

Escobar, Arturo. *Encountering Development: The Making and Unmaking of the Third World.* Princeton: Princeton University Press, 1995.

Fanon, Frantz. *The Wretched of the Earth.* Translated by Constance Farrington. 3rd ed. Harmondsworth, UK: Penguin, 1990.

Fasching, Darrell J., and Dell deChant. *Comparative Religious Ethics: Narrative Approach.* Oxford: Blackwell, 2001.

Forell, George W., and James M. Childs, eds. *Christian Social Teachings: A Reader in Christian Social Ethics from the Bible to the Present.* 2nd ed. Minneapolis: Fortress, 2013.

Foucault, Michel. *The Archeology of Knowledge; and, The Discourse on Language.* Translated by A. M. Sheridan Smith. New York: Random House, 1982.

———. *Discipline and Punish: The Birth of the Prison.* Translated by Alan Sheridan. New York: Vintage, 1977.

———. *The Essential Foucault: Selections from Essential Works of Foucault, 1954–1984.* Edited by Paul Rabinow and Nikolas Rose. New York: New Press, 2003.

———. *Fearless Speech.* Edited by Joseph Pearson. Los Angles: Semiotext(e), 2001.

———. *The Order of Things: An Archaeology of the Human Sciences.* New York: Vintage, 1994.

Frank, Andre Gunder. *ReOrient: Global Economy in the Asian Age.* Berkeley: University of California Press, 1998.

Fretheim, Terence E. *Abraham: Trials of Family and Faith.* Columbia: University of South Carolina Press, 2007.

Frick, Peter, ed. *Bonhoeffer and Interpretive Theory: Essays on Methods and Understanding.* Frankfurt am Main: P. Lang, 2013.

Fung, Yu-lan. *A History of Chinese Philosophy.* Vol. 1, *The Period of the Philosophers.* Translated by Derk Bodde. Princeton: Princeton University Press, 1983.

———. *A History of Chinese Philosophy.* Vol. 2, *The Period of Classical Learning.* Translated by Derk Bodde. Princeton: Princeton University Press, 1983.

Gadamer, Hans-Georg. *Truth and Method.* Translated by J. Weinsheimer and D. G. Marshall. 2nd rev. ed. New York: Continuum, 2004.

Gandhi, Leela. *Postcolonial Theory: A Critical Introduction.* New York: Columbia University Press, 1998.

Gardner, Daniel K. "China's Environmental Awakening." *New York Times,* September 14, 2014. http://www.nytimes.com/2014/09/15/opinion/chinas-environmental-awakening.html?_r=0.

Gayhart, Bryce A. *The Ethics of Ernst Troeltsch: A Commitment to Relevancy.* Lewiston, NY: E. Mellen, 1990.

Geertz, Clifford. *Interpretation of Culture.* New York: Basic Books, 1973.

Girard, Rene. *Things Hidden Since the Foundation of the World.* Translated by Stephen Bann (Books II & III) and Michael Metteer (Book I). Stanford: Stanford University Press, 1978.

Gollwitzer, Helmut. *An Introduction to Protestant Theology.* Translated by David Cairns. Philadelphia: Westminster, 1978.

———. *Krummes Holz-aufrechter Gang: Zur Frage nach dem Sinn des Lebens.* Munich: Kaiser, 1985.

———. *The Rich Christians and Poor Lazarus.* Translated by David Cairns. New York: Macmillan, 1970.

González, Justo L. *The Changing Shape of Church History.* St. Louis: Chalice, 2002.

Gottlieb, Roger S., ed. *This Sacred Earth: Religion, Nature, Environment.* New York: Routledge, 1996.

Gould, Stephen J. "Nonoverlapping Magisteria." *Natural History* 106 (1997) 16–22.

———. *Rocks of Ages: Science and Religion and the Fullness of Life.* New York: Ballatine, 1999.

Graham, A. C. *Disputers of the Tao: Philosophical Argument in Ancient China.* La Salle, IL: Open Court, 1989.

Green, Clifford, and Thomas Tseng, eds. *Dietrich Bonhoeffer and Sino-Theology.* Chung Li, Taiwan: Chung Yuan Christian University, 2008.

Greene, John C. *Darwin and the Modern World View.* New York: Mentor, 1963.

Gregory, Peter N. *Tsung-mi and the Sinification of Buddhism.* Princeton: Princeton University Press, 1991.

Griffin, David R. *Religion and Scientific Naturalism: Overcoming the Conflicts.* Albany: State University of New York Press, 2000.

Habermas, Jürgen. *Justification and Application: Remarks on Discourse Ethics.* Translated by Ciaran P. Cronin. Cambridge: MIT Press, 1993.

————. *The Theory of Communicative Action.* Vol. 2, *Lifeworld and System: A Critique of Functionalist Reason.* Translated by Thomas McCarthy. Boston: Beacon, 1987.

Hardt, Michael, and Antonio Negri. *Empire.* Cambridge: Harvard University Press, 2000.

Hartshorne, Charles. *Anselm's Discovery: A Re-examination of the Ontological Proof for God's Existence.* La Salle, IL: Open Court, 1965.

Harvey, Peter. *An Introduction to Buddhist Ethics.* Cambridge: Cambridge University Press, 2000.

Haught, John F. *God after Darwin: A Theology of Evolution.* Boulder, CO: Westview, 2000.

————. *Science and Religion: From Conflict to Conversation.* New York: Paulist, 1995.

Hefner, Philip. *The Human Factor: Evolution, Culture, and Religion.* Minneapolis: Fortress, 1993.

Heidegger, Martin. *Basic Writings.* Edited by David Farrell Krell. Rev. and expanded ed. San Francisco: HarperSanFrancisco, 1993.

Hessel, Dieter T., and Larry Rasmussen, eds. *Earth Habitat: Eco-injustice and the Church's Response.* Minneapolis: Fortress, 2001.

Hessel, Dieter T., and Rosemary Radford Ruether, eds. *Christianity and Ecology: Seeking the Well-Being of Earth and Humans.* Cambridge: Harvard University Center for the Study of World Religions, 2000.

Hinkelammert, Franz J. *The Ideological Weapons of Death: A Theological Critique of Capitalism.* Maryknoll, NY: Orbis, 1986.

Horkheimer, Max, and Theodor W. Adorno. *Dialectic of Enlightenment.* Translated by John Cumming. New York: Seabury, 1972.

Ingleby, Jonathan. *Beyond Empire: Postcolonialism and Mission in a Global Context.* Milton Keynes: AuthorHouse, 2010.

Ivanhoe, Philip J. "Early Confucianism and Environmental Ethics." In *Confucianism and Ecology,* edited by Mary Evelyn Tucker and John H. Berthrong, 59–76. Cambridge: Harvard University Press, 1998.

Iwand, H. J. *Luthers Theologie.* Edited by Helmut Gollwitzer et al. Nachgelassene Werke 5. Munich: Kaiser, 1983.

————. *The Righteousness of Faith according to Luther.* Edited by Virgil F. Thompson. Translated by Randi H. Lundell. Eugene, OR: Wipf and Stock, 2008.

Jüngel, Eberhard. *God as the Mystery of the World: On the Foundation of the Theology of the Crucified One in the Dispute between Theism and Atheism.* Translated by Darrell L. Guder. Grand Rapids: Eerdmans, 1983.

Kant, Immanuel. *Basic Writings of Kant.* Edited by Allen W. Wood. New York: Modern Library, 2001.

Kaufmann, Stuart. *The Origins of Order: Self-Organization and Selection in Evolution.* New York: Oxford University Press, 1993.

Kellner, Douglas, ed. *Baudrillard: A Critical Reader.* Oxford: Blackwell, 1994.

Kim, Sebastian C. H., ed. *Christian Theology in Asia.* Cambridge: Cambridge University Press, 2008.

King, Robert. *Orientalism and Religion: Postcolonial Theory, India, and "The Mystic East".* London: Routledge, 1999.

Kitamori, Kazoh. *The Theology of the Pain of God.* 1965. Reprint, Eugene, OR: Wipf and Stock, 2005.

Knitter, Paul F. *Without Buddha I Could Not Be a Christian.* Oxford: Oneworld, 2009.

Kolb, Robert, and Timothy J. Wengert, eds. *The Book of Concord: The Confessions of the Evangelical Lutheran Church.* Minneapolis: Fortress, 2000.

Kögler, Hans-Herbert. *The Power of Dialogue: Critical Hermeneutics after Gadamer and Foucault.* Translated by Paul Hendrickson. Cambridge: MIT Press, 1996.

Koyama, Kosuke. *Waterbuffalo Theology.* Maryknoll, NY: Orbis, 1974.

Kremers, Heinz, et al. *Die Juden und Martin Luther, Martin Luther und die Juden: Geschichte, Wirkungsgeschichte, Herausforderung.* Neukirchen-Vluyn: Neukirchener, 1985.

Kuhn, Thomas. *The Structure of Scientific Revolution.* Chicago: University of Chicago Press, 1970.

Küng, Hans. *The Beginning of All Things: Science and Religion.* Translated by John Bowden. Grand Rapids: Eerdmanns, 2005.

———. *Global Responsibility: In Search of a New World Ethic.* Translated by John Bowden. 1990. Reprint, Eugene, OR: Wipf & Stock, 2004.

Lakeland, Paul. *Postmodernity: Christian Identity in a Fragmented Age.* Minneapolis: Fortress, 1997.

Lebacqz, Karen. *Six Theories of Justice.* Minneapolis: Augsburg, 1986.

Levinas, Emmanuel. *Basic Philosophical Writings.* Edited by Adriaan T. Peperzak et al. Bloomington: Indiana University Press, 1996.

———. *Otherwise than Being, or, Beyond Essence.* Translated by Alphonso Lingis. Pittsburgh: Duquesne University Press, 1998.

———. *Totality and Infinity: An Essay on Exteriority.* Translated by Alphonso Lingis. Pittsburgh: Duquesne University Press, 2007.

Lin, Melissa. *Ethical Reorientation for Christianity in China: The Individual, Community, and Society.* Hong Kong: Christian Study Centre on Chinese Religion & Culture, 2010.

Link, Christian. *Schöpfung: Schöpfungstheologie in reformatorischer Tradition.* Vol. 1. Gutersloh: Mohn, 1991.

Lovestock, James. *The Age of Gaia.* Oxford: Oxford University Press, 1988.

———. *Healing Gaia.* New York: Harmony, 1991.

Lull, Timothy F., ed. *Martin Luther's Basic Theological Writings.* Minneapolis: Fortress, 1989.

Lull, Timothy F., and William R. Russell, eds. *Martin Luther's Basic Theological Writings.* 2nd ed. Minneapolis: Fortress, 2005.

Luther, Martin. *The Church Comes from All Nations: Luther Texts on Mission.* Selected by Volker Stolle. Translated by Klaus D. Schultz and Daniel Thies. St. Louis: Concordia, 2003.

———. *D. Martin Luthers Tischreden, 1531–46.* Vol. 1 of *D. Martin Luthers Werke: Kritische Gesamtausgabe: Tischreden.* Weimar: Böhlaus, 1912.

———. *D. Martin Luthers Werke. Sonderedition der kritischen Weimarer Ausgabe. Begleitheft zum Briefwechsel 5, 1529–1530.* Weimar: Böhlaus, 2002.

———. *Luther's Works.* Edited by Jaroslav Pelikan. St. Louis: Concordia, 1955–67.

Lyotard, J.-F. *The Postmodern Condition: A Report on Knowledge.* Translated by Geoff Bennington and Brian Massumi. Minneapolis: University of Minnesota Press, 1988.

Mandel, Ernest. *Late Capitalism.* Translated by Joris De Bres. London: Verso, 1975.

Margulis, Lynn. *Symbiosis in Cell Evolution.* 2nd ed. San Francisco: Freeman, 1993.

Margulis, Lynn, and Dorion Sagan. *Microcosmos.* New York: Summit, 1986.

Marquardt, F. W. *Das christliche Bekenntnis zu Jesus dem Juden: Eine Christologie.* Vol. 1. Munich: Kaiser, 1990.

———. *Eia, wärn wir da: Eine theologische Utopie.* Gutersloh: Kaiser/Gutersloher, 1997.

———. *Theological Audacities: Selected Essays.* Edited by Andreas Pangritz and Paul S. Chung. Eugene, OR: Pickwick, 2010.

Martin-Schramm, James B., and Robert L. Stivers. *Christian Environmental Ethics: A Case Method Approach.* Maryknoll, NY: Orbis, 2003.

Marx, Karl. *Capital: A Critique of Political Economy.* Vol. 1, Book I: *The Process of Production of Capital.* Translated by Ben Fowkes. London: Penguin, 1990.

McCarthy, Thomas. *Race, Empire, and the Idea of Human Development.* Cambridge: Cambridge University Press, 2009.

McFague, Sallie. *Metaphorical Theology: Models of God in Religious Language.* Philadelphia: Fortress, 1982.

Meeks, M. Douglas. *God the Economist: The Doctrine of God and Political Economy.* Minneapolis: Fortress, 1989.

Mencius. *Mencius.* Translated by D. C. Lau. New York: Penguin, 1970.

———. *Mengzi.* Translated by Zhao Zhentao et al. Hunan: Hunan People's Publishing House, 1999.

Metz, Johann-Baptist, and Jürgen Moltmann. *Faith and the Future: Essays on Theology, Solidarity, and Modernity.* Maryknoll, NY: Orbis, 1995.

Miller, Kenneth R. *Finding Darwin's God: A Scientist's Search for Common Ground between God and Evolution.* New York: Harper Perennial, 1999.

Molleur, Joseph. *Divergent Traditions, Converging Faiths: Troeltsch, Comparative Theology and the Conversation with Hinduism.* New York: P. Lang, 2000.

Moltmann, Jürgen. *The Coming of God: Christian Eschatology.* Translated by Margaret Kohl. Minneapolis: Fortress, 1996.

———. *God for a Secular Society: The Public Relevance of Theology.* Minneapolis: Fortress, 1999.

———. *God in Creation: A New Theology of Creation and the Spirit of God.* San Francisco: Harper & Row, 1985.

———. *Theology of Hope: On the Ground and the Implications of a Christian Eschatology.* Translated by James W. Leitch. Minneapolis: Fortress, 1993.

Mongia, Padmini, ed. *Contemporary Postcolonial Theory: A Reader.* New York: Oxford University Press, 1996.

Mshana, Rogate, and Athena Peralta, eds. *The Greed Line: Final Report and Supporting Studies.* Geneva: WCC, 2013.

Murphy, Nancey. *Anglo-American Postmodernity.* Boulder, CO: Westview, 1997.

Nhat Hanh, Thich. *The Moon Bamboo.* Translated by Vo-Dinh Mai and Mobi Ho. Berkeley: Parallax, 1989.

———. *Zen Keys.* Translated by Albert Low and Jean Low. Garden City, NY: Anchor, 1974.

Nisker, Wes. *Buddha's Nature: Evolution as a Practical Guide to Enlightenment.* New York: Bantam, 1998.

Nolan, Patrick, and Gerhard Lenski. *Human Societies.* 10th ed. Boulder, CO: Paradigm, 2006.

O'Brien, Kevin J. *An Ethics of Biodiversity: Christianity, Ecology, and the Variety of Life.* Washington, DC: Georgetown University Press, 2010.

Paley, William. *Natural Theology: Or, Evidences for the Existence and Attributes of the Deity, Collected from the Appearances of Nature.* New York: American Tract Society, 1802.

Pannenberg, Wolfart. *Systematic Theology.* Translated by Geoffrey W. Bromiley. Vol. 3. Grand Rapids: Erdmans, 1998.

———. *Theology and the Philosophy of Science.* Translated by Francis McDonagh. Philadelphia: Westminster, 1976.

———. *Toward a Theology of Nature.* Edited by Ted Peters. Louisville: Westminster John Knox, 1993.

Payutto, P. A. *Buddhist Economics: A Middle Way for the Market Place.* Bangkok: Buddhadhamma Foundation, 1994.

Peacocke, Arthur. *Theology for a Scientific Age: Being and Becoming—Natural and Divine.* Oxford: Blackwell, 1990.

Peters, Ted, ed. *Genetics: Issues of Social Justice.* Cleveland: Pilgrim, 1998.

———. *God—the World's Future: Systematic Theology for a New Era.* 2nd ed. Minneapolis: Fortress, 2000.

———, ed. *Science and Theology: The New Consonance.* Boulder, CO: Westview, 1998.

———. *Science, Theology, and Ethics.* Burlington, VT: Ashgate, 2003.

———. *Sin Boldly: Justifying Faith for Fragile Souls and Broken Souls.* Minneapolis: Fortress, 2015.

Peters, Ted, and Martinez Hewlett. *Evolution from Creation to New Creation: Conflict, Conversation, and Convergence.* Nashville: Abingdon, 2003.

Peters, Ted, and Carl Peterson. "The Higgs Boson: An Adventure in Critical Realism." *Theology and Science* 11 (2013) 185–207.

Polkinghorne, John. *The Faith of a Physicist.* Princeton: Princeton University Press, 1994.

———. *Scientists as Theologians.* London: SPCK, 1996.

Prigogine, Ilya, and Isabelle Stengers. *Order Out of Chaos.* New York: Bantam, 1984.

Pui-lan, Kwok, et al., eds. *Empire and the Christian Tradition: New Readings of Classical Theologians.* Minneapolis: Fortress, 2007.

Rasmussen, Larry. "Bonhoeffer: Ecological Theologian." In *Bonhoeffer and Interpretive Theory*, edited by Peter Frick, 251–67. Frankfurt am Main: P. Lang, 2013.

———. "Is Eco-Justice Central to Christian Faith?" In *Christian Social Teachings*, edited by G. W. Forell and revised by James M. Childs, 414–19. 2nd ed. Minneapolis: Fortress, 2013.

Rawls, John. *A Theory of Justice.* Cambridge: Belknap Press of Harvard University Press, 1971.

Reist, Benjamin A. *Toward a Theology of Involvement: The Thought of Ernst Troeltsch.* Philadelphia: Westminster, 1966.

Rendtorff, Trutz. *Ethics.* Vol. 1, *Basic Elements and Methodology in an Ethical Theology.* Translated by Keith Crim. Minneapolis: Fortress, 1986.

Ricard, Matthieu, and Xuan Thuan Trinh. *The Quantum and the Lotus.* New York: Crown, 2001.

Ricci, Matteo. *The True Meaning of the Lord of Heaven (T'ien-Chu Shih-I).* Translated by Douglas Lancashire and Peter Hu Kuo-Chen. Taipei: Ricci Institute for Chinese Studies, 1985.

Ricoeur, Paul. *The Conflict of Interpretations.* Edited by Don Ihde. Evanston: Northwestern University Press, 1974.

Rieger, Joerg. *Christ and Empire: From Paul to Postcolonial Times.* Minneapolis: Fortress, 2007.

——. *No Rising Tide: Theology, Economics, and the Future.* Minneapolis: Fortress, 2009.

Rivera, Mayra. *The Touch of Transcendence: A Postcolonial Theology of God.* Louisville: Westminster John Knox, 2007.

Rivera-Pagan, Luis N., ed. *God, in Your Grace . . . : Official Report of the Ninth Assembly of the World Council of Churches.* Geneva: WCC, 2008.

Robinson, James M., and John B. Cobb Jr., eds. *The New Hermeneutic.* New Frontiers in Theology: Discussions among Continental and American Theologians 2. New York: Harper & Row, 1964.

Rossing, Barbara R. "River of Life in God's New Jerusalem: An Eschatological Vision for Earth's Future." In *Christianity and Ecology,* edited by Dieter T. Hessel and Rosemary Radford Ruether, 205–24. Cambridge: Harvard University Center for the Study of World Religions, 2000.

Ruether, Rosemary Radford. *Gaia and God: An Ecofeminist Theology of Earth Healing.* San Francisco: HarperSanFrancisco, 1992.

——. *New Woman, New Earth: Sexist Ideologies and Human Liberation.* Boston: Beacon, 1995.

Rupp, E. Gordon, and Philip S. Watson, eds. *Luther and Erasmus: Free Will and Salvation.* Philadelphia: Westminster, 1969.

Said, Edward. *Orientalism.* New York: Pantheon, 1978.

Sanneh, Lamin. *Whose Religion Is Christianity? The Gospel beyond the West.* Grand Rapids: Eerdmans, 2003.

Schweiker, William. *Responsibility and Christian Ethics.* Cambridge: Cambridge University Press, 1995.

——. *Theological Ethics and Global Dynamics: In the Time of Many Worlds.* Malden, MA: Blackwell, 2004.

Sinaga, Martin L., ed. *A Common Word: Buddhists and Christians Engage Structural Greed.* Minneapolis: Lutheran University Press, 2012.

Sittler, Joseph. "Called to Unity." In *Christian Social Teachings,* edited by George W. Forell, revised by James M. Childs, 410–14. 2nd ed. Minneapolis: Fortress, 2013.

Sivaraksa, Sulak. *The Wisdom of Sustainability: Buddhist Economics for the 21st Century.* Edited by Arnold Kotler and Nicholas Bennett. Chiang Mai, Thailand: Silkworm, 2009.

Smuts, J. C. *Holism and Evolution.* 1926. Reprint, Cape Town: N & S, 1987.

Spencer, Herbert. *The Principles of Biology.* London: William and Norgate, 1864.

——. *Social Statics: The Conditions Essential to Human Happiness Specified, and the First of Them Developed.* New York: D. Appleton, 1864.

Spivak, Gayatri Ch. *In Other Worlds: Essays in Cultural Politics.* New York: Methuen, 1987.

Stackhouse, Max L. *Ethics and the Urban Ethos: An Essay in Social Theory and Theological Reconstruction.* Boston: Beacon, 1972.

——. *Globalization and Grace.* New York: Continuum, 2007.

——. *Public Theology and Political Economy: Christian Stewardship in Modern Society.* Grand Rapids: Eerdmans, 1987.

Stern, J. P. *Hitler: The Führer and the People.* Berkeley: University of California Press, 1975.

Streufert, Mary J., ed. *Transformative Lutheran Theologies*. Minneapolis: Fortress, 2010.

Tang, Sui-Keung. "An Ethical Case of 'The Son Concealing the Misconduct of the Father.'" In *Dietrich Bonhoeffer and Sino-Theology*, edited by Clifford Green and Thomas Tseng, 365–93. Chung Li, Taiwan: Chung Yuan Christian University, 2008.

———. "Interpreting Dietrich Bonhoeffer's Theology of Sociality through the Lens of Confucianism Humanism." In *Bonhoeffer and Interpretive Theory*, edited by Peter Frick, 143–58. Frankfurt am Main: P. Lang, 2013.

Taylor, Charles. *Modern Social Imaginaries*. Durham: Duke University Press, 2004.

Tillich, Paul. *Christianity and the Encounter of World Religions*. Minneapolis: Fortress, 1994.

Torrance, Thomas F. *Reality and Scientific Theology*. Edinburgh: Scottish Academic Press, 1985.

———. *Theological Science*. Oxford: Oxford University Press, 1969.

Tracy, David. *The Analogical Imagination: Christian Theology and the Culture of Pluralism*. New York: Crossroad, 1981.

———. *Blessed Rage for Order: The New Pluralism in Theology*. Chicago: University of Chicago Press, 1996.

———. *Plurality and Ambiguity: Hermeneutics, Religion, Hope*. Chicago: University of Chicago Press, 1987.

Trelstad, Marit A., ed. *Cross Examinations: Readings on the Meaning of the Cross Today*. Minneapolis: Augsburg, 2006.

Trinh, Xuan Thuan. *Chaos and Harmony: Perspectives on Scientific Revolutions of the Twentieth Century*. Translated by Axel Reisinger. Oxford: Oxford University Press, 2001.

Troeltsch, Ernst. *The Absoluteness of Christianity and the History of Religions*. Translated by David Reid. Richmond: John Knox, 1971.

———. *Christian Thought: Its History and Application*. Edited by Baron F. von Hügel. New York: Meridan, 1957.

———. *The Social Teaching of the Christian Churches*. Translated by Olive Wyon. 2 vols. 1931. Reprint, Louisville: Westminster John Knox, 1992.

Tu, Weiming. "Beyond the Enlightenment Mentality." In *Confucianism and Ecology: The Interrelation of Heaven, Earth, and Humans*, edited by Mary Evelyn Tucker and John H. Berthrong, 3–21. Cambridge: Harvard University Press, 1998.

———. *Centrality and Commonality: An Essay on Confucian Religiousness*. Rev. enl. ed. Albany: State University of New York Press, 1989.

Tucker, Mary Evelyn. "The Philosophy of Ch'i as an Ecological Cosmology." In *Confucianism and Ecology: The Interrelation of Heaven, Earth, and Humans*, edited by Mary Evelyn Tucker and John H. Berthrong, 187–207. Cambridge: Harvard University Press, 1998.

Tucker, Mary Evelyn, and John H. Berthrong, eds. *Confucianism and Ecology: The Interrelation of Heaven, Earth, and Humans*. Cambridge: Harvard University Press, 1998.

Twiss, Sumner B., and Bruce Grelle, eds. *Explorations in Global Ethics: Comparative Religious Ethics and Interreligious Dialogue*. Boulder, CO: Westview, 1998.

Van Huyssteen, Wentzel. *The Shaping of Rationality: Toward Interdisciplinarity in Theology and Science*. Grand Rapids: Eerdmans, 1999.

Varela, Francisco. "Neurophenomenology." *Journal of Consciousness Studies* 3 (1996) 330–49.

Vattimo, Gianni. *The End of Modernity: Nihilism and Hermeneutics in Postmodern Culture.* Translated by Jon R. Snyder. Baltimore: Johns Hopkins University Press, 1988.

Wang, Yangming. *Instructions for Practical Living, and Other Neo-Confucian Writings.* Translated by Wing-tsit Chan. New York: Columbia University Press, 1963.

Weber, Max. *From Max Weber: Essays in Sociology.* Translated and edited by H. H. Gerth and C. Wright Mills. New York: Oxford University Press, 1958.

———. *Max Weber: Selections in Translation.* Edited by W. G. Runciman. Translated by Eric Matthews. Cambridge: Cambridge University Press, 1978.

———. *The Protestant Ethic and the Spirit of Capitalism.* Translated by Talcott Parsons. Mineola, NY: Dover, 2003.

———. *The Religion of China: Confucianism and Taoism.* Translated by H. H. Gerth. New York: Macmillan, 1964.

———. *The Sociology of Religion.* Translated by Ephraim Fischoff. Boston: Beacon, 1963.

Welch, Claude. *Protestant Thought in the Nineteenth Century.* Vol. 2, *1870–1914.* New Haven: Yale University Press, 1985.

Westhelle, Vítor. *After Heresy: Colonial Practices and Post-Colonial Theologies.* Eugene, OR: Cascade, 2010.

———. *Eschatology and Space: The Lost Dimension of Theology Past and Present.* New York: Palgrave Macmillan, 2012.

White, Lynn. "The Historical Roots of Our Ecological Crisis." Reprinted in *This Sacred Earth: Religion, Nature, Environment,* edited by Roger S. Gottlieb, 184–94. New York: Routledge, 1996.

Whitehead, Alfred N. *Process and Reality: An Essay in Cosmology.* Edited by David Ray Griffin and Donald W. Sherburne. Corrected ed. New York: Free Press, 1978.

Williams, Paul. *Mahayana Buddhism: The Doctrinal Foundations.* London: Routledge, 1989.

Wilson, Edward O. *Consilience: The Unity of Knowledge.* New York: Knopf, 1998.

———. *Sociobiology: The New Synthesis.* Cambridge: Belknap Press of Harvard University Press, 1975.

Wood, Allen, W., ed. *Basic Writings of Kant.* New York: Modern Library, 2001.

Yao, Xinzhong, *An Introduction to Confucianism.* Cambridge: Cambridge University Press, 2000.

Žižiek, Slavoj. *The Puppet and the Dwarf: The Perverse Core of Christianity.* Cambridge: MIT Press, 2003.

Index

www.ingramcontent.com/pod-product-compliance
Lightning Source LLC
Chambersburg PA
CBHW030401270326
41926CB00009B/1210